PENGUIN BOOKS
IDENTITY AND SURVIVAL

As a member of the Indian Police Service, Kirpal Dhillon witnessed at close hand the enormous social, political and administrative changes that swept the country's policing policies. He has been director of police training in the Union home ministry, joint director, Central Bureau of Investigation and director general of police, Punjab and Madhya Pradesh. After retirement, he served as vice-chancellor, Bhopal University.

His published works include two books—*Defenders of the Establishment* and *Police and Politics in India*—and essays on the Indian Constitution, human rights, minority issues and the Bhopal gas disaster. He lives in Bhopal.

PENGUIN BOOKS

IDENTITY AND SURVIVAL

... a member of the Indian Police Service, Kirpal Dhillon witnessed at close hand the numerous social, political and administrative changes that swept the country's police services. He has been director of police training in the Union home ministry, joint-director, Central Bureau of Investigation, and director-general of police, Punjab and Madhya Pradesh. After retirement, he served as vice-chancellor, Bhopal University.

His published work includes two books—*Defenders of the Establishment: Ruler-Police and Policing in India*—and essays on the Indian Constitution, human rights, minorities and the Bhopal gas disaster. He lives in Bhopal.

Identity and Survival

Sikh Militancy in India 1978–1993

KIRPAL DHILLON

PENGUIN BOOKS

PENGUIN BOOKS
Published by the Penguin Group
Penguin Books India Pvt. Ltd, 11 Community Centre, Panchsheel Park,
New Delhi 110 017, India
Penguin Group (USA) Inc., 375 Hudson Street, New York, New York 10014, USA
Penguin Group (Canada), 90 Eglinton Avenue East, Suite 700, Toronto M4P 2Y3
Penguin Books Ltd, 80 Strand, London WC2R 0RL, England
Penguin Ireland, 25 St Stephen's Green, Dublin 2, Ireland
(a division of Penguin Books Ltd)
Penguin Group (Australia), 250 Camberwell Road, Camberwell,
Victoria 3124, Australia (a division of Pearson Australia Group Pty Ltd)
Penguin Group (NZ), cnr Airborne and Rosedale Roads, Albany,
Auckland 1310, New Zealand (a division of Pearson New Zealand Ltd)
Penguin Group (South Africa) (Pty) Ltd, 24 Sturdee Avenue, Rosebank,
Johannesburg 2196, South Africa

Penguin Books Ltd, Registered Offices: 80 Strand, London WC2R 0RL, England

First published by Penguin Books India 2006

Copyright © K.S. Dhillon 2006

10 9 8 7 6 5 4 3 2

ISBN-13: 978-1-04310-036-2   ISBN-10: 0-14310-036-X

Typeset in *Sabon Roman* by SÜRYA, New Delhi
Printed at Presstech Litho Pvt. ltd. Greater Noida

To be, or not to be—that is the question;
Whether 'tis nobler in the mind to suffer
The slings and arrows of outrageous fortune,
Or to take arms against a sea of troubles,
And by opposing end them?

—Prince of Denmark in *Hamlet*

Contents

Foreword

The decade-and-a-half of militancy in the sensitive border state of Punjab posed the gravest threat to India's stability since independence. It is, therefore, hardly surprising that much ink has been spilt in analysing its causes and to a lesser extent its ending. Explanations for the emergence of violence in the Punjab variously focus on Sikh ethno-nationalism, the cultural and economic impacts of the green revolution, the 'hidden hand' of external intervention and the crisis in Centre-state relations, arising from Indira Gandhi's de-institutionalisation of the Congress.[1] Less academic attention has been devoted to the return of the province to 'normalcy' in the mid-1990s. It has been conceptualised by Gurharpal Singh in terms of the state's re-establishment of hegemonic control from overt control.[2] Such writers as Joyce Pettigrew[3] and Shinder Thandi[4] have pointed to the factionalism of the militants, the increasing success of the state's counter-insurgency techniques of criminalisation and infiltration of their ranks, along with the weariness of the rural population, who were victims of both militant and police violence.

Participants in the counter-insurgency have produced

a number of memoirs. The works of D.P. Sharma, Lt-General K.S. Brar and K.P.S. Gill are especially well known in this respect.[5] This volume by Kirpal Dhillon, who took over as director general of Punjab police in July 1984, adds to this growing literature. In terms of its critical awareness and forthright approach, however, it differs markedly from the aforementioned works. Brar blandly endorses the Government of India's *White Paper on the Punjab Agitation* on the army action in the Golden Temple.[6] Gill and Sharma similarly blame the crisis on 'anti-national' forces. The former talks of the 'doctrines of deceit' of the Sikh 'leaders of faith' paving the way for terrorists to occupy centrestage in the politics of the Punjab. There is little sense of history in these accounts. What is even more lacking is critical analysis of the role of the state and the political culture of Punjab. It is precisely these elements that inform and add value to Kirpal Dhillon's approach. He, for example, incisively demolishes the case for the fateful army action on 3 June 1984. The result is a more academically rigorous and intellectually honest account of this traumatic period in the Punjab's history. All that the work shares in common with the other memoirs is perhaps understandable reluctance by its author to delve deeply into the personal role that he played in the drama. The reader is merely provided with tantalising glimpses. Such glimpses are accompanied by acute and sometimes tart reflections on others of the leading *dramatis personae*. In particular, through personal observation, Dhillon reveals Zail Singh's troubled state of mind in the wake of Operation Blue Star.[7]

Dhillon's historical analysis of the onset of the crisis perceptively points to the partition trauma for the Sikh community. He also shares the view of such academics as

Cynthia Keppley Mahmood that an important source of Sikh militancy was the fear of absorption into an increasingly dominant Hindu culture.[8] Paul Wallace links such anxieties with the economic and demographic transformations arising from the Green Revolution.[9] Dhillon also draws into his historical analysis the heightened community expectations arising from the colonial period. Perhaps all that is missing from the impressive argument in the opening chapter is the experience of settlement in the canal colonies of the future Pakistan state and the differences in outlook at the end of empire, arising from these settlers and political elites in the Sikh heartland of central Punjab.

Chapter 2 traces developments during the opening decades of independence, including the creation of a Punjabi *suba* and the relations between the national Congress leadership and the Akali Dal. Dhillon points out that the Centre's policy was based on 'gross ignorance of Sikh history' and insensitivity to 'minority insecurities'. He declares more widely that, 'For far too long, the Indian state had been in the habit of treating grave issues of minority dissent and discontent as mere law and order problems, seeking to address them through the use of sheer force, often turning into state terror'. Dhillon's analysis is largely in keeping with mainstream academic opinion on the role of Indira Gandhi's advisers in precipitating the Punjab crisis. This may surprise readers who can recall that at the time of his appointment, the media portrayed him very much as Indira Gandhi's man.

Another strength of the analysis is the awareness that the new boundary arrangements after 1966 increased the scope for tensions in the region and provided opportunities for the Centre to play off the interests of Haryana and Punjab. Dhillon also, in this chapter, introduces the role of Zail Singh, which he displays in a very unflattering light. He is indeed depicted throughout the volume as fishing in Punjab's troubled waters. His conflict with Darbara Singh and his early patronising of Bhindranwale, in order to undermine the Akali Dal, are highlighted as key factors in the Punjab's descent into violence. The latter element has been reflected upon by a number of scholars. Dhillon is also at one with such writers as Gurharpal Singh, when he points out that Akali demands for rectification of political and economic grievances were always more vociferous when they were out of office. He also perceptively reveals that the Centre sought to portray the Akali agitation as solely 'a religious-based stir' and to play down the 'diverse political, economic and territorial issues affecting the interests of all Punjabis.' Finally, he is strongly of the opinion that the Centre had considerable responsibility for the failure of successive rounds of talks with Akali leaders. This is very much in keeping with the view of journalist Patwant Singh, who played an unsuccessful mediatory role.[10]

Another important variable in Dhillon's state-centric analysis is the disabling of the Punjab's administrative responses, because of 'large-scale politicization and factionalism'. Throughout his volume, in contrast to some former state functionaries, Dhillon displays a realistic—if not downright cynical—awareness of corruption and of the political culture it spawns. He also pulls no punches when he writes of the 'traditionally oppressive Punjab police' and its ruler-supportive role, a trait that continues to define police operations even in post-colonial India. This is marked by 'a habit of excessive servility and submissiveness to political and civilian officialdom and disdain and disregard for the community and public institutions in general'. Strikingly, Dhillon admits to police lawlessness and recognises that this gave 'a fillip to militant activity' and promoted 'a sense of revulsion among the mass of the people'. He reserves greatest criticism, however, for the army action in the Punjab from 3 June onwards, which resulted in a 'major intensification of militancy and terrorism in the region'. One of his first actions as incoming director general of Punjab police was to advise that the army be relieved 'of their civil commitments'.

The author indicates that he took up his posting with a clear mandate. This was to contain the ongoing violence, examine the reasons for the police failure to deal with the violence in its formative stages, address the growth of militancy arising from police 'fake encounters' and minimize the sense of panic amongst the Hindus, who were leaving the countryside for the relative safety of Punjab's towns. This agenda reflects Dhillon's reform-minded approach to policing, which was seen throughout his career and in subsequent publications. He set about attempting to halt the decay in police administration in Punjab arising from political interference by serving on the R.V. Subramaniam reform committee as its member secretary. He also sought to gain the trust of the local cadre of officers, some of whom were resentful at his being parachuted into the state through a policy of active touring. This was also accompanied by a 'hearts and minds' strategy, which unfortunately soon foundered, 'as I realized that the Indian state was not particularly interested in looking at peaceful and constructive solutions to the untidy mess it had so deftly created'.

Dhillon's narrative does not in itself give credence to the many conspiracy theories which surround the events in the Punjab during this troubled period. His frank uncovering of the seamier side of governance, however, judiciously reveals how such theories abound, when they concern such pivotal events as Blue Star and the assassination of Sant Longowal. The recrudescence of violence following the latter's death resulted in the undermining and eventual dismissal of Surjit Singh Barnala's Akali Dal government on 11 May 1987. Dhillon was replaced earlier in March 1986 as Director General of Police by J.F. Ribeiro. The latter was to introduce the controversial 'bullet for bullet' policy, which rather than ending the militancy encouraged more young Sikhs to join the armed insurgents.[11] It was only under Ribeiro's successor K.P.S. Gill that the militants were finally defeated. Kirpal Dhillon is, however, critical of both Gill and Ribeiro for pursuing 'strategies that tended to promote a culture of illegitimate, brutal and possibly venal policing among their subordinates'. Dhillon rightly points out how the police acquired vested interests in the perpetuation of violence, a view that found considerable support in contemporary media reports, among them a well-known weekly, which stated that, 'the end of terrorism was literally the end of a multi-crore industry'. He also questions whether the resort to such tactics of state terror could root out militancy in the long term, or merely 'eliminate the current crop of militants'.

The author returns to this theme in the final chapter. Many academic observers are aware that most of the key political grievances that the Sikhs perceive as genuine have not been addressed and for this reason, it is possible that there could be a future recrudescence of violence. It is nevertheless a highly unusual assessment for a former police chief. 'Let us not forget', Kirpal Dhillon affirms, 'that though militancy and extremist violence have been eliminated, deep-seated political grievances remain unresolved'. This mature judgement marks out the work for its objectivity and detachment, with the writer basing his argument on historical perspective and logical precision, rather than merely proffering apologetics on behalf of the state. In this respect, it departs significantly from the views contained in some other accounts of the Punjab counter-insurgency operations.

IAN TALBOT

University of Southampton, UK

Preface

Before my name was finally cleared by the Union home ministry for posting to the Punjab as director general of police in June 1984, I appeared twice before Prime Minister Indira Gandhi for what were termed as briefing sessions. I had already met her security adviser and other senior functionaries in the government, mostly for advice—but also for a subtle kind of vetting of my credentials for the top job in the troubled state.

I was visibly ill at ease when ushered into her presence, although the prime minister was at her gracious best. After a few preliminary remarks, she asked me about my previous postings and why I thought I would be able to competently handle the grave situation then developing in Punjab. After describing as best as I could how I perceived the situation, I asked her how the government expected me to discharge my duties in the border state.

By the time the meeting ended, it seemed to me that the PM was fairly satisfied with its outcome. Then, she smilingly remarked, 'But people tell me you are a very decent man.' The expression she used in Hindi was *'Lekin log kehte hain ki aap bahut sharif hain.'* As if *sharafat*, or decency, was hardly the best of virtues for a police chief in the kind of situation then obtaining in the country in general—and Punjab in particular!

The PM's remark just about summed up what the establishment thought of enlightened policing practices. Most educated police officers are generally regarded as misfits in the Indian police. The upshot is that under the sheer weight of popular perceptions, officers laboriously shake off their reputations as refined and compassionate human beings so as to pass muster as pragmatic and tough police leaders. Archaic concepts of control and superintendence frustrate any well-meaning attempt to correct many systemic aberrations.

As a class, policemen are believed to look at aggressive behaviour as a symptom of criminality and malfeasance. In fact, a successful career is largely contingent upon shedding all commitment to human rights and democratic imperatives. A police recruit must first thoroughly and consciously dehumanize and desensitize him/herself. It follows that a refined sensibility, compassion and empathy have no role to play. Living and working in a sordid environment, cheek-by-jowl with the dregs of society, a neophyte policeman tends to soon lose his faculty to distinguish between a habitual criminal and a hapless victim of social injustice who is impelled by circumstances to overstep the boundaries of law in order to impel the authorities to take note of his grievances, real or perceived.

Then, in post-colonial societies of Asia and Africa, the police are still largely governed by colonial enactments and attitudes, dating back to the mid-nineteenth century. All over South Asia, governments swear by what is called *hard policing*, in which police organisations and personnel are thoroughly conditioned to divest themselves of all humane and civilised concerns for the suspects and victims of crime.

The point that I am trying to make is that the persistent refusal of the Indian political and bureaucratic classes to take note of the enormous changes taking place all over the world in the art and science of law enforcement has led to grave distortions in the handling of crime and criminals by the police. Not only has police performance in day-to-day crime-control tasks plunged to abysmal levels, the Indian police has also proved hopelessly inept in coping with the expanding span of extremist violence and insurrectionary movements. Policing policies and processes that still reflect mid-nineteenth century values and attitudes, as embodied in the Indian Police Act of 1861, breed a culture of law enforcement grossly at odds with present-day social prerequisites.

Moreover, militancy and extremist violence are not purely a law and order problems, which can be contained merely by the use of deadly weaponry. Sikh militancy in Punjab continued to be treated as a mere law and order problem even though it showed all the characteristics of a political movement. Later, when Rajiv Gandhi did open a dialogue with moderate Sikh leader Sant Harchand Singh Longowal (president of the Akali Dal), it failed to carry conviction, because by then a sense of anger and resentment had seized the Sikhs. Whether an honest political approach at the outset and positive and constructive policing in the post-1986 phase of acute militant activity would have saved the situation remains wide open for history to assess.

Years of study and introspection have gone into the making of this book. As the Punjab police chief in the wake of Operation Blue Star, I was witness to many vital developments in an action-packed era, both at the political and the administrative level. But my very proximity to the crucial events then taking place in the state and in Delhi precluded an objective appraisal of the situation. Moreover, my status itself acted as a barrier to free flow of information and inputs from all but governmental organisations and from a few unofficial sources. Two decades have gone by. With the benefit of hindsight, I am able to view the episode in perspective. I have also had occasion to study some analogous militancies in other parts of the world and hold discussions with scholars and police leaders on the subject in India and abroad.

All such inputs have deepened my understanding of the aetiology and management of militancy and extremism in multicultural and multi-ethnic societies. It seems to me that India is especially vulnerable to eruption of major militant and insurgent movements and will continue to be so in the foreseeable future, given the proven ineptitude of its political and bureaucratic leadership. The growing acceptability of a combative form of ultra-rightist ideologies among the country's Hindu majority has immensely added to the problem.

*

In a work of this nature, it is difficult to individually identify all those who helped me in pursuing this study by freely sharing their perceptions and experiences on the subject. Needless to say that a theme as complex and multi-dimensional as a minority insurgency can hardly be handled except through a judicious process of consultation and feedback for gathering inputs and developing insights. For this purpose, I met with fairly representative sections of politicians, civil servants, police officers, journalists and political analysts, many who were part of the administrative or political set-up or were otherwise involved in the process. I could not find a way to elicit the views of any former militant, for obvious reasons, much as I would have liked to.

To all of my interlocutors I am deeply beholden in more senses than one. I must, however, make a specific mention of some to whom I owe a special debt of gratitude. My long-time friend, Prof. J.S. Grewal, a former vice-chancellor of Guru Nanak Dev University, Amritsar and a distinguished historian was a constant source of inspiration and advice on many intricate issues concerning Punjab and Sikhism. Dr Birinder Pal Singh of Punjabi University, Patiala, the author of a most readable and analytical book on the discourse of violence, Prof. Pritam Singh of Oxford Brookes University, UK and Prof. Indu Banga, an eminent historian and teacher in Punjab University, Chandigarh formed the academic resource pool for me to draw upon to clarify and organize the approach and argument of my presentation. P.H. Vaishnav, who served as the Punjab chief secretary during a very critical phase of militancy, gave me free access to some of his personal papers on the subject, which helped me recall events relating to the period much before I was posted to the state. Belonging to the Punjab cadre as he did, Mr Vaishnav's account carried a special seal of authenticity. N.N. Vohra, another Punjab cadre IAS officer, then my colleague in the state as the principal secretary, home and later to occupy two of the most important posts in the Union government, shared with me his views and experiences of those traumatic years in Punjab. Several Punjab police officers, who worked with me as district superintendents at the height of militancy and would later head the state police, were most forthcoming on issues that only grass-roots officers can be acquainted with. Two of them, A.A. Siddiqui and S.S. Virk, merit my special thanks. There were many more, at the time occupying highly sensitive posts, who did not want to be identified by name but whose inputs were nevertheless of great value to me. I sincerely acknowledge their contribution.

I am deeply grateful to Prof. Ian Talbot, an eminent historian and writer specializing in South Asian affairs, for writing the foreword. More so because Ian and I share a profound interest in post-Partition developments in the two Punjabs, one in India and the other in Pakistan. I am also greatly beholden to Prof. Upendra Baxi, a former vice-chancellor of Delhi University and an internationally renowned law teacher, for doing a remarkably candid and perceptive analysis of the subject in the form of an introduction to this book. Besides being a discerning observer of contemporary events and intensely committed to countless social causes, Prof. Baxi is an amazingly thoughtful individual and a sincere friend. Prof. Richard W. Ward, director, Institute for the Study of Violent Groups and associate vice-president for research, Sam Houston State University, Huntsville, Texas, USA and David Washbrook, Department of South Asian History, St. Anthony's College, Oxford, UK, offered to go through the manuscript and write blurbs despite many other pressing commitments. I am deeply obliged to them.

At a more personal level, no writer can do much writing on a sustainable basis without complete and unconditional spousal acquiescence and support. A sullen and inattentive husband, preoccupied with his writing most of the time, can hardly be the dream on which conjugal relationships can be nurtured. Obviously, it entails an element of immense sacrifice for a wife to suffer a husband, who remains locked in his study for hours together only to show up after repeated calls for a meal or some other errand. My wife, Sneh, bore the ordeal wonderfully well. I sincerely appreciate her loving care and support. I am also thankful to my daughter, Preeti, whose passion for surrounding herself with books far exceeds her fondness for jewelry and clothes, unlike most persons of her age, procured for me some very useful reports on the 1984 Sikh carnage in Delhi, which were otherwise impossible to obtain.

KIRPAL DHILLON

Bhopal

Introduction

Non-partisan and conscientiously researched contemporary histories of the insurgent movement occur infrequently in India. Access to reliable information of critical events of organized political violence poses massive difficulties that subsequently pale into insignificance when one tries to make 'sense' (both in logical and passional languages) of insurgency and 'counter-insurgency' operations. How may a historian relate the somewhat easily understandable current triggers for state and insurgent violence to wider narratives of its causes and histories? How may any history-writing proceed conscientiously to read the deep structures of insurgent action, in terms of its *original intention/ purpose*? How may the craft of history provide the best possible narrative of the radically heterogeneous character of the insurgent movement lived within the everyday labours of insurgency and the material labours of governance aimed at its repression? Rebel solidarity, as Ranajit Guha educates us,[1] necessarily remains fractured by violence-within (that is annihilating violence directed at its own cadres, animated by suspicions of disloyalty and betrayal of this intention) and violence-without (that is annihilating violence directed to state actors and bystander civilians). How may a historian of insurgency decode the logics of this violence? Further, how may 'we' ever further fully speak, in this context, to the subordination or even disarticulation, of women's feminist presence, voice, and participation in some canonical narratives of insurgency and counter-insurgency?[2] These and related questions invite attention to areas of immense perplexity, which no reductive reading may ever fully explain. Such readings remain rife with propagandist truths, bedeviling further, in complex ways, the tasks of a historian of insurgency.

We ought to note some commonalities or homologies among the statist and insurgent discourse. If the statist discourse renders it awesomely easy to describe insurgent actors as the enemies of the 'nation' and 'people' and to castigate them as *outlaws*, the insurgent discourse likewise, and with some coequal order of cruel felicity, fully and fiercely returns the same compliment to state managers and agents. If the statist discourse develops various regimes of bio-political (encounter killings/custodial torture and tyranny) power directed to annihilate insurgent actors, the insurgent discourse as well reproduces new technologies of mass violence. Each seeks to disrupt and destroy the other's justificatory languages. Insurgent actors seek to represent the *rule of law* talk as masking so many *regimes of terror*. In turn, state managers and agents resolutely signify insurgent action as the practice of collective political violence for *its own sake*, divested of any redemptive political cosmology. In both these processes, violence of 'pure means', the 'Divine violence', as Walter Benjamin so unerringly named this, presides over the varied regimes of insurgency and counter-insurgency operations. At stake, then, remain practices, on both sides, of destruction of what Pierre Bordieu famously names as 'symbolic capital'.

Further, if state–sponsored reductive readings extravagantly forfeit the potential of understanding insurgent violence as carrying messages for some amelioration of the *rottenness* (as Benjamin describes this[3]) at the very core of constitutionally presented ways of practising 'representational'/'deliberative' politics, pro-insurgency reductive readings gloss over the irrationality and the horror of some of its own practices of mass violence and even 'terror'. They choose to follow the notion propounded by Shaheed Bhagat Singh in his little-read tract *A Philosophy of the Bomb*, which described 'terror' as 'propaganda by deed'. However, Bhagat Singh did not celebrate any total erasure of the distinction between political targets and civilian populations.

In contrast, non-reductive modes of reading both insurgent and state violence seek to understand the pathologies of extreme violence on both sides[4]. Such readings thus further invite some agonizing attention to the place and character of violence in doing 'politics'. Insurgency, at least partially, thrives parasitically[5] on the quotidian violence of the state and law, which in turn it aggravates. If the rebel thus seeks to castigate governance as itself criminalized, and the state as a manifest order of class-based violence, thus extricating her from the 'placenta of common crime'[6], the state and its law seek to restore the pre-natal condition by representing the insurgents as dangerous criminals. Not so curiously, then, state power seems almost to require states of permanent insurrection for the reproduction of legitimate governance credentials. In a deep inversion, then, insurgent violence stands appropriated as business as usual. Both forms of public, total, and destructive violence seem to reproduce themselves (in the words of William Blake) a 'fearful symmetry'. Both combine to produce a 'pathological nation'.[7] Reading insurgency then, I suggest, remains at least as arduous as reading the state and its law.

Kirpal Dhillon's narrative here invites us to a close and agonized attention to these concerns by a scrupulously detailed account of Sikh 'militancy'. He deserves our profound readerly gratitude for re-situating these concerns.

II

Any presentation of the formative contexts of the roots of insurgency remains notoriously prone to political provocation, state persecution, and often both. The tasks and risks of historical narrative remain thus infinitely complicated. Because insurgent actors openly articulate sustained collective political violence (deploying the means and celebrating ends of death and destruction) as way to achieve 'justice', or at least as so many modes to combat structurally imposed political injustices, the official discourse and state managerial constructed Indian political vocabulary of governance describes these as 'outlaws' variously in terms of 'anti-social' and 'anti-national' elements. And the Indian media uses this phrase-regime that so dreadfully often announce the massacre of 'anti-social' elements by 'anti-national elements' and in turn of both by the police and paramilitary forces. Thus emerge various and viciously anonymous, and even unnamable, orders of some abiding casualties.

Indeed, and shockingly, official reports even now continue to refer to the 'Naxalite-*infested* areas', as if insurgent actors were mere *vermin* worthy of speedy and lawless bio-political annihilation. As far as I know, this vicious political entomology that after all assimilates protesting Indian citizens to the category of political *insects* has gone unchallenged even in the activist discourse. The 'vermin' of course is occasionally brought to a roundtable of negotiations, as it were, in the Diet of Worms; but all this does not divest 'it' of this essentially ontological entomological 'status'. The power of anti-insurgency discourse at the very least creates and marshals a distinction between *citizens* entitled at least to the uncertain promise of the rule of law and '*terrorists*' to whom may be owed, by democidal definition, not a tattle of constitutional solicitude.

All this, and more, complicates further the telling of the stories concerning the dialectical relationship between 'national integration' and 'development' and 'insurgent violence'. If the former deploys the languages of contemporary human rights norms and standards as languages of *governance*, the latter deploys these as facilitating acts/performatives of *insurrection*[8]. State managers, and their normative cohorts, contest insurgent violence in the name of national unity and integration, the ekta and *akhandata* of India that is constitutionally christened also as Bharat; in contrast human rights and social activist practices castigate 'state terrorism' that proceeds to construct justifications for contemporary Indian statecraft bereft of any historically 'real' concern for justice.

In either case, though differentially, at stake remain some futures of human rights. The statist discourse marshals the languages of collective human security, human rights, and national development. The insurgent discourse renews, at least in part, some 'cargo cult' visions of social redemption and justice. The apex judicial actors, uneasily and unenviably placed alongside both, typically engage in some 'one-step-forward, two-steps-backward' type moves. They remain inarticulate and quiescent before a dreadful

59th amendment of the Constitution that suspends for Punjab a time-bound denial of even the minima of right to life. The much-vaunted Indian judicial activism stays thus fully situated within the comfort zones that pursue human rights only when consistent with the state-ordained security regimes. Likewise, even as the Indian media commodifies collective political violence as the hardcore pornography of power, it, at the same moment, also ambivalently enables articulation of concern at the myriad forms of escalating state and insurgent violence.

In such a zodiac, any act of contemporary history-writing/reading insurgency as a way of making a wider political statement concerning structural injustices runs the risk for its intrepid authors of some involuntary membership of the communities, constituted by some dragnet security legislations that criminalize whatever a regime may consider as supportive of, or 'harbouring', 'terrorists'. In the process, stand some unwholesomely generated grammars of two kinds of 'citizenship': the 'democratic' Indian citizenry contrasted with the 'outlaw' citizenry, defined and legislated by the dragnet security legislations. Overall, conscientious historians of insurgency now risk a global Guantanamo-type universal global citizenship.[9]

However, conscientious historians of insurgency, loyal to their task and craft, must perforce run such narrative and existential risks by directing attention to the intertwining ways in which histories of governance, especially in post-colonial, and now post-socialist, societies, variously and intransigently construct and install several and multifarious histories of insurgency. Such historians may, as already noted, now perforce run the risk, in a Guatanamo world, of some officially indictable prosecution as supportive, even of 'glorification' of 'terrorism'. It is not clear how state-independent ways of historical knowing that trace the 'causes' of pre- and post-histories of insurgency may fully now negotiate the newly emergent global regimes of violent state and dominant civil society censorship. By the same token, their art and craft may allow no moment of convenient repose from the agonizing task to explain the 'roots' of insurgency. Understandably, then, while the narratives of 'good governance' vigorously flourish, those concerning the logics of insurgency remain globally sparse.

Against this officially ordained register of the atrocious erasure of public memory, we all ought to welcome Kirpal Dhillon's endeavor in unfolding some causal 'histories' of Sikh 'militancy'. He here offers a clear–sighted, lucid, and painstaking exploration of causes, careers, and some continuing aftermaths of 'Sikh militancy'.

That 'history' navigates several itineraries of difficult-to-decipher histories of the anti-colonial, or self-determination movements, if only because the official histories describe these as endangering 'national unity'. Dhillon traces some histories of the constitutional promises and betrayals. Was it, indeed, the case that some pre-independence national movement promises to the Sikh communities were foredoomed to some ultimate betrayal in the Nehruvian regime? Likewise, was it the case that within-nation political translations of devolution of power remained, after all, directed to pre-empting secessionist confrontations? How may we further grasp the several ways of the politics of regime expediency as contributing to the more radical manifestations of an 'ethno-nationalist' impulse?

All this further raises the all-important interrogation concerning serious readings of constitutional 'promises' and 'betrayals'. Far too many communities of promise have suffered eventual and wholly unconscientious betrayal but only a few of these have historically marshalled the power of 'constitutional insurgency' as a mode of setting things 'right'. How may we understand and explain why some communities exposed to the past-colonial as well as millennial injustices emerge as militants, waging, as it were, acts of 'war' against the Indian 'state', while others remain quiescent with their un-constitutionally ordained political *fate*, even *destiny*? Further, may we regard the militarization of Indian governance practices as a *cause* rather than an *effect* of political insurgency? Perhaps, it would be rewarding to read Dhillon as offering some important contextual clues concerning why this may actually happen to be the case.

Moreover, at stake in insurgency and counter-insurgency movements/operations remain some practices, translating *citizens* possessed of the guaranteed human rights and fundamental freedoms into 'colonial'/'neocolonial' subjects. This constant conversion remains a notable feature of the post-colonial (and now post-socialist) conjunctures. Put shortly, as Dhillon here remarkably suggests, we stand confronted with the sovereign issue concerning taking *citizenship seriously*. How may we fully grasp the logics and languages of post-colonial constitutionalism that rest on, and thrive upon, some magical belief systems, which ever so fully entrench the notion that the principle of self-determination exhausts its historic potency with the attainment of 'independence'?

Finally, and without being exhaustive, arise some further concerns about the violent graduation, as it were, of the within-nation 'autonomy' movements into 'secessionist' ones. The Indian Constitutional development suggests, of course, some scrupulously grudging regard for the still expansive scope for the principle of within-nation development of the principle and detail of Indian 'federalism'. This, at the same moment, 'accommodates' some regional autonomy movements while thoroughly 'outlawing' forms of 'secessionist' movements. This difficult political articulation verges on what Gayatri Spivak names variously as 'failed decolonization'[10]. Even so, the Indian democratic experiment and experience may not as yet fortunately attract the globally hegemonic discourse of 'failed states'.

But all this remains only a part of the story. The standpoint of the pioneers of subaltern insurgent discourse—a staggeringly and proliferatingly varied repertoire of articulate/disarticulated voices—constitutes everywhere archives of histories of betrayal of the original constitutional promises. Dhillon conscientiously traces this perception in his narrative of the 'Sikh militancy'. Other contrasting narratives stand presented by the enduring 'Naxalite' movement, and the 'secessionist' movements in the North-East and Kashmir.

Kirpal Dhillon accomplishes, with some remarkable narrative success, a difficult task: providing a narrative of a recent insurgent moment/movement in Indian history that he names as 'Sikh militancy'. As already noted, the task remains haunted by some extraordinary difficulties. Even so, I believe that he thus makes an important contribution for any serious understanding of the dialectics of what I may here name, following Antonio Negri, as *constitutional insurgencies*. I read the work in your hands as offering an honest citizen's guide seeking to expand our knowledge and understanding of such critical events.

III

Kirpal Dhillon offers a kind of ringside view of Sikh insurgency spanning the period 1978-1993. His perspective is that of a privileged actor, a conscientious police official, who, in a superannuating moment, as a proud citizen of India, reflects upon both the lived post–'Operation Bluestar' national policing moment and its long aftermath. Surely, he offers a most informed, and often anguished, narrative of policing insurgency in a milieu in which a corrupt and violent sovereign remains fully determined to use police powers to save dilapidated political regimes. Dhillon does not so describe the performances of sovereign militancy, and remains more guarded in his diction, preferring instead to carefully archive the province of chance and necessity that characterized some indeterminate forms of political decision-making. Indeed even as noting fully the venalities of national politics, Dhillon still allows a rather wide margin of appreciation for 'honest' mistakes of judgement. Even so, I believe, that this text remains productive of labours of reading that fully suggest the power of interlocution that finally disrupts regime-produced production of political truths.

Dhillon's narrative concerning his own elevation to Punjab in those troubled days reminds me of what Giani Zail Singh, as the then incumbent Union home minister, told an incoming police chief of Delhi. The latter narrated to me, in a confidential moment, which I now breach, what Gianiji said to him: '*Khyal rakhna, agar aapka danda giraga tau hamara jhanda giraga!*' (Lit: if your baton falls, so will our flag!) In a further breach of posthumous confidence, I may here add that when later I asked Gianiji, occupying then a more exalted constitutional position, whether he actually said this, he confirmed this in an entirely unperplexed way! Policing, in contemporary Indian conjuncture, thus epitomizes the extraordinarily strange relationship between the *danda* and the *jhanda*!

The work in your hands provides unusual, even

extraordinary, bouquets of narrative insights in the ways of 'governance' as 'insurrection' and 'insurrection' as 'governance'. Each defines the other, often in terms of the Holocaustian regimes of the practices of cruelty of the insurgent and constitutional players/actors alike. The dividing line between constitutional *Veerappans*[11] (those that maximize power and wealth in the name of the Indian impoverished) and some self-proclaimed constitutional 'have-not' Robin Hood type Indian citizenry (insurgents that thrive on not dissimilar promises), remains historically almost wafer-thin. Together, and cumulatively, and in some poignant cumulative contemporary Indian historicity, they violently test and tease the promise/ betrayal of the Indian constitutionalism.

Surely no one may afford to ignore this new archive embodying some previously unavailable and yet fully reliable information concerning 'Sikh militancy' and the scrupulous knitting together of a larger narrative concerning the political economy of the Indian governance. Nor may anyone concerned with democratic future of India any longer afford to remain complicitly uninformed by this narrative.

Dhillon narrates the ways in which official histories of insurgencies sanctify orders/disorders of regime desires that sanitize and 'justify' an enormous order of violence in the name of collective human security. Thus stands here offered the art and craft of history, contesting 'history' written from the standpoint of the *daroga*, as Ranajit Guha witheringly named this narrative practice of 'colonial historiography'.

A compelling merit of this work lies in transcending neo-colonial narratives of insurgency. Put another way, I read Dhillon as offering some order of empathetic understanding of the ensemble of insurgent actors, and their recourse to violent means, posing in the process a finally 'both-to-blame' kind of analysis of the 'logics' of governmental and insurgent actors. Some readers of this work may not be satisfied with this approach; yet, a salient merit of work lies in illustrating some severe difficulties of understanding and judgement concerning the causation of insurrection and repression. This achievement comes by no means easy even to professional historians; yet, Dhillon accomplishes this remarkably as a former top cop aspiring to be a historian. In so doing, he offers an unusual message: the province of writing reflexive histories of collective political violence constitutes and remains a conjoint arena of the labours of understanding by conscientious citizens and professional historians. Even when the latter class of epistemic actors may regard the labours of the former as furnishing mere *raw materials* for their endeavors, Dhillon here surely furnishes *embarrassment de riches*.

IV

Any careful reader of this work must stumble upon, and straddle along, the difficult choice—the politics of naming that Dhillon makes through the title of the book. 'Militancy' relates to, in some crucial ways, to the politics of insurgency but does not entirely summate it. 'Militancy' signifies at best, and also at worst, the language of governance. 'Insurgency', in a stark contrast, delineates acts/performances of resisting unconstitutional governance as structurally violent and 'unlawful'/'unjust'. Poignantly, the languages of state and insurgent violence remain incommensurable. And this aggravates in the play, and war, of contrasting languages of 'saintly' and 'secular' governmental and social actors. Importantly, Dhillon gives body and voice to these different languages and discourse. But the spiritual saints and secular savants often produce the same history of tyranny: thus 'Sant' Bhindranwale with cruel felicity reproduces some post-histories of the 1975-77 anti-constitutional Emergency proclamation and regime. We must not fail to note here the fully at work politics of acquisitive mimesis (to which René Girard drew our attention in a different context[12].)

Dhillon brings home that 'Sikh militancy' remains an irreducibly heterogeneous phenomenon, an archive of many different colonial pre-histories and post-colonial post-histories. He thus suggests that we may not ever fully grasp 'militancy' in terms of some violent triggers, outside the residues of lived and felt historic injustices. Kirpal Dhillon thus remains a good navigational guide, precisely because he promises no false safe harbours of understanding. All this, then, signifies a considerable, and at places, a compelling achievement.

For our author, the practices of cruel venality of national governance furnish an *important* leitmotiv but only offer a *part* of the story. No doubt, some real-life histories of insurgency problematize the practices of regime consolidation and state formative practices; however, crucially, Dhillon offers us some ways of dialectical understanding of how these regime-serving practices of power, at the same moment, foment insurrection as well as seek to contain/combat it. Both the 'host' (the Indian state) and the 'parasite' (the insurgent) continue to complement each other.

Put another way, here also remain offered some 'whodunit' type narratives concerning Operation Blue Star and Operation Wood Rose, the former more poignantly known than the latter. Yet, put together, these emplot and enact some stories of vicious spiral of collective establishment and insurgent political violence, which also resonate in the blighted arenas/regions of violent Indian 'development' elsewhere. The learned author fortunately remains conspicuously, and in my view happily, 'not guilty' of any mindless fidelity to some cruel canons of 'political correctness'. He deflates some contemporary claims, offered co-equally by the army generals and time-serving civilian advisers that sculpt different violent 'landscapes of memory', and orders of 'justification', concerning these, and indeed other myriad, violent operations.

Dhillon scrupulously archives for us many national policy-making puzzles. What other clear and compelling evidence exist that may, in the eye of history, 'de-justify' Operation Bluestar? How may we access any understanding of the alternatives for the sustained orders of violence encoded by 'Operation Wood Rose'? How may we arrive at some historic understanding of their perpetual aftermaths and aftershocks? What further messages this may be said to have carried for the *habitus* of Indian militarized governance at other sites? How may we understand the origins and aftermaths of the expediently induced Rajiv Gandhi-Sant Longowal 'accord'? Was the killing of the Sant an aspect of the politics of some rather vicious conjoint orders of the establishment and insurgent politics of 'assassination'? Who 'gained' and 'lost' through the enactment of such emplotted political violence on either side? All this raises, in turn, some far-reaching issues concerning the practices of *politics of assassination*, or put another way, *assassination as politics*, a violent estate installed at the very bleeding heart of both 'good' governance and 'good' resistance practices.

For all these, and related reasons, I commend to you this superbly poignant work. Its message remains inestimable in terms of what, after all, the 'Sikh militancy' dared to seek to achieve, and what it failed to, but also in terms of those that any insurgent movement may likewise seek or fail to achieve in a hyper-globalizing India of the contemporary moment and in not dissimilarly constructed registers of governance and insurgency elsewhere equally in post-colonial/post-socialist regimes. As befits any narrative of contemporary historicity, this work raises far too many questions that it may actually, after all, respond in any conclusionary, and authoritative, mode. I do not think that the author aspires to any such stunning order of achievement. Yet, this narrative traces some future histories of understanding, and in some fascinating everyday detail, of an unfolding scenario. It suggests the importance of revisiting Indian constitutionalism, long before 9/11 and also amidst its subsequent global aftermaths. Dhillon provides much precious ground for tracing some anticipatory Indian pre-9/11 histories of the two contemporary 'terror' wars—the 'war *of* terror' and the 'war *on* terror'. He thus, with further poignancy, summons us all to a more informed understanding of the now distinctly emerging messages emanating from some now universalizing histories of the two 'terror' wars.

UPENDRA BAXI

University of Warwick, UK

1

The Backdrop

In retrospect, it seems rather odd that the outbreak of Sikh militancy in the 1980s should have taken the Indian state somewhat unawares.

Apparently, neither the Central nor the state intelligence agencies had anticipated the scale and sweep of the flare-up. But the growth and intensification of Sikh militancy in India at that particular juncture in history was not a mere flash in the pan, unrelated to the collective historical experience and perceptional backdrop of the Sikh community.

In contrast, significant segments of Indian intelligentsia recognized the nature and genesis of the many grievances and concerns of the community that prompted a section of them to embark on a course of confrontation with the Indian state, although they also felt acutely uneasy at the turn of events. The ruling Congress party, under the formidable leadership of Indira Gandhi, however, appeared to view the Punjab developments in a different light. Because of many interrelated and complex factors that will emerge in the course of this study, the Sikh discontent and its fallout in terms of disorder and turmoil in North India came to be viewed by the Indian state as posing a different kind of challenge, both qualitatively and quantitatively, from that in other parts of the country, such as the north-east and Kashmir. For unlike in those regions, the Sikhs had always been regarded by their compatriots as an amiable people, highly unlikely to turn instigators of extremist violence. The application of any excessively harsh measures in Punjab, a prominent mainstream region of the country, therefore, would have caused acute anxiety and unease among the many minority segments of the Indian people.

Several socio-political grievances of the Sikh community that had remained unaddressed before independence acquired a new stridency after independence. The consequential Sikh discontent and disillusionment with the Indian state offered a fertile new field for Pakistan to exploit, which that country soon proceeded to do, an exceedingly alarming development for the Indian state, especially because several other disgruntled minority groups too were getting restive. Since past experience had shown that, in many respects, Sikh discontent was the most difficult to handle, the Indian establishment possibly thought that if the Sikhs could be subdued, all other nascent insurgencies in various parts of the country would disappear on their own.

Such a view of the developing situation in the Punjab in the early 1980s must have brought Mrs Gandhi under intense pressure from her close advisers to deal with the so-called Sikh grievances and the incipient militant movement it was fuelling, with a heavy hand. Regardless of the veracity of these reports, large sections of the Sikh community seemed to implicitly believe in them. Subsequent happenings would further reinforce the distrust and suspicions the community had come to entertain against the Congress party, then synonymous with the Union government. The deployment of central security forces in large numbers in the state also made the Sikhs somewhat uneasy, though it is unclear if such large-scale placement of central armed forces in the Punjab also envisaged an assault on the Golden Temple in Amritsar, the holiest of holy Sikh shrines, or this became necessary because of the mishandling of the problem in early stages.

If indeed the Indian state intended to use the army to restore a semblance of normalcy in the region in the face of mounting Sikh alienation, a suitable climate had to be created in the country to make such a course of action acceptable to various shades of opinion across the political spectrum. It was probably in pursuit of such a goal that the ruling establishment made use of Sant Jarnail Singh Bhindranwale, head of a hitherto obscure Sikh seminary at Chowk Mehta in the border district of Gurdaspur, and his growing band of militant followers, to devise a policy of slyly maligning the community in order to build a national consensus against the alleged secessionist plans of the Sikh leadership, in league with a hostile neighbour.

Such anti-Sikh projections would continue to be subtly promoted in various sections of the Indian people with a view to devising a broad coalition of all the nationalist political forces, or what came to be termed as the national consensus against supposed Sikh designs to destabilize the crucial border region. This may have been considered necessary in order to make an army assault on the Golden Temple look unavoidable and justified.

In a more significant sense, the June 1984 army action

4 Identity and Survival

in Amritsar, Operation Blue Star, also marked a general hardening of attitude of the Indian state towards movements for voicing minority dissent and discontent, regardless of which political party held office in Delhi. With rightist Hindu ideologies acquiring greater acceptability among the country's majority Hindus, forming almost 84 per cent of its population and seeking to assert their primacy in the country's power structure, India's many minority segments, whether religious, linguistic or ethnic, have faced a growing threat to their distinct identities and, indeed, to a secure space to grow and develop as equal citizens of this great country.

*

Considering that in its long history, the premier Sikh political party, the Akali Dal, had never allowed any of their numerous political and religious struggles, starting with the gurudwara movement of the 1920s, to turn violent, how did Bhindranwale suddenly come to so totally dominate the Sikh political discourse in the early 1980s? Either the issues that now troubled the small Sikh community were much more critical to them or there were other factors or players, which sought to so enfeeble the Akali leadership as to let the initiative pass out of their hands.

During the later phases of Sikh militancy, I happened to frequently interact with socially and politically aware groups of citizens in the course of my travels in the country. I must confess that I was shocked at the extent of ignorance and misinformation about the subject prevailing even among the more alert sections of the people, especially in the southern and eastern Indian states. While some degree of insularity and ignorance about happenings in distant regions is not unexpected in a vast country such as India, despite the vast range and reach of the electronic media, the scale of misperceptions among the bulk of the people as to why the Sikhs had chosen the course of open confrontation with the state was amazing. This could probably be ascribed to the media blitz let loose by the central government after the return of the Congress party to power in 1980, apparently to prepare the country for Operation Blue Star, the groundwork for which was allegedly being put in place for some time[1].

There were also rumours that the Indian army had actually been preparing for an assault on the Golden Temple in the course of their tactical exercises in some north Indian cantonments, complete with a replica of the Temple. If true, this could point to two possibilities: either the operation was premeditated or the army was only exercising abundant caution that every professional army must exercise in such matters to remain in a state of maximum preparedness if at all such an operation became necessary. All the same, large sections of the people were intrigued and, indeed, deeply troubled at the phenomenon of a relatively prosperous community like the Sikhs, so far looked upon as spirited soldiers and defenders of the motherland, suddenly turning into a band of fierce and brutal terrorists.

*

This chapter is intended to look at some more important factors that apparently led to a sudden and, by all accounts, an unprecedented outburst of Sikh militancy in the region at that particular moment in history. For this, we will have to approach the subject at two levels. One, briefly trace the broad framework of Sikh religion and history, especially the construction and consolidation of a distinct Sikh identity. And two, recall some of the more significant political events, before and after the country's independence and partition, that shaped the course of Sikh politics.

Some basic knowledge of Sikh religion and history is necessary also to properly grasp the nature of Sikh militant violence, which naturally is heavily coloured by the self-perception of those who wield it as a political weapon to gain power and recognition. Equally, some appreciation of the nature of the *other*, in this case the Indian state, too is essential. For, the choice of means, techniques, strategies and tactics as well as the selection of targets is determined not only by the ideology of the primary actors but also by the nature and character of the perceived enemy, his conceptual framework as well as the socio-cultural milieu in which violence is executed[2].

As a religious faith, Sikhism originated in a deeply turbulent and chaotic age. Attempting to formulate a radically different religious doctrine in a society torn between an overly defensive and ritualistic Brahmanism and an aggressive state-sponsored, proselytizing Islam, the new religion, called Sikhism, carried a spontaneous appeal to a confused and disconsolate people. The founder of the creed, Guru Nanak, born in the late fifteenth century in the Muslim-ruled Punjab, deeply troubled by the prevailing climate of oppression, injustice, inequality and disharmony, expounded a compassionate and tolerant monotheistic faith, bearing some similarities to the (Hindu) Bhakti and (Islamic) Sufi movements, though from its very inception, it clearly was a separate, self-contained and distinct set of beliefs.

The new religion, with its message of universal brotherhood and down-to-earth tenets, found an instant appeal among many segments of a socially and religiously divided populace and would soon draw adherents from all over India, Hindus and Muslims alike. For, its three basic precepts of *nam japo*, *kirt karo* and *wand chhako* (meditation on God's name, honest labour and sharing the fruits of such labour with other fellow beings) carried a firm ring of sincerity and honesty that most intricate Hindu creeds lacked.

The new faith also attracted the wrath of the ruling classes, both in Punjab and in Delhi, who saw in the incipient Sikhism a powerful threat to their dominance. In the course of the next two centuries, while Nanak's mission was carried further by his nine successors, brutal repression let loose upon the new converts would mount sharply with each change of regime and by successive raiders from beyond the country's north-western borders. Two of the ten Sikh Gurus were tortured to death for refusing to convert to Islam under threat of execution. In the process, the essentially pacifist and catholic faith propagated by Nanak also underwent a radical transformation to assume militant, defiant and excessively self-assertive traits, first under the sixth Guru, Hargobind, and then during the far more troubled times that confronted the tenth Guru, Gobind Singh, who was required to build up an equally effective response to the escalating levels of oppression and religious bigotry on the part of the ruling establishment. This development was to play an important role in the 18th and 19th centuries in re-drawing of religious and political boundaries in north-western India.

Guru Gobind Singh, a notable warrior-statesman of his times, who lost his entire family in his many battles against an oppressive state, infused a dynamic new spirit of militancy and audacious courage among the Sikhs by creating, in 1699, a select order of the Khalsa (the pure) brotherhood. His lifelong fight against tyranny and injustice would predictably invest his teachings with deeply political overtones. This Guru was also a prolific writer and a poet of considerable merit, who used Persian, Sanskrit and the contemporary idioms of Hindi and Punjabi to give expression to the lofty idealism that suffused most of his religious and political philosophy. The bulk of his work was in heroic verse, in keeping with the underlying philosophy and ideology that he propagated. Although the essential unity and integrity of the basic tenets of Sikhism remained intact throughout the period of its evolution from the first to the tenth Guru, the very nature of challenges faced by the community during the period did nevertheless impart a new spirit of defiance that came to distinguish the Khalsa Sikhs from the early followers of Sikhism as preached by Nanak.

The *Dasam Granth*, a compilation of Guru Gobind Singh's major works, broadly encapsulates his vision of the political struggles that the community must wage to secure a place of honour in the polity. From Nanak's simple and pacifist faith to a set of radical and protestant, even militant, beliefs, as expounded by the tenth Guru, the new religion had, indeed, traversed a vast sacred space. Thus, the appeal and attraction that the new faith acquired for a varied constituency, in an era of religious intolerance and persecution, was not unexpected. Ironically, it was these self-same newly acquired traits of indomitable courage, assertive self-confidence and determined opposition to an unjust polity, which would expose the community to a long period of maltreatment and oppression.

For much of the eighteenth century, the Khalsa Sikhs were subjected to organized and repeated pogroms by state functionaries. Their villages were torched, rewards were set on their heads and their means of livelihood systematically destroyed. Most Muslim rulers, often actively supported by their Hindu officials, regularly wreaked atrocities on them in deliberate attempts at what would these days be known as ethnic cleansing. Two such massacres find prominent mention in Sikh history under the name of *ghallugharas*, one in May 1746 when Nawab Yahya Khan slaughtered over 10,000 Sikhs and the second and considerably more lethal one at the hands of the Afghan raider Ahmed Shah Abdali in 1762, also referred to as the *wada ghallughara* or the great massacre. This high-spirited community, however, not only survived, it even managed to bring large areas in central Punjab under its occupation, and finally to consolidate these small principalities, towards the end of the 18th century, to form the huge Sikh kingdom of Ranjit Singh over north-west India and present-day Afghanistan.

The Sikh killings of June and December 1984, during Operation Blue Star and later as a sequel to Mrs. Gandhi's assassination in Delhi, are sometimes referred to as the third *ghallughara*, though somewhat self-consciously. Many Sikh organizations, including some political parties, do observe the anniversary of Operation Blue Star in the first week of June every year as the *ghallughara* week.

*

It was these traits of unyielding resistance and enduring courage in the face of unrelenting persecution during the early stages of its evolution as a distinct religious community that were largely responsible for shaping typical Sikh attitudes to life and adversity. Several extraordinary qualities marked the Khalsa personality, among them a sense of unshakable self-assurance, persistent and defiant courage and a kind of tough sullenness in confronting injustice and cruelty—qualities mainly acquired in decades of living virtually on the brink of death. Their supremacy in Punjab for several decades in the 18th and 19th centuries, despite their small population, also bred in them the highly assertive traits of audaciousness, supreme self-esteem and a firm belief in their destiny as a people born to rule.

The British Indian government, appreciative as it was of the strong support it received from the Sikhs during the events of 1857, proceeded to deftly draw on the many socio-political developments in the post-1857 period to win the support and allegiance of the community in governing this vast land. For one, it successfully worked on the Sikh psyche to cultivate in them a feeling that they were a group of chosen people with intrinsic claims on special rights and privileges, regardless of their small numbers. Major A.E. Bastow of the Sikh regiment, the author of an official handbook for the Indian army published in 1899, dwells on the subject in some detail.

As he puts it, 'The reorganization of the Bengal army, which followed the Mutiny, led to a complete change in its class constitution. The Hindustanis of the Regiment, which had either revolted or been disbanded were replaced by the Sikhs, Dogras, Punjabis and Pathans, of the levies raised by Lord Lawrence and the history of India since that time bears ample testimony to the military qualities of these races...The soldierly qualities of the Sikhs have been fittingly recognized in the extent to which they have been employed in the Indian army, in which on the outbreak of the {First World} War, they numbered 33,000 out of 174,000, or somewhat less than 1/5th of the total strength'. Further that 'the Sikhs in the Indian army have been studiously *notionalized* or encouraged to regard themselves as a totally distinct or separate nation...The good services of the Army in buttressing the crumbling edifice of Sikh religion has been acknowledged by orthodox Sikhs'.[3]

The reference in the last sentence is to the very strict instructions to Sikh soldiers to rigorously abide with religious injunctions in the matter of keeping their hair unshorn. In a way, the departure of the British from the Indian subcontinent and several other post-independence political developments, to be gone into later in this chapter, brought the Sikh community face to face with the bitter reality of demographic compulsions in the new polity for the first time in their short history. Such a realization would soon induce in them a rather unsettling frame of mind as they had now to learn to survive in a political system where numbers were all-important.

A minuscule religious minority had, therefore, to cast its net wide to come up with alternative strategies to face the new predicament, arising out of a radically changed situation. One option that readily came in handy, which also conformed to the modern idiom of a multi-cultural and multi-religious India, was the renewed and more focused assertion of a separate identity, which had been a subject of ardent debate within the community right since the eighteenth century, but more intensely after the advent of the Arya Samaj in the late nineteenth century.

*

Appropriate management of minority aspirations and distinctive identity are critical to peace and order and good governance in a multicultural society like India's. It is even more so in the case of the Sikhs because of the special position they thought they had been accorded in the Punjab by the British. A perceived threat to their distinct identity in the new Indian polity would breed a deep sense of disenchantment with the Congress party, which would henceforth shape all Sikh political strategies. Further, the identity question, being principally rooted in a grave existential dilemma, acquired a special place in all Sikh political transactions. It will, therefore, help greatly in understanding the nature and extent of Sikh militancy; if we start with a historical retrospect to define the process of construction of a distinct Sikh identity and the characteristic Sikh psyche.

In their zeal to glorify Sanskrit, the language of the ancient Indian classics and sacred texts, the Arya Samaj started treating the local language, Punjabi, with the disdain usually reserved for a vernacular dialect, and sought to distance the Hindus from their mother tongue and, as a corollary, also from their cultural roots. To counter the Arya Samaj arguments belittling Sikhism, their Gurus and the Punjabi language, which also happened to be the language of their holy books, the Sikh leadership started the Singh Sabha movement, which soon came to gather substantial support in the community. Apart from its purely religious concerns, the new movement was also closely committed to propagate the characteristic Sikh values and way of life, through works of literature and other means. This objective was well accomplished by the appearance on the literary scene of several committed writers, of which the most prominent was Bhai Vir Singh.

A sizeable volume of fiction, prose and poetry produced by these writers sought to invest their Sikh characters, both men and women, with extraordinarily heroic traits. Brought up on such literary fare and exposed to a sweeping religious revitalization, the younger Sikhs soon became even more intensely conscious of an identity, essentially separate and distinct from that of the Hindus, a development that would materially alter the Hindu-Sikh equation for all time to come.

However, the identity question was by no means a purely nineteenth century phenomenon, though it did assume a special stridency following the widening of the Arya Samaj support base in the Punjab. There is a long historiography tradition in which the Sikhs figure as a distinct community, different from Hindus and Muslims, as representing the third *panth* (religio-political community) and eighteenth century Sikh literature also fully supports that premise. But the matter really started occupying centrestage in the nineteenth and early twentieth centuries. A fierce debate was generated by two books published in early 20th century. The first book with the overtly provocative title *Sikh Hindu Hain* (The Sikhs are Hindu) was an obvious corollary and affirmation of the Arya Samaj claim that the Sikhs were but an offshoot of the Hindus and, thus, had no claim to being a distinct community. The other book, called *Ham Hindu Nahin* (We are Not Hindu) by a Sikh scholar, Kahn Singh Nabha, was in the nature of a rejoinder to the former on behalf of the Sikhs, which, incidentally, remains a classic statement of a separate Sikh identity. Originally written in Hindi, this book was clearly meant to primarily address a Hindu audience. In support of his thesis, the writer marshals extensive arguments, which are comprehensive in scope, relating as they do to scriptures, religious doctrines, the modes of worship, the code of conduct, the rites of initiation and passage, the character of the Sikh *panth* and the consciousness of separate identity, which he claims pre-dates the Khalsa era, as having emerged in the sixteenth and seventeenth centuries.

The raging debate on the Hindu-Sikh question during

the gurudwara reform movement of the 1920s and the course of Sikh political discourse in subsequent decades also substantially validated Nabha's projections on the identity issue. Although, Nabha viewed the Sikh identity as inclusive of *sahajdhari* Sikhs (who do not wear their hair unshorn), later social and political dynamics would play an important role in making the Khalsa identity as the dominant Sikh identity in the nineteenth century.[4] The colonial rulers quickly recognized this fact and shrewdly proceeded to exploit it for their imperial advantage. Such a course of development must have given rise to the notion of a close symbiotic relationship between the Sikhs and the British rulers, smugly claimed by sections of Sikh aristocracy.

Clearly, the identity issue had become a crucial factor in all political developments in Punjab, culminating in Indian independence and, in a more traumatic sense, the partition of the province. While analyzing the events of the decade of militancy and violence in Punjab, it is important not to lose sight of the Sikh sensitivities in this regard. It is in this context that the phenomenal upsurge of Bhindranwale's popularity among the Sikh masses, especially in the countryside, needs to be viewed. Significantly, the impact of his arguments with respect to the primacy of identity and the threats faced by the community in that respect would not remain confined to the masses—it also left a deep impression on sections of the Sikh intelligentsia.

Quite clearly, post-independence Sikh political strategies have been substantially influenced by the need to keep the issue of a distinct identity in the forefront, in order to achieve political power in the new democratic dispensation. Identity questions would become even more central to governance in later years, when rightist Hindu parties would acquire political supremacy at the Centre and in several states and would set about systematically imposing their patently homogenizing policies in a bid to bring the many minority populations, religious and otherwise, into what they termed the national mainstream, a process that would cause a great deal of alarm in many parts of the country, especially its peripheral regions. Such homogenizing policies would, however, be pursued as ardently by the Congress as the BJP, except while the latter did it in the name of Hindu rashtra, the former employed the secular idiom of national unity and solidarity.

As the Indian freedom movement gathered momentum in the second and third decades of the nineteenth century, it became vital for the Sikhs to be accepted as a political—not merely a religious—community. In the intensely overcharged political climate of the times, no significant minority was prepared to be taken for granted. Communitarian nationalism became the preferred mode of political discourse in the newly emerging Akali-Sikh leadership. In other words, the latter would considerably radicalize the process of identity-articulation, earlier taken up by the Singh Sabha movement and the other politico-religious formations like the Central Sikh League and the Chief Khalsa Diwan. Such a tactical stance found frequent expression in political perceptions and their articulation in the 1930s and 1940s during a period of heightened political activity in the subcontinent. The Sikhs were prepared to struggle for independence along with other Indians, Hindu or Muslim, but not as an appendage of another *qaum*, a relationship perceived by them as politically disadvantageous.

The term *qaum*, loosely translated as a nation or nationality, has been the cause of much misunderstanding as to the political objectives of the Akali party, but even more importantly of the various militant movements. The identity question, which had traumatized the community during most of its existence, became more intense as the country raced towards independence and partition in the 1940s. The Sikh leadership was now faced with a very difficult choice indeed as to its future course of action, and the hectic pace of events made it important that the choice be made perceptively, prudently and speedily. The predicament faced by the community at this juncture needed to be resolved soon to forestall the highly baneful consequences of a probable submergence in a Hinduized India or a sure annihilation in an Islamic Pakistan.

*

It was these assumptions and concerns, emanating from threats to religious identity, which first precipitated the process of transformation of a religious into a political community, a process which came into full play as the spectre of a sovereign Pakistan loomed large during the closing years of World War II. It may be noted, however, that the Congress party never accepted this proposition and continued to treat the Sikhs as a religious, not a political, community. A lavishly-illustrated booklet published by the Union government titled *The Sikhs in their Homeland India* shortly after Operation Blue Star asserted this in so many words. The Punjab, annexed by the British colonial power in 1849, remained unique as the only region in South Asia where three major religious communities—Muslims, Hindus and Sikhs—went through a process of simultaneous mass politicization and communitarian solidification in the ninety years of British rule.

In the wake of movements for socio-religious reform

and with religion determining the apportionment of political privileges between different communities on the basis of census figures, an intense competition between Hindus and Sikhs to expand their recorded populations had commenced in right earnest by the beginning of the 20th century. This would lead to redefinitions and magnification of communities and sharpening of mutual suspicions. Even language was communalized; Hindus declaring Hindi and Muslims Urdu as their respective mother tongues, leaving the universally spoken Punjabi to be owned only by the Sikhs. This would become a major divisive issue between Hindus and Sikhs in post-partition Indian Punjab, and lead to a further bifurcation of that state with many deeply unsettling consequences, as we shall see later. A deliberate disowning of the linguistic link with fellow Punjabis by the Hindus would also cause a degree of cultural estrangement and a drift away from a shared heritage of Punjabiat or a collective Punjabi cultural tradition.

Right after the gurudwara movement, Sikh political parties had taken to using religious identity, reinforced by the linguistic factor, as an ideological-political medium to formulate their political strategies, a process that would become even more pervasive in the 1930s and 1940s, when all segments of the Sikh community, except the communists and leftist intelligentsia, felt greatly exercised over the Muslim League's Lahore resolution of 1940, vaguely worded as it was, demanding some kind of sovereign autonomy, bordering on virtual separation of Muslim majority provinces from the rest of India. Sikh apprehensions were further heightened by its endorsement by the Congress, implicit in the so-called CR Formula.[5]

The communal award of 1932 and the scheme of provincial autonomy four years later, as provided for in the Government of India Act, 1935, as its full political

implications unfolded, when Indian ministers assumed
office in 1937, had also considerably upset the Sikhs.
Since they then formed no more than 13 per cent of
Punjab's population as against 55 per cent Muslims and
32 per cent Hindus (Census 1941), they could hardly
make population figures a basis for claiming a share in
any post-independence political settlement. They feared
that in the proposed Pakistan their distinct religious identity
and culture would be smothered, their economic status
endangered and their political ambitions repressed. Their
opposition to the Pakistan idea was total, based as it was
on their experience of unrelenting persecution under the
Mughal rulers, except during Akbar's reign. This was now
vehemently articulated by them from all available
platforms. Sikhs of all political shades and opinion shared
the community's misgivings, as the fateful 1940s journeyed
towards independence and partition. The most vocal and
consistent protests emanated from the Akali Dal, the
oldest religio-political organization of the Sikhs. By 1945,
it had established itself as the sole political party
representing the community. Interestingly, the Communist
Party of India supported both the concept of a Sikh
homeland as well as the demand for Pakistan, while
upholding the right of self-determination of the various
nationalities inhabiting the Indian subcontinent, under
what came to be known as the Adhikari thesis.

*

Lacking the requisite demographic clout, the Sikhs sought
to base their claims to a share of political power in post-
partition India on several other factors. They formed
almost 23 per cent of the British Indian army though they
were less than 2 per cent of the Indian population,

contributed 40 per cent to the provincial exchequer in the Punjab in land revenue and irrigation tax. They had the highest rate of literacy and managed 400 self-financed educational institutions. Almost 80 per cent of Indians who took part in the freedom struggle and ended up in British jails or on the gallows were Sikh. It was invidious and improper, therefore, according to this line of reasoning, to reckon the intrinsic importance of the community in accordance with the fallacious western notions of democracy, viewing people merely in terms of majorities and minorities. So went the drift of their arguments for a greater share in any post-independence dispensation. For, their major concern in the early 1940s was basically to ensure an honourable status for themselves within a united India, free from communal domination in their sacred homeland of the Punjab. The Akali Dal, in fact, went out of its way to stress that the Sikhs did not want Khalistan or Sikh Raj but visualized a joint political future for the three religious communities in the Punjab, but under a federal set-up. Until 1944, Sikh leadership saw no problem living honourably in a free and united India, which provided equal and fair opportunities to all citizens, irrespective of their minority or majority status. They considered freedom from communal domination in a multi-religious and multicultural society like India's of prime importance.[6]

Such an approach, however, did not seem adequate after 1944, when the partition of India appeared to have become a distinct possibility. In that year, the all-party Sikh conference asked for a status of equality with Hindu and Muslim nations. If Pakistan came into being, the Sikh *qaum* would necessarily have to demand an autonomous state of its own, though the precise character of such a state was left somewhat vague. Simultaneously, they also placed it on record that their first preference would still be to live as an integral part of a multi-national but united India, sharing political power with other *qaums*. This position became unsustainable after 1946, when the Muslim League secured 428 out of 492 Muslim seats in the provincial assemblies and all the Muslim seats in the Central assembly, on the slogan of Pakistan (*The Political History of Pakistan* by Zahid Choudhary in Urdu, Nigarshat Publishers, Temple Road, Lahore).

In the Punjab, although the League had won nearly all the Muslim seats, it was denied the opportunity to form a ministry, despite being the single largest party. On the other hand, after a brief spell of Governor's rule, a coalition government, comprising of Unionist party, the Akalis and the Congress, was sworn in. Incensed at this turn of events, the Muslim League launched a massive agitation in favour of partition, incidentally the first mass movement by the party in Punjab. This agitation carried special import because it successfully rallied the bulk of Punjabi Muslims behind the concept of Pakistan, an ideology which had never secured a popular mandate until then. This was even more significant because ranged against the Muslim League were not only the Unionists and the Congress but also a number of Islamic outfits, as for instance the rabidly religious Majlis-e-Ahrar and the Deobandi conservative Jamiat-ul-Ulma-e-Hind. The League agitation, however, did succeed in galvanizing a large majority of Punjabi Muslims in favour of Pakistan, though it would later be hijacked by unscrupulous elements and degenerate into partition riots and internecine violence.

Now that the creation of Pakistan looked imminent, another change of stance by the Akalis became necessary. In their representations to the British cabinet mission, then visiting India to find a broadly acceptable formula to reconcile the increasingly conflicting demands being made by Indian political parties (April-May 1946), the Sikh leadership claimed that the Sikhs had all through history been a separate nation with a distinct culture, identity, world-view and political objectives. The Khalsa of Guru Gobind Singh, formed to fight the Mughals and other dominant powers of the time, was essentially a political concept, a fusion of his followers into a nation based on religion and ideology. Right from the time of the sixth Guru, Hargobind, the community had fought for temporal—and hence political—causes in addition to purely religious ones, and had acted as an organized political entity in much of geographical Punjab. The gurudwaras were centres of Sikh national life and the holy Akal Takht at Amritsar, the seat of the Sikh national will and power. Sikh nationhood was further strengthened by a shared historical experience and common language, literature, locale and customs (almost all of them, in fact, were shared by all Punjabis, including Hindus and Muslims; claimed differences were obviously being advanced merely for political gain). They could thus no longer accept the concept of an overarching Indian nation, promoted by the Congress in which Hindus, Muslims, Sikhs and others were required to merge their separate identities, relegating a sovereign, conquering and dominating people like the Sikhs to an inconsequential minority. The Sikhs could not live and grow as a nation in accordance with their historical and political ideals as weaker partners under a Muslim or Hindu majority state.[7] It needs to be mentioned at this stage that an acute sense of anxiety with regard to what were called special Sikh interests pervaded all Sikh movements and to safeguard them, by whatever means, remained the principal concern of all Sikh organizations, whether religious or political, before or after partition.

*

The Sikhs were unhappy with the Congress party too for its disregard of their interests as a distinct religious community in the Lucknow Pact (1916), Motilal Nehru report (1928) and the communal award (1932), though it was still seen as the trustee of national honour and self-respect. By 1946, relations between the Congress and the Akalis had deteriorated to such an extent that the party was now clearly seen as the Hindu Congress, totally unmindful of the interests of Sikhs in soon-to-be-partitioned India, a stance similar to the Muslim League's. Nehru, who had acquired some proximity to the Sikh leadership during the gurudwara reform movement in the early 1920s, seemed to have promised a special status to the Sikhs in a free India. He came close to defining such a special status at least twice, once in a statement at a Congress convention in Bombay on 7 July 1946, reported by the *Statesman*: 'I see nothing wrong in an area and a set-up in the north where the Sikhs can also experience the glow of freedom', and again in a speech at the annual Congress session at Calcutta in December 1946, in which he visualized 'a special set-up in the north-west of India where the Sikhs are also able to enjoy the glow of freedom'.

As later events would show, these statements could only have been designed to pre-empt any deal between the Sikhs and the Muslim League to prevent the partition of Punjab, which looked imminent at the time. It seems that a group of Punjab civilians, known as the 'friends of Punjab', Pendral Moon and Major Short among them, busily sought to find a way to prevent the impending break-up of the province by interceding with the Akalis and the Muslim League leadership. Jinnah and Liaquat Ali Khan reportedly agreed to the formation of a Sikh homeland in Eastern Punjab as part of a federal Pakistan

and an option to secede after five or ten years, if they so
wanted.

When this did not find favour with Sikh leaders,
Pendral Moon and Mushtaq Ahmed Gurmani of the
Muslim League, then the prime minister of the Muslim
princely state of Bahawalpur, sent a fresh set of proposals
to the Sikhs on 29 June 1947, offering:

(1) A separate unit of Eastern Punjab with rights in
    the central government of Pakistan equal to any
    other unit such as Sind and West Punjab
(2) Special privileges for the Sikhs in West Punjab,
    and
(3) Special privileges for the Sikhs in Pakistan as a
    whole. Giani Kartar Singh, then a prominent Akali
    leader, was in favour of accepting the offer, but
    Tara Singh and others decided against it. Nehru
    would never forgive the Giani for that indiscretion.

Another attempt was made to soften the Sikh leadership
on the idea of giving up their demand for Punjab's
partition by a prominent Punjabi leader, Sir Feroz Khan
Noon, but the long historical experience of the community
made a credible Sikh-Muslim relationship of the type
being projected by the Muslim League all but inconceivable.
That the Sikhs did implicitly believe in the legitimacy of
their claim to a special status in independent India,
howsoever repugnant to the spirit of democracy it would
appear to others, is clear from the refusal of the two Sikh
members of India's constituent assembly to affix their
signatures to the final document, stating, 'The Sikhs do
not accept this Constitution. The Sikhs reject the
Constitution Act', a gesture which in a way disassociated
the community from the future constitution of the country.

*

Through the 1940s, the primary concern of the Sikhs, as articulated by the Akali Dal, was to ensure that they would not become subject to Muslim dominance in the Punjab. To achieve this objective and to prevent the whole province becoming part of Pakistan, they employed different strategies from time to time. The underlying aim of all their various demands, including the unrealistically-worded concept of Azad Punjab, was to save the region between rivers Yamuna and Chenab, their cherished homeland and holy land, from becoming part of Muslim-ruled Pakistan. What they tried to secure then was not a Sikh majority state, which was then a demographic impossibility, but an area in which no single community was in a position to dominate and in which Sikh political, economic and cultural interests could be safeguarded. By the end of 1945, it had become clear that Indian independence would inevitably be accompanied by the partition of the subcontinent. This realization made the Sikh community in the Punjab extremely restive and alarmed at the prospect of having to live as future citizens of the Muslim state of Pakistan. This was not unexpected, founded as it was on their historical experience of oppression under most Muslim rulers in Punjab.

The end of World War II in 1945 vastly quickened the pace of events, which forced the Congress and the Sikh leadership to seriously explore possible options to save at least some part of the Punjab from being included in Pakistan. This led to the demand for the division of the Punjab along sectarian lines. Significantly, the demand for a 'Sikh state' never became a mass-goal until much later, and that too in a somewhat vague manner. Most of the time, it was probably used as a bargaining counter in political parleys and was thus qualitatively different from the demand for Khalistan raised by a few individuals, mostly living abroad, at a later stage.[8] The division of Punjab thus became a joint Akali-Congress demand as independence and partition became imminent. Even a casual analysis of the dilemmas faced by the Sikh leadership in their efforts to safeguard Sikh interests at critical junctures would be enough to recognize the limited options available to them in this regard. Strangely, the key elements that shaped their policy initiatives to address the principal concerns, demands and grievances of the community in colonial times remain unchanged even after independence. A careful reading of the Anandpur Sahib resolution of 1973 and its further amplification in 1978 would spell out the Sikh perspective in the matter.

*

The Shiromani Akali Dal (*dal in* Punjabi means organization), was set up in 1920 to lead the agitation for wresting control of the Sikh gurudwaras from hereditary *mahants* (priests) in a prolonged but non-violent struggle. Hailed as a major non-violent mass movement in British India, the Gurudwara movement clearly demonstrated the moral supremacy of passive resistance over brutal state repression. The Akalis could, thus, be regarded among the pioneers of the satyagraha mode of India's freedom struggle. Right since its birth, the Akali party remained the principal Sikh political voice, both before and after independence, though some other Sikh groups too were in the field for the same purpose. The Akali agenda, covering the protection of not only the religious integrity of the community but also its social, economic, cultural and political interests, too remained unchanged. By its pre-independence stance of resolute opposition to the concept of Pakistan as originally conceived, the Akalis had helped bring about the partition of Punjab, along with the Congress. They also probably engineered the transfer of populations with not a little help from the Sikh princely states, to improve the percentage of Sikh population in East Punjab, so as to improve their chances to secure political power.

Independence and partition had altered the political configuration in the Punjab in many significant aspects. For one, British colonial power and the Muslims ceased to be important factors in Punjab politics. The transfer of populations had raised the proportion of Sikhs to Hindus in Punjab, roughly to the same level as that of Hindus to Muslims in pre-independence Punjab. Certain contiguous areas had also acquired a Sikh majority character so as to enable them to be considered as Sikh areas. With Urdu no longer a competitor, Punjabi could now form the basis for the establishment of a Punjabi-speaking state or Punjabi *suba*, as the Akalis fondly christened it.

However, the bitterness and acrimony that marked the creation of the Punjabi *suba* left a lasting legacy of suspicion and distrust between the Sikhs and the Congress party, which would generate strong new pressures in the community to look for different political strategies to achieve their goals, in a way forcing them to consider many hitherto untried modes of political mobilization, though militancy and violence did not then seem to feature among them. It was Bhindranwale who opted for extremist violence as an instrument of demand fulfillment. However, though he frequently spoke about the freedom of the Sikhs, whether he genuinely believed in Khalistan or a separate and sovereign Sikh state remains unclear. The closest he ever came to talking about it publicly was when he declared, 'We are not in favour of Khalistan nor are we against it. We wish to live in India but would settle for a separate state if the Sikhs did not receive what he regarded as their just respect'.[10]

He is also reported to have made another significant remark that the day Indian army enters the Golden Temple complex, the foundations of Khalistan would be laid. Perhaps, Operation Blue Star was just such an event that would precipitate much of the post-1986 militant activity, as it turned out later.

*

As we have seen, the political and electoral policies pursued by the Congress party in the Punjab, especially during the years following the trifurcation of the state in 1966, turned out to be a major factor in setting the course of Sikh militancy in India. For one, the denial of a Punjabi-speaking state when all the major Indian languages had been so accommodated and the Sikhs had to struggle for ten long years to secure such a state, would deeply colour their perceptions of mainstream political parties. It was not as if Punjabi was a minor language or that it was not extensively spoken in the region. Only, Punjabi Hindus had by and large chosen to disown it as their mother tongue for various political and sectarian reasons until after the formation of the Punjabi *suba* (state) in 1966, as is evident from a comparative study of census data from 1941 onwards. In the 1991 Census, for example, 81 per cent of Punjab's population declared Punjabi as their mother tongue.

The alienation of the Sikh community dating back from the country's partition itself was further reinforced by the manipulative manner in which the state was partitioned between Punjab, Haryana and Himachal Pradesh, leaving several Punjabi-speaking areas in the latter two states. This happened because Punjabi Hindus in several areas of the state that were now excluded from the new Punjab had claimed Hindi as their mother tongue.

Much later, most Hindu leaders and the leading Hindu party, the Bharatiya Janata Party, would realize the folly of their refusal to declare Punjabi as their mother tongue. For otherwise, no Punjabi-speaking state could have had a Sikh majority. This was ruefully admitted by a senior BJP leader of Amritsar in a meeting with me some time in April 1985, when I had to fly to Amritsar in a special aircraft to look up R.L. Bhatia, a senior Congress leader of Amritsar, who had been seriously injured in a militant attack. Bhatia survived the attack and went on to become a minister in the Union government soon afterwards, and the Governor of Kerala two decades later. The importance of Bhatia to the Congress party at that particular juncture, however, lay in his alleged proximity to Bhindranwale as it was through him, among others, that the top Congress leadership kept in touch with the Sikh extremists right until the end.

*

We must at this stage examine the grievances of the Sikh people. It is not easy for members of a majority community to understand, much less empathize with, the insecurities that often trouble minority segments in a country as vast and as diverse as India. It is particularly difficult for the Hindus, who constitute a brute majority of over 83 per cent of the country's population (Census 2001). Since the Sikhs had always been viewed in the rest of the country as an affluent and cheerful people, who had generally been doing rather well for themselves, it was considered inconceivable that they could have had any grievances.

That a community could be comparatively well off in economic terms and still remain discontented to the extent of bearing arms against the state needed a lot of explaining to a puzzled society.

Their minuscule percentage in the total Indian population in independent India made the Sikhs inconsequential in the overall political power structure of the country. As one of the many minority sections in a vast and heterogeneous land, they had to make do with whatever came their way in the democratic polity of the country, dominated by the majority Hindus. The huge loss of lives and prosperous estates suffered by the Sikhs in the partition-related genocidal rioting, before and after Indian independence, was an enormous jolt to their proverbial aplomb and self-esteem. Since the Congress was the principal political party in the forefront of the Indian freedom struggle, the community held the Congress leadership primarily responsible for its travails and tribulations, thus severely undermining their faith in the foremost party of governance in independent India. What made the collective sense of hurt even more painful was that it was the same Congress party, which had inherited the post-colonial Indian state, with all its grandiose paraphernalia of pomp and show and the instruments of power, from the departing British. This would induce a highly unsettling mental and emotional framework of attitudes, stemming from religious insecurity, political marginalization and economic discrimination, in the small but assertive Sikh minority. Such worries and concerns were further compounded by several other factors such as a progressive rise in educated unemployment, fragmentation of holdings, diminishing returns from the green revolution, curtailed recruitment quotas in the defence forces, now linked with population percentages and shrinking opportunities of emigration to foreign lands for various reasons.

The net effect of such a collective sense of resentment and restiveness in the community would soon lead to a radical shift in the balance of power between the moderate elements in Sikh politics and the hardliners. However, so long as the Akali party retained its political supremacy in the Sikh community, it did not allow any movement for redress of grievances to turn violent. The militant and terrorist movements that overwhelmed the state, as indeed major parts of north India, could take root only after the Akali party, the long-time political voice of the community, was itself enfeebled, through some ill-conceived political skullduggery by a few top-level Congress leaders, now a well-established fact of recent Indian history. However, regardless of its root causes, sustainable militant violence must also possess a logic of its own, even though such reasoning may sound somewhat far-fetched to others. So what was this logic? We will attempt to find out presently.

*

While the Indian media and intelligentsia strove laboriously to discuss the probable roots of Sikh militancy, periodic debates in Britain's Parliament focused on what some members thought were the chief causes of the alienation of the Sikh community after independence. Terry Dicks, a conservative MP from Hayes and Harlington, was one of the more vociferous British MPs cutting across party lines, who took up the so-called Sikh cause in right earnest. While speaking on the subject in a debate on 29 November 1991 in the House of Commons, he made significant references to the moral responsibility of the British government to intervene in the ongoing state repression in the Punjab. According to him, 'In 1947, when India obtained its independence, it was the British who accepted a guarantee by the Hindus, who made 84 per cent of the population, that the self-determination of the Sikhs in the Punjab would be recognized. On that basis, the British government granted India its independence. Unfortunately for the Sikhs, the British government has done nothing to enforce the guarantee and successive Congress party dominated governments have been able to ignore the pledge...The failure of the Indian government, aided and abetted by Britain, to keep their word has led the Sikh people to call for their own independent state.'[10]

The British government, however, maintained a meticulously correct political and diplomatic stand on the issue, somewhat supportive of the Indian state. This was only natural and in conformity with the rules and conventions of international conduct, invariably dictated by mutual give and take.

*

History bears out that all the protests and agitations led by the Akalis in pursuit of their objectives were always peaceful and non-violent. How, then, did large sections of the community accept and approve, at least for some time, the assumption of militancy and terrorism as a mode of political mobilization, and the Akali leadership turn into a mute, or more likely impotent, witness to the occurrence? Surprisingly, the many factors that led to the conversion of an essentially peaceable and non-violent mode of demand-articulation into a wide-ranging orgy of militant violence did not immediately attract the attention of many scholars and social scientists. Most contemporary writings turned out to be first-off-the-block kind that failed to present a reasoned analysis of the phenomenon. A few that brought a historical perspective to bear on their analysis came later.

Two writers, both foreigners, however, appeared to break fresh ground in their appraisal of the Sikh militant movement, its ideological underpinnings and the broad framework of Bhindranwale's arguments, and sought to look at the unfolding chronicle of Sikh militancy in some depth. Both deserve to be mentioned here. One was Mark Juergensmeyer (1988), who tried to explore the logic of religious violence in the Punjab through an analysis of the recorded speeches of Sant Bhindranwale, the acknowledged source of inspiration for all the earlier militant groups. Juergensmeyer was primarily concerned with the linkages between religion and violence, which to his mind were central to militant violence in the Punjab until then. He found a definite relationship between the two variables. 'Since religious language is about the tension between order and disorder, it is frequently about violence'.[11] Disorder is thus inherently violent. He suggests, 'By identifying a temporal social struggle with the cosmic struggle of order and disorder, truth and evil, political actors are able to avail themselves of a way of thinking that justifies the use of violent means.'[12]

The other writer was Joyce Pettigrew (1995), who undertook an elaborate analysis of the militant violence in the state with the help of interviews she conducted with eleven young members of one of the more prominent groups, the Khalistan commando force (Zaffarwal), whom she called the children of Waheguru.

Inarguably, the idiom of Bhindranwale and the mainsprings of what he advocated were firmly rooted in the Punjab soil and Sikh history, but his formulations were hardly dissimilar to those of other clerics elsewhere.

'Much of what Bhindranwale has to say in sermons of this period, however, might be heard in the homilies of clergies belonging to any religious tradition anywhere on the globe. He calls for faith—faith in time of trial—and for the spiritual discipline that accompanies it',[13] notes Juergensmeyer. Pettigrew, however, postulates that, 'In the democratic societies of the West, these values would not be termed religious but would rather be described as civil libertarian and socialist. His (Bhindrawale's) primary objective was to undercut the spread of consumerism in family life.'[14] That is why the earliest converts to his preaching were the Jutt women in the villages, who had for long experienced suffering and oppression at the hands of their drunkard menfolk. She thought that the blame for the rise and rapid expansion of militancy in the Punjab rested squarely on the Indian state for pursuing manipulative and iniquitous strategies leading to state terror in addressing the grievances and demands of the Sikhs in post-independence India.

Evidently, Sikh militancy in its early phases was inspired by Bhindranwale and his views, often expressed in picturesque, if somewhat crude, Punjabi. Most secular historians tend to overlook the vigour of the militant streak that sets apart Sikhism from all other Indian religions. For one, there is no place in it for ahimsa: the use of force for a righteous cause is fully accepted and has the Guru's absolute approval. It is no accident that of the ten gurus, five kept armies, organized militarization and confrontation with an oppressive regime. The wearing of *kirpan* is meant to be a constant reminder against reversion to pacifism and monasticism and ignoring social responsibility towards fellow beings. The concept of the *sant-sipahi* or saint-soldier, for instance, is unique in this religion as enjoying the utmost esteem in the community.

'Ideologically, the *sant-sipahi* or whole-life concept is based on the view that cultures that fail to provide for moral moorings, which can be applied by religion, so as to enable the society to meet the challenges of destructive and aggressive forces of life, inevitably decay into dichotomy, involving monasticism, *sanyasa* and other-worldliness as the path of salvation and unbridled greed and injustice in the empirical life".[15]

It is in this context that one has to view the reverence that Bhindranwale came to enjoy after his death in Operation Blue Star. He was obviously being equated with a *sant-sipahi* in the collective consciousness of the community. Vinod Sharma, a senior journalist, reported how an old man, on seeing the sacred Akal Takht completely destroyed during Operation Blue Star told his grandson: 'That is where the Sikh *mahapurukh*, Sant Bhindranwale*ji* Maharaj, laid down his life in defence of the *Panth*. *Puttar*, we have to avenge the insult' (*Hindustan Times*, Delhi, 14 August 2005). Axiomatically, Sikhism does not distinguish between religion and politics and has, in consequence, been the target of much misconceived disparagement over the years.

The Indian state, on the other hand, viewed the developments taking place in Punjab as the 1980s decade unfolded in a very different light. While at one level, it looked at the events as purely negative and separatist, even secessionist, and attributed the spread of militant thinking on the part of sections of Sikh youth to misplaced zeal and malevolent guidance by certain disgruntled Akali politicians, at another level, it considered the militants as criminal gangsters, instigated by Pakistan to subvert Indian national unity and integrity as part of a well thought-out plan to avenge its defeat in the 1971 war, culminating in the formation of Bangladesh. Such characterization was not only widely propagated through government and allied media, it also got fairly vividly reflected in the formulations and writings of some contemporary scholars. The acts of terrorism were described as isolated, individuated, self-centred and confined to a narrow fringe of the community, thus losing sight of the internal linkages and mechanics of the movement.

In consequence, the administration generally tended to ignore the obvious, and later well-substantiated, classical dynamics of the militant movement, whether proactive or reactive, which clearly constituted a definite and well-defined language of violence. The inability or unwillingness to comprehend and accept the innate linkages between the perceived grievances of the community and militant acts, and a failure to view the movement for what it was—as an integral whole at least until 1987—seriously confused the state response for its containment, except by frequently over-stepping the boundaries of law and legitimacy. Such controversial strategies would, in fact, unduly prolong the agony of the people and, in the end, leave several questions unanswered.

2

The Exposition

Looking back half a century, it is clear that of the three religious communities in Punjab that became hapless victims of partition-related turmoil and violence, it was the Sikhs who suffered the most, having been ousted for ever from their homes in the thriving canal colonies and commercial centres in west Punjab, now part of Pakistan, and leaving behind the bulk of their gurudwaras, now virtually inaccessible because of extreme antagonism between the two new countries. It would be decades before Sikhs could travel once again to Pakistan to visit their holy places and acquire some voice in their management.

For one, the Punjab was the only region where they formed a significant proportion of the population and which had been for them the embodiment of the vision of both a homeland and a holy land in their brief history. Naturally, therefore, their emotional attachment to the land of the five rivers as well as its language and culture was much deeper than that of the Hindus. Of course, the Punjabi Hindus too suffered gravely in the partition-related riots, arson and plunder and the agony of displacement was no less distressing for them, though in the matter of lives lost Sikhs suffered the most. As it happened, the majority of Sikh refugees, especially those from the agrarian sector, chose to relocate in the then east Punjab, although quite a few belonging to the trading classes proceeded further to Delhi and beyond in search of suitable openings in trade and industry. So while the Hindu migrants preferred to settle down primarily in Delhi and other industrial and commercial centres across the country, Sikh refugees generally opted for a new beginning in east Punjab itself.

Was the exercise of different options by the Hindus and Sikhs in this matter determined simply by pragmatism, or did it connote any deeper value judgment on the part of the Hindu refugees? Two assumptions come to mind in this regard. Did the preference of the Hindu migrants to seek re-settlement in states and cities with predominant Hindu majorities at this juncture imply that they wanted to pre-empt any more migrations in future, in case Hindu-Sikh relations deteriorated at some future date? Or were they merely looking at better opportunities in larger and more prosperous areas, not then available in small, undeveloped east Punjab? It is important not to dismiss such speculation as a mere afterthought. This writer knows quite a few Hindu migrant families who took a conscious decision not to set up house in east Punjab, though ample attractive options were on offer from many of their Sikh friends. For the deep-rooted, though so far mostly understated differences between the two communities on the question of Hindi and Punjabi, were undeniably becoming more volatile with each passing year.

In a different context, the fact that the bulk of Sikh trading classes chose to relocate in Delhi and some other big cities outside of Punjab, while those engaged in agricultural jobs settled in east Punjab would, at a later date, tend to divide the Sikh community itself into two fairly distinct blocs, the agricultural class of Jutt Sikhs holding a dominant position in Punjab and the non-Jutt trading classes or the Bhapa Sikhs in control of Sikh political and religious institutions outside Punjab, each with its respective priorities and agendas. This too was an important development inasmuch as the Akali-Sikh leadership would now increasingly pass into the hands of Jutts in the Punjab and Bhapas in Delhi and the rest of India, a process that would severely undermine the collective capacity of the community to safeguard Sikh interests in the overall Indian context.

The growing dissociation between the Jutt and non-Jutt Sikhs would become more discernible from 1960s onwards, when Sant Fateh Singh replaced Master Tara Singh as president of the Akali Dal, an event that also marked the final switch from urban to rural leadership in the community. Such a reapportionment of political primacy in the Sikh leadership would significantly determine the shape of all political struggles in the post-1966 Punjab, but especially influence the nature and course of Sikh militancy in the post-Bhindranwale phase. The non-Jutt elements were fairly active in the pre-Blue Star phase of the movement. But after the catastrophic events of 1984, almost the entire Sikh militant movement in the Punjab came to be dominated by the Jutt Sikhs. This fact too needs to be expressly noted because a unique culture of violence and retributory violence permeates the

Jutt tradition and the social milieu in which he lives. The enormously fragmented nature of Jutt society would, in due course of time, lead to the fragmentation of the Sikh militant movement and the setting up of a number of *panthic* committees, often with different and mutually hostile agendas.

It is not as if the major militant groups were unaware of the dangers that disunity in their ranks posed to the movement, making them vulnerable to police pressures and infiltration. There were frequent attempts, therefore, by the more influential of the *panthic* committees to bring about some unity of purpose and tactics between different groups. Once again, the essentially fragmentary nature of Jutt society would ensure that all such efforts proved futile, with the many contextual differences among various militant groups, in fact, becoming more marked with the passage of time. This would greatly help the security forces in exploiting inter-group tensions and rivalries and setting off frequent internecine clashes, in order to finally seize the initiative and deal with the various militant groups one by one.

*

But we are straying into the future. Let us go back to the enactment of the Government of India Act of 1935, which intensified the political discord between the Congress and the Muslim League, now led by M.A. Jinnah, at one time a prominent Congress leader. The prospects of a united India gaining independence from the British colonial power noticeably receded. This would significantly re-determine the Congress perspective on the finer contours of a future India and set the tone for the crucial pre-independence negotiations between the British government, the Congress and the Muslim League after the end of the War in 1945. The escalating likelihood of partition required the Congress to ingeniously rework its earlier position on the question of minority identities, which had all through been central to its policy framework so as to attract all the diverse Indian peoples to actively participate in the country's freedom struggle and to assuage minority apprehensions and concerns. The party now started looking at a unitary system for an independent India rather than a federal set-up it had been advocating all along. Later, partition and the unprecedented violence on both sides of the new borders that preceded and followed it, would require an alarmed Congress party leadership to provide for a strong Centre in the new Indian Constitution. This was in sharp contrast to its long-held view that a federal polity would best suit the imperatives of a pluralist Indian nation.

Although outwardly still claiming to speak for all Indians, the dominant party of the freedom movement and now the principal party of governance would increasingly shift focus from its secular past to a Hinduistic view of nationhood, in which the diverse minority communities were urged to adopt the values and beliefs of the so-called mainstream India, which in essence meant the cultural and political paradigms of the central Hindi-speaking states. This school of thought gained increasing ascendancy within the Congress leadership after the death of Jawaharlal Nehru in 1964, especially in the face of mounting popular disenchantment with the socio-economic policies of the Congress party in the aftermath of Indira Gandhi's Emergency regime. Perhaps, it was not sheer coincidence that both the principal political outfits, the Congress and the Bharatiya Janata Party (BJP), harped on the need for minority and subaltern communities to join the so-called Indian mainstream, the former in the name of national solidarity and the latter for the greater glory of Bharat Mata and the Hindu nation. Apart from other post-partition compulsions, the Indian political leadership also perceived vital electoral advantages in wooing the majority Hindus by whatever means, as they formed almost 83 per cent of the Indian population.

Understandably, such a clean break with the concept of an inclusive kind of Indian-ness on the part of mainstream political parties caused not a little alarm and anxiety among the country's numerous minority communities, some of them even staking claims to a sub-national status. Ironically, while the minority claims of separate and distinct identities remained largely dormant during the long colonial rule, the advent of independence and a democratic system of governance acted as catalysts in reinforcing such assertions. This was natural given that while the new constitution provided for all the trappings of democracy, which would promote a heightened awareness of their rights and privileges among the minority segments, the operational and administrative inadequacies and distortions that soon crept into the system due to the failure of the political and bureaucratic hierarchy to completely break with India's colonial past, made any fulfillment of minority aspirations hostage to political and electoral compulsions of the two principal parties of governance.

When the various mechanisms for demand articulation by the minority populations, integral to a genuine democratic structure, failed to meet their aspirations to grow as equal and respectable citizens of this great country, discontent and frustration set in, triggering a number of militant movements and insurgencies in parts of the country but mainly in the north-east and the north-west. Denied adequate space to preserve and nurture their distinct cultural and ethnic genius and threatened by the fast emerging consensus between the two principal political parties on the criteria that defined mainstream Indianness, the minority assertions of separate and distinct identities assumed extra stridency. Hindutva, rapidly gathering momentum in the central Hindi heartland of the country, was sure, in due course, to pose a grave threat to their very existence as distinct peoples, proud of their history and culture.

Let us now recapitulate some important events that marked the second partition of the Punjab in 1966. As already mentioned, the rejection of the demand for a Punjabi *suba* in 1956, when the entire country was reorganised on a linguistic basis, caused a deep sense of hurt in the Sikh community at being discriminated against and unfairly treated by the Indian leadership, which the Akali party under Master Tara Singh was quick to exploit for political gains. This was also projected as a clear betrayal of the 'glow of freedom' promise held out to the Sikhs earlier by Nehru in the run-up to India's independence. Instead of a Punjabi *suba*, what was mooted in 1957 was a proposal to effect a notional division of the state into two regions, one Punjabi-speaking and the other Hindi-speaking, with each region being served by a sub-legislature dealing with some subjects like health and education transferred to them from the state assembly list. Called the regional formula, its primary purpose seemed to be to address the Sikhs' sense of outrage. Assembly constituencies of Ropar, Morinda and Chandigarh falling under Ambala district of the Hindi region, were included in the Punjabi region, with Punjabi as its official language. The Chandigarh capital project area was not included in any of the two regions, pending the process of its delimitation and notification as a full-fledged Assembly constituency. In the interim, its representative was to sit in the Punjabi regional committee.

If followed sincerely, this arrangement could have served as the first step in creating an agreeable ambience in the Sikh community to help promote a positive dialogue with the Akalis to arrive at a more broad-based accord, an acceptable via media without resorting to the division of the state. This would also have helped in curbing the growing acrimony between Hindus and Sikhs and averting the ill effects of Punjab's bifurcation a few years later. However, this was not to be, and it soon became clear that the failure of the regional formula was only a matter of time as the Arya Samaj and the rightist Hindu party, the Jan Sangh, later to be reborn as the Bharatiya Janata Party (BJP), which had not taken kindly to the formula from the very beginning, now chose to launch a statewide 'Save Hindi' agitation.

The extent of hostility between the two communities, which had together borne the main brunt of violence at the hands of murderous Muslim mobs at the time of partition barely a decade ago, could be gauged from the slogans shouted by agitators on both sides. While a section of Hindus coined the picturesque slogan of '*Kachh, kara, kirpan, dhak diyange* Pakistan', the other side responded equally vehemently by the counter-slogan of '*Dhoti topi Jamuna paar*'. So while the former vowed to push out the Sikhs across the border to Pakistan, the latter wanted the Hindus to be thrown across the river Jamuna, the perceived boundary of the Punjabi *suba* or the Sikh homeland of old. Though the Hindi agitation petered out by December 1957, failing to get the regional formula scrapped, it did considerably embitter Hindu-Sikh relations.

The Akalis regarded the Hindi agitation as largely Congress-inspired, validating their anti-Congress bias and adding to the community's feelings of discrimination at the hands of the Congress-ruled Centre. After the bilingual state of Bombay was also bifurcated into Maharashtra and Gujarat in 1960, Punjab remained the only state in the country that was not linguistically reorganised. This would considerably reinforce the resentment and feelings of injustice already troubling the Sikh community, and worsen the relations between them and the Indian establishment.

With the failure of the regional formula, the Akalis under Master Tara Singh reverted to their earlier demand for a Punjabi *suba* with renewed vigour. They also considerably intensified their verbal attacks on the Congress, which was bluntly depicted as a Hindu party, reminiscent of the pre-partition days, openly accusing not only the Congress party but also the Indian state itself of favouring the state's majority Hindus and working against the interests of the Sikh community. The then Punjab chief minister, the redoubtable Partap Singh Kairon, one of the most astute, as also highly unscrupulous and ruthless, politicians of his time, and a close confidant of Prime Minister Jawaharlal Nehru, sought to beat the Akalis at their own game by trying to win over the Sikhs politically. He also freely employed the state's coercive power to malign the Akali party and wear down the momentum of their agitation. Probably for the first time in history, the Punjab police, led by the charismatic Deputy Inspector General Ashwini Kumar, forced their entry into the Golden Temple complex to arrest some Akali leaders, a step that would unfortunately set the pattern for many such intrusions in future.

Far from weakening the agitation, such blatant misuse of state machinery to crush the movement, in fact widened its appeal among the Sikh masses, who would become more emotionally involved in the agitation. However, even though sustained state repression had considerably diluted the initial intensity of the Akali agitation, the search for an alternative plan in place of the regional formula became imperative for the Indian authorities. This was even more necessary in view of the growing opposition of the Punjabi Hindus to accepting Punjabi in the Gurmukhi script as the language of administration and education, even in the Punjabi region.

A rather comic episode occurred relating to the *suba* agitation and the fast-unto-death undertaken by Akali leader Master Tara Singh in the premises of the Golden Temple complex in 1961. He had taken a vow before the holy Granth Sahib that he would give up his fast only after the government agreed to form the *suba*. As it happened, the fast extended to more than two months without the Master, an old hand at engaging in countless struggles for the fulfillment of his community's many demands, showing any noticeable loss of weight or girth. He was alleged to have been generously partaking of the holy *prasad*, which as a true Sikh he was bound by faith to consume. The Master's fast was shown up as a farce even more because at about the same time another Akali leader, Darshan Singh Pheruman, actually breathed his last while on hunger strike for the same cause. Master Tara Singh had to finally give up not only his fast in some disgrace, but also the leadership of the Akali Dal.

That the rapid political decline of the veteran Akali leader thereafter would have far-reaching consequences for the course of Sikh politics in subsequent years became apparent soon after. Sant Fateh Singh, who now replaced him as the president of the Akali Dal, undertook another fast-unto-death but with a clear warning that he would immolate himself if the demand for the *suba* was not accepted by a certain deadline. This technique seemed to work and Indira Gandhi, now the prime minister of India, relented sufficiently to declare her readiness to finally accede to the Akali demand for a Punjabi-speaking state. Whether the Master's fast was really a charade or the whole thing was orchestrated by the crafty chief minister and his advisers to disgrace the old warhorse of Sikh politics would never be fully known. The replacement of the Master by Sant Fateh Singh also marked the decline of the Khatri/Arora urban Sikh leadership and its gradual substitution by Jutt Sikhs from rural backgrounds. The Sant was believed by some people to be actually a plant in the Akali Dal, organized at the instance of Partap Singh Kairon, himself a Jutt.

The sabotage theory may be a myth, but the fact remains that the course of Sikh politics would never be the same again. Some ten years later, another Sikh Congress leader and a former chief minister of Punjab, this time a non-Jutt, would engage in a similar exercise, with the full approval of the top Congress leadership, to cajole another Sant, though of a very different disposition, to undermine the authority and credibility of moderate Sikh leaders for a different and much more sinister purpose.

*

The Akali demand for the formation of a Punjabi *suba* was finally conceded by the government in 1966, when Indira Gandhi succeeded Lal Bahadur Shastri as prime minister. The decision, however, failed to satisfy the Akalis. This was mainly due to the exclusion of Chandigarh and some other Punjabi-speaking areas from the new Punjab, and lingering doubts over a just allocation of Punjab river waters. Punjab felt it had exclusive and rightful claims as a riparian state. It also caused considerable apprehension among Punjabi Hindus as to their future in a Sikh majority state.

In order to stave off the possibility of living in a Sikh majority state, the Hindu parties, probably backed by the Congress, now put forward a demand for *maha* Punjab or greater Punjab, to be formed by merging three neighbouring states of Punjab, Haryana and Himachal Pradesh. However, the die had been cast, and the long-awaited *suba* of the Akalis did take shape in 1966, though hardly conforming to their vision. The Chandigarh capital project area was kept out to become a Union territory, with both Punjab and Haryana allowed to set up their capitals in the city. The control and management of the Bhakra Dam headworks on rivers Satluj and Beas, over which the Punjab sought to assert exclusive riparian rights, were vested in a centrally-controlled management board. The Akalis were also peeved at the exclusion of several Punjabi-speaking areas from the new state, which they would contemptuously refer to as a *subi* not a *suba*.

Mrs Gandhi's award on Chandigarh, delivered some time later in response to Akali protests and agitations, made the confusion worse confounded. According to this award, Chandigarh will be transferred to Punjab, but in exchange the latter must hand over the fertile areas of Abohar and Fazilka to Haryana. Further, since Fazilka would have been an isolated pocket within Punjab, it was to be connected to Haryana by a corridor passing through Punjab territory along the Indo-Pakistan border. This move was mischievously projected by interested elements as signifying the lack of trust by Delhi in the patriotic credentials of the Sikhs in relation to Pakistan. The gains in political and sectarian terms to the Congress party that were expected to follow the formation of a Punjabi *suba* thus failed to materialise, as the whole exercise was conducted in a clumsy and maladroit manner, a pattern that would often be replicated in the future.

It seems that political leaders have a penchant for supporting apparently innocuous but highly motivated strategies in dealing with critical and emotive issues agitating the minorities. Such tactics would continue to mark the handling of Sikh discontent and alienation right up to the catastrophic events of 1984 and after.

As Indira Gandhi was the supreme leader of the Congress party during much of the period that saw Sikh militancy grow in intensity and range, it might be legitimate to speculate about her attitude towards the community. Was she indeed indifferent, even hostile, to Sikh aspirations for a more assured future in the new dispensation? Did she resent their uppishness in putting forth new and—as they would probably appear to her—somewhat bizarre demands every now and then to be followed by *morchas* (protest marches) and other forms of agitation? Interestingly, the Akali Dal was the only party in the whole of India that continued to oppose Mrs Gandhi's Emergency regime throughout the 20 months it remained in force by offering daily arrests at Amritsar, which must have riled her no end. But then, what to make of her alleged fondness for her two Sikh security guards, who later shot her out of anger and outrage at Operation Blue Star?

That she strongly disliked the Akalis was not the best kept secret of the times, especially after their reaction to her highly implausible award on Chandigarh. In a one-to-one meeting this writer had with her in her office in Parliament House, some time in August 1984, she expressed herself very strongly against the Akalis and their alleged propensity for vacillating and undependable behaviour. It

is unclear whether she was, in fact, as anti-Sikh in her
beliefs as the Sikhs came to regard her on account of her
discernible pro-Hindu bias in the handling of the Punjab
question in 1966. In her autobiography *My Truth* (1981)
she went on record to express the Congress view that the
formation of the Punjabi *suba* amounted to letting down
the Punjabi Hindus, who had been voting for the Congress
party all these years, a highly ill-advised statement to
come from the prime minister of a nation characterized by
extraordinary diversities.

Sardar Hukam Singh, a highly respected Sikh leader,
one of the two Sikh members of India's Constituent
Assembly, was deeply upset by some of her actions during
the time he presided over the Lok Sabha as its Speaker.
Gulzari Lal Nanda, the then Union home minister, believing
that Hukam Singh was opposed to the formation of the
Punjabi *suba*, had persuaded Prime Minister Lal Bahadur
Shastri to appoint him as chairman of a parliamentary
committee to deliberate the tricky issue. Mrs Gandhi, then
the minister of information and broadcasting, however,
did not fully trust Hukam Singh in this respect and, along
with Y.B. Chavan, urged Shastri to speak with Hukam
Singh so that the committee did not submit an unhelpful
report, which could cause considerable discomfiture to the
government of India. Even as a cabinet minister, she
apparently enjoyed a good deal of influence with the
prime minister. Sardar Hukam Singh was hurt by the
move and felt acutely resentful of the implied insinuations
against his integrity as the Lok Sabha Speaker.

Many years later, Hukam Singh would recall the
entire episode in an article published in the *Indian Express*
of 11 April 1983 under the title The Other Side, in the
context of Mrs Gandhi's disclosures in *My Truth*. He also
revealed in that article that while he did not think the

suba would be in the long-term interest of the Sikhs, at the stage it was being debated there was no option but to accept the Akali demand.

There were also reports that the Congress went out of its way to induce the Hindus to declare Hindi as their mother tongue in Census 1961. This was the second time after independence when the Punjabi Hindus by design disavowed their mother tongue in favour of Hindi, the first being the Census of 1951. Interestingly, the proportion of Punjabi-speaking people in Punjab had been showing a declining trend since the Census of 1891, with the Arya Samaj doggedly campaigning in favour of Hindi against Punjabi. So a large number of Punjabi Hindus were in any case recording Hindi as their first language.

Another powerful factor now came into play. This was the fear of a second partition of Punjab, which appeared to be a looming possibility, given the shrill tenor of many statements made by the Akalis under Master Tara Singh. It may be recalled that the latter was freely indulging in separatist rhetoric while holding out threats of *morchas* and other forms of coercive action in the years immediately following the partition of the province in 1947. A second partition was projected by the Hindu leadership, whether belonging to the Congress or the Jan Sangh, as implying another displacement for the Hindus, with all its associated suffering and hardship, which they naturally wished to forestall at any cost. By recording Hindi as their mother tongue, they wanted to effectively disprove the Sikh claim that the Punjab was a unilingual state, and thus preclude any possibility of the formation of a Punjabi *suba*. On its part, the national leadership too felt considerably alarmed by the Akali stance, as the gory events of the partition days were still fresh in the minds of people. The overly anti-Punjabi posture of the Hindus did not endear them to the Sikhs, a development which would further distance them from Hindi, which they had until then been learning with some enthusiasm.

Was the Congress attempt to persuade Punjabi Hindus to record Hindi as their mother tongue in 1961 meant to invalidate the criteria earlier followed in delineating the boundaries of Hindi and Punjabi regions in 1957? The Sikhs, in any case, came to believe implicitly in such an assumption when Mrs Gandhi's government, disregarding the principles followed in 1957, made Census 1961 the sole basis for the 1966 bifurcation of the state into Haryana and Punjab. This would virtually lead to the creation of two perpetually hostile neighbours in the region, forever at each other's throat on some pretext or the other. If it was the river waters dispute one day, it would be territorial claims next. The extent to which Haryana chief minister Bhajan Lal and some of his successors would go to spite the Sikhs was apparent from the step-motherly treatment given to Punjabi in Haryana schools. For, despite Punjabi being the language of first choice for the largest number of people in that state, next to Hindi, Haryana would recognize Tamil or some other such distant language as the second language in its schools rather than Punjabi.

Bhajan Lal, several times chief minister of Haryana and pioneer of the noble art of defections in Indian politics, who set a record of sorts by walking out of one ruling party to join another along with his entire cabinet, so as not to have to give up the loaves and fishes of office, took some sort of sadistic pleasure in needling the Sikhs now and then. He would continue to prove a stumbling block in all attempts at finding a solution to the Punjab problem, whether by Mrs Gandhi during the four years that she ruled the country after her return to power in

1980 or her son Rajiv, who succeeded her as prime minister or, indeed, at any other time in subsequent years.

Whether by design or otherwise, the Union government's approach to finding a workable solution to the unfolding Punjab crisis in the early 1980s smacked of clumsiness, short-sightedness and lack of vision. Its Punjab policy, if indeed there was such a policy, was marked by gross ignorance of Sikh history and tradition and a manifest insensitivity to minority insecurities in a country where the majority community dominated many times over. Generally regarded as the most dynamic of Indian prime ministers, next only to her father Jawaharlal Nehru, Indira Gandhi's handling of the many conflict situations in the country's peripheral regions, whether in the north-east or the north-west, left much to be desired. It is not without reason, therefore, that she goes down in history as the most inscrutable of Indian prime ministers.

*

Far from easing the political tensions in the region, the division of Punjab in 1966, in fact, greatly expanded the areas of conflict and confrontation between the Akalis and the central Congress leadership. It also led to a reorientation of political agendas in Punjab and Haryana. For one, the Punjab Congress now started siding with the Akalis on many of their demands like territorial disputes and river water claims, which were now perceived as basically Punjabi issues, not merely Akali grievances. The Punjabi Hindus would also soon realize that the state's partition had chiefly benefited the Hindi-speaking Haryanvis, who had now got a separate state of their own, while the erstwhile Hindi lovers of the residual Punjab had now to perforce take to learning and working in a language they had so far been disowning as a mother tongue, that too in Gurmukhi script. They would continue to resist this imperative for as long as they could, the educational institutions run by the Arya Samaj being in the forefront. DAV College Jalandhar, for example, would rather be affiliated to the centrally-controlled university in Chandigarh than the one in Amritsar, named after Nanak Dev, the first Sikh Guru. However, all of them had to ultimately fall in line in due course, prompted also by some judicial verdicts.

On the other hand, large communities of Punjabi-speaking Hindu refugees, living in the new state of Haryana since the country's partition in 1947, were practically sidelined in political terms by the original inhabitants of the land. The wheel, it seemed, had come full circle and the entire tactical policy so far pursued by the anti-Punjabi language brigade, from Gulzari Lal Nanda to the Mahasha (Arya Samaj) press of Jalandhar, seemed to have collapsed. The Akalis got their *suba*, though somewhat truncated, where they could finally come to power in accordance with the new democratic norms. Ironically, the very strategies employed by the Congress and the Hindu leadership to keep as many areas with Punjabi Hindu majorities as possible out of the reorganized Punjab had made the latter a Sikh majority state. Incidentally, the chief beneficiary of Punjab's second partition was neither Punjab nor Haryana but the hill state of Himachal Pradesh, which came by quite a few Punjabi-speaking areas like Kangra and parts of Hoshiarpur district to considerably enlarge its territory, among strong rumours that Union home minister Gulzari Lal Nanda, a Punjabi Hindu settled in Gujarat and an influential Congress leader of the Nehru era, had played a significant role in keeping the new Punjab as small as possible. However, the realization came too late.

The many inter-state claims and counter-claims between Haryana and Punjab would test Mrs Gandhi's political acumen to the maximum. It is clear that the frequent wrangling arising out of territorial claims, allocation of river waters and the status of Chandigarh city, among others, were the product mainly of the inept manner in which the process of bifurcation had been carried out. The ever-expanding span of distrust and hostility between Haryana and Punjab would keep Mrs Gandhi fully occupied in the delicate task of reconciling the clashing interests of her party in the new states, as well as retaining support of the electorate. Evidently, it was not an easy task even for her, accomplished as she was known to be in the art of shrewd political management. For, strongly ranged against each other were her party people in Haryana and Punjab, who had now adopted differing, almost irreconcilable, positions on all contentious issues. This would soon oblige her to explore whatever viable alternatives were available, based either on merit or political considerations tailored to suit Haryana, and aggravating the Punjab situation. Any effort at resolving the many disputed issues that might precipitate discontent in Haryana was likely to cause disaffection in the Hindu electorate spread over the whole of North India, so she considered it more prudent to sacrifice the interests of Punjab farmers. The most intractable of these disputes related to the allocation of river waters, which we will take up now.

*

Since a large majority of people in Punjab and Haryana were dependent on agriculture for their livelihood, the river waters issue had come to acquire deep emotional overtones in both states. A fair and mutually acceptable allocation of waters of the Punjab rivers to the successor states of Punjab and Haryana was, therefore, an extremely difficult matter and needed to be resolved in an atmosphere of mutual trust and accommodation. It also required the Union government to approach the issue without being constrained by electoral compulsions and without appearing to take sides. However, in the then prevailing climate of suspicion and hostility, it was precisely these resources that were in short supply. Even if plenty of water was available in the Punjab rivers to fully satisfy the requirements of both the states, there was another claimant, Rajasthan, which had already been allocated 8 million acre feet (m.a.f.) out of 15.85 m.a.f., that is more than half the available water, under the Indus Waters Treaty between India and Pakistan, as a result of the World Bank's arbitration in the late 1950s. In the event, only a limited quantity of water was available for distribution between Punjab and Haryana, which would lead to endless, often rancorous, but unproductive negotiations between the two states under the supervision of the Union government. Punjab claimed a major share of the waters on the basis of being a riparian state, as also to meet its huge irrigation needs.

Since river waters formed part of the state list in the Constitution, Punjab claimed an over-riding share in the waters of its rivers. The requirements of non-riparian states could be accommodated only after its own present and future needs were fully met, it argued. In any case, if it had to share the waters of its rivers, none of which were inter-state, it should also be given a share of Jamuna waters. Haryana asserted that since its share of water was being used by the Punjab so far because the Satluj-Jamuna canal could not be constructed, Punjab's grievance about the so-called *loss* of water under the award was baseless.

Disregarding the protests and objections from the Akalis and acting under sections 78, 79 and 80 of the Punjab Reorganization Act, 1966, which had made non-riparian states eligible for allocation of waters of the Punjab rivers, the Union government issued a notification on 24 March 1976, allocating 3.5 m.a.f. each to Haryana and Punjab, besides 8 m.a.f. to Rajasthan, 0.2 to Delhi and 0.65 to Jammu and Kashmir out of a presumed availability of 15.85 m.a.f. water, based on 1921-45 flows. To add insult to injury, the notification also stipulated that if more water was to be available in future, all of it would go to Haryana. The Congress chief minister of Punjab, later to become Union home minister and the first Sikh President of India, thanks to his open and frequent professions of loyalty to the Nehru-Gandhis, meekly accepted the seemingly unequal award. This verdict would set off a chain of rallies and agitations by the Akalis and, for some time, also by the Marxists, that would spill over well into the next decade and become a major cause of discontent in Punjab. Later, Punjab would challenge even the constitutional validity of sections 78, 79 and 80 of the Punjab Reorganization Act.

Obviously, the most appropriate option under the circumstances would have been to leave the matter to a judicial verdict, which would have allowed tempers to cool down and facilitated a judicious decision. However, the electoral compulsions in Haryana and Rajasthan, always a prime consideration with political parties, had led the prime minister to declare the above-mentioned award during the Emergency regime of 1975-77, allotting equal quantities of water to Punjab and Haryana, although the latter state was much smaller in size.

As was to be expected, the award was perceived by the Akalis as grossly unfair. Gurdial Singh Dhillon, a long-time Congressman and a cabinet colleague of Mrs Gandhi, feebly argued that it would be difficult to implement such an award by the Punjab chief minister. Her imperious response was that in that case she would find a chief minister who would be able to do so.

Not yet fully reconciled to the changed situation brought about by the division of the state, and unable to break out of their past fixations, the Punjabi Hindu leadership, based mostly in Jalandhar and in control of the Mahasha press, continued to directly and indirectly oppose what they still considered to be merely Sikh demands rather than those of the state as a whole. Stimulated by such a mindset, Virendra, a prominent Arya Samaj leader of Jalandhar and, along with Lala Jagat Narain of the Hind Samachar group of newspapers, widely known for his anti-Sikh biases, affirmed in an article published in the *Indian Express* that the Punjabi Hindus had nothing to do with the river waters dispute. He and his colleagues in Jalandhar obviously did not realize the full impact of the award on Punjab's economy and consequently on its social cohesion. For, if the award was implemented in full, Punjab's agricultural productivity would be hit hard by the reduced availability of water for irrigation. With the bulk of Sikh population dependent on agriculture, nothing could be more provocative to them than Virendra's article. However, the likes of Virendra would soon become voices in the wilderness as soon after the formation of the Punjabi *suba*, the bulk of Punjab's Hindus would come to realize the full range of the their responsibilities towards the new state and their Sikh fellow citizens. And though the Arya Samaj leadership and the Mahasha press did not readily give up their earlier attitudes and biases against what they still considered Sikh demands, the bulk of the Hindu political spectrum, including the Jan Sangh-BJP, would begin to extend support to the core issues raised by the Akali party. Such cooperation would later widen considerably and, in due course, lead to formation of coalition governments by the Akalis and the BJP, much to the chagrin of the Congress leadership. They would also soon come to realize that their refusal to acknowledge Punjabi as their mother tongue and a studied indifference to Punjab's claims on its river waters had not been in their long-term interests.

With the Congress party losing the 1977 elections soon after the end of internal emergency imposed by her about two years before, Mrs Gandhi lost power. The Janata government that replaced the Congress was also not particularly interested in supporting Punjab against Haryana because a prominent Jat leader of western UP, now Union home minister, had turned a strong champion of Haryanvi interests in his quest for enlarging his constituency among Haryana's influential Jat community. (A distinction needs to be made between Sikh Jutts of the Punjab and Hindu Jats of Haryana). Having lost all hope of obtaining any support in its quest for a more acceptable deal from the new political alliance at the Centre, the Punjab government under Parkash Singh Badal, the Akali chief minister in an Akali-Janata Dal coalition, formed after the dismissal of the Congress government of Giani Zail Singh, repudiated the central notification of 1976 regarding the allocation of river waters and approached the supreme court of India for a judicial verdict. This was just as well, otherwise Punjab's claims on its river waters would have been lost for ever under the law of limitation.

However, soon after the Congress came back to power, after the premature demise of the factious Janata regime in 1980, Darbara Singh, the chief minister of Punjab, withdrew the case from the supreme court, obviously under the direction of his party leadership. Haryana too withdrew its petition from the apex court soon after. Both the states as well as Rajasthan now gave full authority to Mrs Gandhi to resolve the issue. Consequently, the chief ministers of Punjab, Haryana and Rajasthan, all belonging to the Congress party, signed a fresh agreement on 31 December 1981. According to this agreement, Punjab was allocated 4.22, Haryana 3.50, Rajasthan 8.60, Delhi 0.20 and Jammu & Kashmir 0.65 m.a.f. water. The total availability of water was now revised upwards to 17.17 m.a.f., ostensibly on the basis of flow series of 1920-60, a stratagem that would later be employed again to make the Rajiv-Longowal accord palatable to the Akalis. Although Punjab put up some resistance, though in a somewhat feeble manner, on the ground that the fresh allocation was based on erroneous calculations of the flow series, chief minister Darbara Singh bowed to the dictate of his party high command and accepted the award. Apart from the fact that Darbara Singh would never be able to live down the ignominy of putting his signature to this manifestly unfair agreement, what was even more unfortunate was that the award and the manner in which it was arrived at would become another searing indicator of the central government's discriminatory attitude towards Sikh-majority Punjab.

As elections to the Haryana legislature were scheduled for early 1981, electoral compulsions again came into play to determine the future course of action. Prime Minister Indira Gandhi decided to ostentatiously launch the construction of the Satluj-Jamuna link canal to carry Haryana's share of water from the Punjab rivers to its fields. An elaborate ceremony was arranged in a Punjab village on 8 April 1982, in the face of strong opposition from the Akalis and the Communist Party of India

(Marxist) or CPI-M, which reiterated its resolve to jointly thwart its construction by all means at its disposal. This was a clear enough warning of the provocative nature of the project and its divisive potential, but the establishment went ahead with the function, except that the time fixed for Mrs Gandhi's function was changed to foil opposition protests at the site. The Akalis and the CPM commenced the *morcha* in full strength from 16 April when volunteers from both the parties in their thousands responded enthusiastically to the call. This agitation, known as the *Nehar Roko* or 'block (the digging of) the canal' *morcha*, would prove to be the starting point of a series of such protest agitations by the Akalis in the early 1980s.

The link canal, however, could never be completed and all construction work would come to a standstill soon due to stiff opposition to the project from successive Punjab governments, whether Congress or non-Congress, in spite of repeated intercession by the higher judiciary. More than two decades later, a Congress chief minister of the state would get an enabling legislation unanimously passed by the Punjab Assembly to annul all agreements regarding the sharing of river waters so far entered into by the state of Punjab. Some feeble noises were made by the central Congress leadership against the step taken by Punjab, but they soon died down. Haryana's reaction was on expected lines. All the accompanying sound and fury, however, failed to change the overall picture. The Centre was content to make a reference to the apex court for directions where Haryana too lodged a fresh petition. That is where the matter rests for the time being (May 2006). Further work on the link canal remains suspended. The incomplete portion of the canal in Punjab's Ropar and Patiala districts has to be guarded night and day by security forces against attempted breaches by Sikh protestors. During the militancy years, such breaches were a fairly common occurrence.

To the dismay of the Congress party, all the fanfare accompanying the formal inauguration of the work for the construction of the link canal failed to win the Haryana elections for the party, although the wily Bhajan Lal still managed to get into the chief minister's chair, thanks largely to his proven talent for engineering defections and an overly obliging Governor. He would later show his profound sense of gratitude to his bosses in Delhi by indulging in some highly provocative acts against the Sikhs during the Asian Games in 1982 and at other times. More of this later.

In a very basic sense, the river waters dispute between Punjab and Haryana is a product of history to the extent that the two partitions of the state, first in 1947 and then again in 1966, contributed substantially to its progression. The pre-partition undivided Punjab was an integral whole in all respects, but especially in the matter of its river systems. That intrinsic *wholeness* got fractured as a consequence of division of the country in 1947. The mechanics of the partition process left the Indian part of Punjab with heavily depleted irrigation resources from the rivers that fell to its share. On a rough estimate, while the Indian Punjab inherited some four million acres of cultivated land under irrigation, that is, 26.8 per cent of such area in the undivided Punjab, it received only 15 per cent of the total irrigation potential. This degree of impoverishment in the matter of irrigation resources in a predominantly agricultural society alone was sufficient to cause an almost pathological attachment to river waters in the new state. Since the western region of the new state was populated by Sikh agricultural classes, Hindus being engaged mostly in trade and business, the river waters issue thus acquired a patently sectarian character as Punjabi Hindus would have hardly lost sleep over an issue of little concern to them. Mr Virendra's article in the *Indian Express* was a clear reflection of such an attitude.

It would take another few years before the Punjabi Hindus realized all the implications of the matter and it ceased to be an exclusive Sikh concern. That is why the Hindu BJP voted with the Congress and the Akalis in 2004 to unanimously pass the Punjab Termination of Agreements Act to protect the interests of the state in the matter of its river waters. It is difficult to predict the future course of events, although it is fairly certain that Punjab will not easily give up its stand in view of the very heavy stakes involved. More than any other issue, the river waters dispute has emerged as the most emotive unifying factor in the Punjab and needs to be very carefully handled, taking into account all its various dimensions— technical, cultural, civilisational, historical, emotional, economic and administrative. It is vital that it is not allowed to become an instrument merely of political manipulation in order to win elections or to sideline an important minority like the Sikhs. One way out is, of course, to leave the matter to the good judgment of the higher judiciary, which still enjoys high credibility ratings among all sections of the people. Though the process may be time-consuming, its decision is sure to facilitate an acceptable settlement. It needs to be remembered that this particular issue has triggered several agitations and militant activities during the last two decades and its potential for the revival of militancy in the state is rated very high by intelligence agencies.

*

In their relentless pursuit of power, South Asian political parties routinely resort to a variety of manipulative practices. One such tactic is to utilise the powers vested in the President of the republic or the state Governors to dismiss duly elected state governments on grounds which can always be rigged with handy inputs from intelligence agencies. In common parlance, such unprincipled political moves are known as political *dadagiri*, or bullying. The formation of the Punjabi *suba* in 1966 had fired the Akali ambitions to seek to secure political power in the new state through the electoral route, as envisaged in the country's democratic dispensation. It would not be long, however, before they came to the unhappy conclusion that the formation of the *suba* was no guarantee that the much more resourceful Congress party would let them rule the state, even if they came to power through democratic means.

The first legislative elections after the formation of the *suba* were held in February 1967, which returned an Akali-Jan Sangh coalition government to power under the chief ministership of Gurnam Singh, a former high court judge and by all accounts a man of impeccable credentials to provide a clean and effective administration. This was the first non-Congress government in the Punjab, as in many north Indian states—and by all indications, it appeared to be performing fairly well in all respects. Hindus, who had so far been feeling distinctly uncomfortable in the *suba*, now started breathing easy due to their participation in administration and power-sharing. There was also a perceptible drop in the separatist rhetoric of the Akalis, who were showing signs of maturing into a responsible party of governance. However, not used to being out of power for long, the Congress would soon lose patience and take resort to the by now well-known weapon of engineering defections to bring down the Akali-Jan Sangh government. In less than a year, that is by November of the same year, Lachhman Singh Gill, an Akali minister, was inveigled into leaving the party along with sixteen others to take over as chief minister with the support of the Congress legislature party.

The new chief minister was shrewd enough to recognize that the Congress needed him more than he needed the Congress, and did not allow the latter to ride roughshod over him to rule by proxy. Although he did not last long in the chief ministerial chair as the Congress withdrew support to his faction in August 1968, Gill was able to greatly accelerate the pace of development in the state. His chief achievement, however, lay in forcing Punjabi in Gurmukhi script down the throats of an unenthusiastic bureaucracy as the sole official language in the secretariat and heads of department offices. Any infringement of the government directives in this regard was met with heavy penalties.

Fresh elections were held in February 1969 after a brief spell of President's rule, when Akalis came back to power with a big majority. Gurnam Singh again took over as chief minister. In his second tenure, he felt strong enough to stand up to the dictates of the Sikh politico-religious establishment headed by Sant Fateh Singh, who had acquired considerable influence among the Sikh masses as the principal architect of the Punjabi *suba*. Unable to defy his party leadership for long, Gurnam Singh was replaced within a year as the leader of the Akali legislature party and chief minister by Parkash Singh Badal. The Congress once again instigated defections, this time choosing the very same Gurnam Singh to lead a group of 26 defectors out of the ruling coalition. Badal was, however, smarter, and prevailed on Governor Pavate to dissolve the Assembly before his ministry could be voted out on the floor of the House. The state was placed under president's rule once again in July 1971. In the general elections of January 1972, the Congress party again came to power and ruled the state until 1977, with Giani Zail Singh as chief minister.

*

A school drop-out from a small town in the tiny Sikh princely state of Faridkot in the Punjab, the Giani had started life as a *granthi* (priest) in a local gurudwara and went on to become the general secretary of the town's Akali *jatha* (party). He was reported to have been convicted to four years imprisonment for embezzlement in 1939[1], which was later sought to be passed off as conviction on political grounds, a common enough subterfuge in the country for the purpose of claiming the status of freedom fighters and the privileges linked to that status. Soon he was sucked into the popular movement against the whimsical rule of the Raja of Faridkot. This would bring him to the notice of Jawaharlal Nehru, whose entry into the state to participate in a political conference in 1946, was barred by the Raja. The Faridkot agitation, it may be mentioned, was inspired more by the *gurudwara* agitation of the 1920s than the Praja Mandal, which was closely aligned with the Indian National Congress and functioned as its adjunct in most Indian princely states. Zail Singh would, henceforth, try to copy Nehru by wearing an *achkan* (long coat), complete with a rose in the buttonhole. Well-versed in Sikh scriptures due to his early upbringing, he was far more practised in the art of using the Sikh religious idiom for political ends than many of the Akali politicians of his times, except possibly Gurcharan Singh

Tohra. Widely known for his fondness for the good things of life and one of the most intriguing and crafty politicians in the state, the Giani would regularly put his vast earthy common sense to maximum use in his many political battles with the Akali leadership to beat them at their favourite game of evoking religious metaphors to win over the Sikh masses.

Although belonging to an artisan class and coming from a modest background, he became the first and only non-Jutt Sikh chief minister of Punjab, a state with a marked Jutt domination in both its principal parties. Far from feeling handicapped on this account, he ruled the state with supreme self-confidence, secure in the knowledge that he enjoyed the fullest trust of Mrs Gandhi, the all-powerful prime minister and president of his party. In a bid to steal the Akali thunder, he went out of his way to emphasize his deep commitment to the many symbols and traditions of the Sikh *panth* and did much more to bring diverse Sikh religious rituals and practices to the forefront of Punjab's collective consciousness and organized more functions in memory of Sikh Gurus than any Akali chief minister had ever done. That all this was being done in pursuance of political goals is another matter. In any case, the Giani was candid enough to admit as much in unguarded moments. Among such demonstrative acts was the construction of a state highway, cutting across a so-far undeveloped region of the state, to commemorate the famed journey of the tenth Sikh Guru in 1704 from Anandpur Sahib to Damdama Sahib, two of the most revered Sikh sites, on his way to the Deccan, where he was destined to die at the hands of hired assassins.

Unfortunately, his proximity to the top Congress leadership and his soaring political ambitions would also tempt him to seek to eliminate the Akali party altogether as the political voice of the Sikh people. Presumably, the top Congress leadership would have jumped at the Giani's proposition and the mechanics to bring about the political downfall of the Akalis, considering that the Akalis were the only political outfit that agitated against Indira Gandhi's emergency regime throughout the 20 months it remained in force. The manipulative genius of this master-practitioner of realpolitik would now come into full play, and a plan would be devised, with the tacit approval of the prime minister's younger son and some of her other close advisers, to rope in an up-and-coming Sikh preacher, who probably had his own problems with the Akalis, to upstage the latter and cut back their support in the Punjab countryside. Much has been written about this unholy alliance between the Congress and Jarnail Singh Bhindranwale for the express purpose of putting the Akali party out of reckoning in the state's politics forever. As it turned out, the plan succeeded eminently in suppressing the moderate voice of the Sikh community for several years, a development for which the people as well as the state would have to pay a very high cost indeed, as we shall see later.

However, for the time being, Zail Singh rode tall in the Punjab and continued to steadily consolidate his position in national Congress politics by continually swearing unstinted loyalty to Indira Gandhi. When the latter returned to power as prime minister in 1980, Zail Singh was appointed Union home minister, a position of considerable importance and influence in view of mounting instability and turmoil in several parts of the country, not excluding his own home state of Punjab, then ruled by chief minister Darbara Singh, one of his strongest opponents in the Congress hierarchy. As Union home minister and enjoying the full confidence of and proximity to the centres of power in Delhi, nothing could restrain the Giani from doing everything in his power to make life difficult for Darbara, both administratively and politically, to prove that the latter was an inefficient administrator and an inept politician. A major part of the blame for allowing a well-administered state like the Punjab to slip into conditions of lawlessness and anarchy in the early 1980s before being sucked into one of the most lethal militant movements in the world, must be placed at the doors of these two politicians, both from the Congress party, and the indifference or unwillingness of the top brass in the party and the Union government to bring them to heel.

One of the more serious instances of the kind of atrophy that had seized the state law-enforcement machinery as a result of such divided loyalties in the state administration was the appalling failure of the police and the magistracy to react effectively when Deputy Inspector General of Police, A.S. Atwal was shot in the Golden Temple in 1983, in full view of the police and magistrates on duty. We will deal with the subject in detail later.

*

All militant movements are complex in character, with their own special dialectic. With the advantage of hindsight, the clash between the Nirankaris and a radical Sikh group, the Akhand Kirtani Jatha, in Amritsar on 13 April 1978, resulting in the death of 13 Sikhs, appears to be the single most prominent episode that would set off a chain of events leading to what would turn out to be a prolonged confrontation between the Indian state and a section of the Sikhs. Founded as a puritan sect of the Sikhs in the nineteenth century, the Sant Nirankaris had split into two factions by 1947, one setting up headquarters at Agra and the other at Delhi. The latter group was able to secure a strong foothold in the corridors of power in Delhi through its sundry political and bureaucratic linkages. Primarily a Sikh sect, Hindus too started joining it in large numbers after the country's partition, thus pushing the sect away from mainstream Sikhism. As resolute supporters of the emergency, the Nirankaris had forged close links with many Punjab Congress politicians and bureaucrats, in the bargain earning the hostility of the Akalis, who continued to agitate against it throughout the period it remained in force. They had also come in for severe criticism from Damdami Taksal, the Sikh seminary where Jarnail Singh Bhindranwale had had his initiation and over which he was later to preside, for some of their rituals considered sacrilegious to the Sikh faith.

The Taksal, located at Chowk Mehta in Punjab's Gurdaspur district, was an esteemed Sikh religious institution, set up to train young Sikhs in scriptural and canonical studies to build a specialist cadre of priests and religious teachers. It was probably because of its location in Gurdaspur that militant violence first made its appearance in Gurdaspur and Amritsar districts. It will not be correct, however, to attribute the antagonism between the Taksal and the Nirankaris entirely to the ascendancy of Bhindranwale in the Taksal and Sikh politics. His mentor Sant Kartar Singh had already set the ball rolling by denouncing their activities and beliefs as blasphemous to the Sikh faith, which had even led to some clashes between the two in the nearby areas. Although the Sikh religious establishment virtually treated the Nirankaris as apostates and heretics, they had been able to attract a sizeable following in the Punjab and outside, among them a number of high government officials, both Hindu and Sikh.

It is not improbable in the kind of unstable political conditions then obtaining in the state for some of these officers to try to influence governmental decisions in some crucial matters. The grant of permission by the district authorities to the Nirankaris to hold their convention in Amritsar, the principal seat of Sikh religion and politics, on a day that coincided with Baisakhi, a most important day in Sikh history, would probably fall in this category. For, it is extremely unusual for a prudent district magistrate to act in such a manner, in view of the long history of conflict and confrontation between the Nirankaris and a sizeable section of hard core Sikhs, then under Bhindranwale's influence. The Akali party, as the principal partner in the ruling coalition in the state, was already under considerable pressure to take effective political and other action against the Nirankaris for propagating a heretical creed. They were, however, loath to act strongly because their coalition partners, the BJP (erstwhile Jan Sangh) were not altogether averse to exploiting the issue to keep the Akalis engaged in sorting out their inner party conflicts. Never known for taking a bold stand, likely to threaten their ministerial positions, the Akalis dithered, thus allowing the matter to soon get out of control.

There is reason to believe that the decision to permit the Nirankari conference at such a sensitive venue and juncture by the Amritsar district magistrate could only have been determined either by outside pressure or due to failure to apply his mind to the crucial issue. In either case, he was guilty of gross negligence and misjudgment, leading to a major breach of public order, to say the least. It is also highly unlikely that he would have sought a report from the district police before grant of sanction for the meeting. For no police superintendent in his senses would have recommended such a course of action, unless he too was acting under pressure. We know from reliable sources that the deputy commissioner of the neighbouring district of Gurdaspur, Niranjan Singh, belonged to the Nirankari sect, as probably did the then state chief secretary. Then there were sundry other unseen hands in Delhi and Chandigarh, both among politicians and bureaucrats, who were interested in aggravating conflict situations in the state in pursuance of their own devious objectives. The case of the Amritsar district magistrate acting in a palpably irresponsible and imprudent manner in such a vital matter reflects the degree of trivialization of the instruments of state policy and its implementation, especially in the sphere of law enforcement.

Such persistent decline of state instrumentalities would finally lead to the virtual collapse of the entire state structure in the next decade to usher in an era of turmoil. If such crucial pillars of state power and the rule of law as district magistrates and police chiefs become creatures of powerful politicians and unscrupulous seniors and compromise their commitment to the basic charter of their duties, both public order and the security of state, the two imperatives to which the modern state structure is supposed to owe its very existence, are bound to come under grave threat. That is exactly what happened in the Punjab after the initial fuse was lighted by the Baisakhi clash of 1978 in Amritsar.

Let us take a close look at the episode itself, probably the most significant of the many that led to the decade-long militancy in the region. Sikhs traditionally celebrate the historic event every year by gathering in large numbers in the Golden Temple at Amritsar, where religious congregations and discourses are held, calling pointed attention of the audience to their glorious history and the spirit of sacrifice and valour displayed by the Khalsa to defend panthic values and traditions, whenever it came under threat from disbelievers and detractors. The Nirankaris were at that very juncture being projected as posing just such a threat to the purity of the Sikh faith by the Taksal chief and his followers. No Punjab cadre officer could have been so ignorant as not to realize the grave risks involved in allowing such a convention to be held at Amritsar in the climate then prevailing in the state and in the face of the extreme position taken by not only Bhindranwale but also by a section of the Akalis, led by that master manipulator, Gurcharan Singh Tohra.

It may be mentioned that even after the permission had been granted, the Punjab government had been approached by some well-meaning individuals to rescind it and ask the organizers to change the venue. However, the compulsions of coalitional politics and perhaps a directive from Delhi negated all such efforts. With the amplifiers installed all around the Nirankari convention site relaying what the people gathered in the Temple considered a heretical anti-Sikh creed, Bhindranwale was under intense pressure from his fanatical followers to retaliate strongly against such provocative goings-on. It did not take long for the crowds of devotees gathered there for the Baisakhi celebrations to get embroiled in the commotion and create an awkward situation for Bhindranwale, well on his way to secure a dominant position for himself in Sikh politics and project the Akali leadership as a bumbling and power-hungry set of politicians, incapable of safeguarding Sikh interests and purity of the panthic legacy from many anti-Sikh forces, among them the Nirankaris.

Such a situation was custom-made for exploitation by the Congress leadership in Delhi to surreptitiously lend a hand in provoking a confrontation between the two sides and prompt Bhindranwale to seize the initiative from the Akalis at this significant moment. It may be recalled that the former was already being zealously wooed by Zail Singh and Sanjay Gandhi and would soon be inveigled into opposing the Akali candidates in elections to the Sikh Gurudwara Prabandhak Committee (SGPC) and the panchayats. He would later actively canvass for R.L. Bhatia and Sukhbans Kaur Bhinder, Congress candidates from Amritsar and Gurdaspur parliamentary constituencies in the 1980 elections.

Later, when the pressure from the congregation mounted amid slogan-shouting and some exchange of blows, Bhindranwale offered to go to the site of the convention in order to protest against the anti-Sikh utterances of the Nirankari leaders. He was, however, dissuaded from doing so by some well-wishers. According to some versions, however, the Sant grew somewhat nervous at the prospect of a confrontation and opted out on some pretext or the other. Instead a group of Sikhs, including some members of the Taksal, led by one Fauja Singh, an employee in the Punjab agriculture department and a prominent member of the Akhand Kirtani Jatha (those who recite the holy *Granth*) proceeded to the venue of the Nirankari meet to protest. What happened afterwards is unclear. While the protesters complained that the Nirankaris attacked them with swords and firearms, the latter accused the Sikhs of armed assault on the meeting with a view to killing their guru, Gurbachan Singh, and described their action as self-defence. However, the melee ended in the death of 13 Sikhs, which would lead to a prolonged strife between the Sikh political and religious establishments and the Nirankaris. But even more importantly, the clash will also, in a short span of time, propel Bhindranwale to emerge as the tallest Sikh

leader in the state. The Akalis will henceforth be content
to play a subsidiary role in the state, though they will
continue to make efforts to regain the initiative The
reported participation of some senior Punjab government
officials in the Nirankari convention must also have
encouraged the Nirankari people to take the bull by the
horns. Police investigations later revealed that the attack
on the Sikhs was led by a man on horseback and took
place some 250-400 yards away from the conference
venue, and the attackers were armed. They were obviously
determined to teach the Sikhs a lesson and settle their
protestations once and for all with deadly force[2].

The ruling Akali party, no longer able to maintain a
stance of masterly inactivity, now acted at two levels. On
the religious front, a *hukumnama* or religious decree was
issued on 10 June 1978 from the Akal Takht, the supreme
seat of temporal power, sanctified by the sixth Guru,
Hargobind, requiring the Sikhs to sever all social relations
and marital alliances with 'those Sikhs who have become
a part and parcel of this hypocritical and heterodox so-
called Nirankari organization and with their leader,
Gurbachan Singh'. On the administrative side, a special
investigation team was set up to pursue the criminal case,
registered against Nirankari guru Baba Gurbachan Singh
and 63 others. The investigation came to the conclusion
that the attack on the Sikhs was in pursuance of a
conspiracy, hatched by a number of accused persons,
including Baba Gurbachan Singh. Accordingly, all the
accused were taken into custody except the latter, who
was arrested later in Delhi, but only after obtaining
clearance from no less a person than then Prime Minister
Morarji Desai. Two of the accused persons turned
approvers. Later, the case was transferred for trial to
Karnal in Harayana as the accused persons feared threat
to their lives.

The case ended in acquittal on January 1980, thus strengthening Bhindranwale and his expanding band of supporters in the belief that Sikhs could never get justice in a Hindu India. Bhindranwale himself was transformed overnight into a celebrity leader of the community, soon to reduce the entire traditional Sikh leadership to a helpless bunch, thus substantially fulfilling the long-desired Congress objective in this regard.

The case failed in court due to the inability of the Punjab authorities to ensure that the prosecution witnesses were not suborned by interested parties in distant Karnal and the adverse ambiance created by the local people with the connivance of Haryana police. However and more importantly, it was the evidence tendered by Lala Jagat Narain of the Hind Samachar group of newspapers, that clinched the issue. In his deposition, he refuted the entire prosecution theory by claiming that the 13 Sikhs had, in fact, died in police firing. Jagat Narain had been persona non grata with the followers of Bhindranwale for quite some time due to his relentless campaign against their leader and defending the Nirankaris' right to freedom of expression and faith in a democratic polity. His staunch disapproval and censure of the causes espoused by Bhindranwale in his many editorials had made him extremely unpopular with them, to say the least. His evidence in the Karnal court, leading to the failure of the case against the Nirankaris, further compounded the hostility of the Bhindranwale camp towards him and his family-held group of newspapers. The Punjab government, now headed by Darbara Singh of the Congress, declined to file an appeal against the acquittal, even though the prosecution had made out a well-reasoned case for the same. Bhindranwale now went on the offensive, declaring from every available platform that since the Hindu government had failed to render justice in the case where 13 Singhs had lost their lives, he would see that the killers are brought to book by whatever means. As if on cue, Baba Gurbachan Singh was shot dead on 24 April 1980 in the Nirankari Bhawan in Delhi.

To his devotees, he was the embodiment of divinity and *jagat pita*, or father of the world. His murder in the national capital expectedly shocked not only his followers but also the entire establishment. The act was projected as an open challenge to the Indian state, marking a serious breakdown of law and order in the country. The Central Bureau of Investigation (CBI) was entrusted with the case, which soon unearthed the conspiracy and arrested the main accused Ranjit Singh. The case was successfully prosecuted by the CBI and ended in conviction of Ranjit and a few others. A few years later, the same Ranjit Singh would be appointed the head priest of the Akal Takht, a position of immense prestige in the Sikh religion. This is not unusual, as this is how the community traditionally demonstrates its high regard for those of its members, who, in its judgment, have avenged a perceived wrong to the *panth*, even though the state might have found them guilty of a criminal offence and awarded the prescribed punishment. In a way, this would also become a precedent for the future when a large number of militants killed by security forces, as well as the killers of Indira Gandhi, would be posthumously accorded high ceremonial honours.

Lala Jagat Narain was shot dead on 9 September 1981 while on his way to Jalandhar after attending a function in Patiala. His son Ramesh Chander met the same fate on 12 May 1984. The entire establishment of the Hind Samachar group, including many in its editorial staff and the sales network, continued to be targeted during the whole period of militancy. An important spin-off of the 1978 Nirankari-Sikh clash in Amritsar was the emergence of Sant Bhindranwale as the most popular mass leader of the Sikhs and the initiation of a process of steady decline of mainstream Sikh leadership.

*

We have already referred to the Sikh institution of Damdami Taksal and the rapid rise of Sant Jarnail Singh Bhindranwale in its hierarchy. It remains to be mentioned that its then chief, Sant Kartar Singh, nominated him as his successor in preference to his son, Amrik Singh, obviously because he saw in him a more doctrinaire successor. Amrik Singh remained his life-long associate, both meeting their death during Operation Blue Star in 1984. Bhindranwale's career in the Taksal and then in the Sikh politico-religious hierarchy, after the Baisakhi clash in Amritsar, was swift and, in some ways, unexpected. Several factors must have played their part in the process, among them the manipulative practices of the Congress leadership and the inbuilt weaknesses of the Akali party, along with their intense craving for political power at all costs. The ordinary Sikhs were thoroughly disillusioned with them as they were neither able to provide good governance nor safeguard their religious or political interests. To make matters worse, the party was steeped in corruption and the *jathedars*, who controlled the party structure at the district and lower levels, were virtually unlettered and uncouth. The 1978 clash between the Nirankaris and a section of the Sikhs would further alienate them from the mass of the Sikh people for their failure either to prevent the mishap or to take effective action afterwards. Being the dominant partner in the coalition government in Punjab, this was the least that the community expected from them.

On the other hand, it was Bhindranwale who appeared to have sensed the mood of his people and wrested the initiative from the Akali-led government in the matter of truly and strongly voicing the Sikh demands and aspirations. His clear-cut affirmation of the injustice meted out to the Sikhs in the Baisakhi episode in Amritsar, couched in his typical rustic and forthright idiom, would create an instant rapport with the Sikh masses. It was this constituency that would provide the mainstay of the militant movement in the years to come.

Having lost the advantage to Bhindranwale and his revivalist line, the Akalis reverted to the Anandpur Sahib resolutions of 1973 and tried to beat the former at his own game of fundamentalist rhetoric. However, it was too late and in a matter of less than two years, they would lose political power in the state to the Congress. As is their wont, once out of office, the Akalis once again became vociferous campaigners for rectification of many Sikh grievances and fulfillment of their demands put forward from time to time. A period of mutual wrangling and unseemly tussles between the two sides, each trying to upstage the other, would now follow, with the Akalis frequently coming out second best. The Akali party would itself split among many factions, directing their ire more often at each other than at the Congress, obviously an immensely enjoyable spectacle for it. Not until the late 1990s would the battered party regain political power in the state, once again with the BJP as its coalition partner.

For the present, however, Bhindranwale's stars were clearly on the ascendant. In the wake of the Nirankari clash, he had emerged as the authentic defender of the honour and integrity of the *panth*. He had vowed to

avenge the killings of Sikhs and it did not take him long
to prove that he was true to his word. As a first step,
Nirankari Bhawans all over the state were *gheraoed* (a
Hindi word meaning laying siege and blocking all ingress
and exit from the target site) and threats of physical
assaults were allegedly freely held out to the followers of
the Nirankari creed. Bhindranwale was taken into custody
by the Punjab police for interrogation in connection with
the murder of Baba Gurbachan Singh in Delhi, because he
had allegedly promised 'to weigh the killers in gold' for
their signal service to the *panth*. But he was soon let off,
presumably on advice from Delhi. The police also wanted
to examine him in the Lala Jagat Narain murder case. By
that time, however, he was away in Mumbai and Delhi,
travelling through Maharashtra, Rajasthan, Madhya
Pradesh and Haryana, accompanied by his band of heavily
armed retainers in a well-appointed bus. The magnitude
of his presumed proximity to powerful elements in the
Union government and the Congress party pre-empted
any police action against him for breach of several sections
of the Indian Arms Act and other relevant provisions of
law. According to some police officers, then in service, the
signals from Delhi were treated with due deference and, in
some places in Rajasthan, the caravan was suitably escorted
by local police teams to the next destination, not an
unlikely practice with Indian police forces, still functioning
in an overly servile mode with respect to those in power.

To the large number of his simple and ingenuous
admirers in Punjab and elsewhere, these events were a
clear indication that he was a person to reckon with in the
corridors of power, even in the national capital. Among
his mentors in Delhi was Jathedar Santokh Singh of the
Delhi Sikh Gurudwara Parbandhak Committee, another
of Giani's favourite Sikh leaders, who too was suspected

of extremist links and was later to be killed by them. On receipt of information that, on his return journey, Bhindranwale was to stay for some time at a gurudwara in Chando Kalan village in Haryana, a Punjab police party under DS Mangat, then a deputy inspector general of police, was rushed there to take him in custody for interrogation in the Lala murder case. However, the quarry fled the scene before Mangat's arrival, apparently having been tipped off by persons or agencies allegedly working at the behest of Zail Singh and the Haryana government. In the event, while the Sant made his way successfully to the heavily-barricaded gurudwara in Chowk Mehta, eluding the special police arrangements made all over the state for his arrest, the Punjab police posse vented their anger and frustration by beating up people all around and setting fire to the property. They would later be charged with intending to eliminate the Sant in an *encounter*, not an implausible accusation in view of the reputation of the Punjab police in that dubious department. The police party was also blamed for setting fire to some holy books and generally vandalizing the gurudwara. Sikh militants would later take revenge by killing Mangat's son.

Safely ensconced in the relative security of his headquarters in Chowk Mehta, Bhindranwale now set his own terms for his surrender and arrest, to which the authorities, considerably more cautious after the Chando Kalan fiasco, meekly agreed. On 20 September 1981, the day chosen by him for his surrender, he came out of the gurudwara after addressing a large religious gathering, which included a number of Akalis as well as pro-Congress Sikh leaders from Delhi like Santokh Singh, and offered himself for arrest in an environment of much religious fervour and slogan-shouting. With the situation threatening to go out of control due to the excitement and ardour prevailing among the crowd, the police opened fire, killing some 12 people. This provoked a great deal of violence by his followers, in which a police official lost his life. His followers firmly believed that he had been falsely implicated. Apart from setting off a great deal of resentment and anger in the Sikh masses, the arrest inspired at least one retaliatory terrorist act within a few days of that event, when an Indian Airlines aircraft was hijacked on 29 September by Dal Khalsa, a radical Sikh organization of long standing.

The theatrical style of his arrest and the way in which he was seen to be dictating terms to an all-powerful Punjab police would greatly reinforce his mystique and charisma in the eyes of ordinary Sikhs and help him in acquiring a reputation for invincibility as against the mighty Indian state. The bulk of the Sikh people, especially in the rural areas, not aware of the support and patronage freely extended to him by Zail Singh, the Union home minister, and the powerful state agencies under his control, came to invest him with superhuman traits and capabilities. Soon, his no-nonsense and brusque style of sermons, delivered in unpretentious Punjabi with a flavour of its own, would become enormously popular in the Punjab countryside and even a casual drive through the villages would furnish enough evidence of his growing popularity and influence among the Sikh masses. In a couple of years, he would acquire such an air of inviolability that the Sikh masses stubbornly refused to believe that he had indeed been killed in Operation Blue Star and remained confident that he would soon resurface to lead the community in those troubled times, much in the manner that large segments of Indian people continued to hope for the return of freedom fighter Subhash Chandra Bose.

It may not be far off the mark to assume that a large segment of the Sikh community saw in Jarnail Singh Bhindranwale an authentic sant or saintly personage carrying on a relentless struggle against the oppressive forces of imperialism, directed against the small Sikh minority, which readily brought to mind the sacrifices of Guru Gobind Singh in an earlier age. The concept of *sant-sipahi* or saint-soldier is deeply rooted in Sikh tradition and occupies a special place in the collective Sikh consciousness, particularly in times of crisis for the community. That could be the most rational explanation for Bhindranwale's rapid rise in the Sikh hierarchy that also coincided with the escalation of anti-Congress sentiment in the community.

Some social analysts have sought to relate the phenomenon of Bhindranwale's swift rise to a position of centrality in Sikh politics to Punjab's green revolution, brought about by the modernization of agricultural techniques in the early 1970s and its degenerative effects on the economy, sociology and cultural values in the countryside. Dr Pritam Singh of Oxford Brookes University, who has dealt with the subject at length, thinks that such modernization affected the Punjab countryside in two ways, one progressive and the other degenerative. While 'the progressive form expressed itself in the erosion of obscurantist beliefs and values and the spread of modern ideologies like Marxism... (its) degenerative form—the other facet—was the product of the differentiated nature of economic prosperity generated by capitalist transformation of agriculture, the disruption of old social ties, the cultural trauma caused by the dislocation of the old forms of life and the fracturing of the moral-ethical norms. This degenerative form of modernization expressed itself in the menacing spread of alcoholism, smoking, drug-addiction, pornographic literature, lewd music and vulgar cinema'.[3]

Also, and expectedly, religious revivalism of the type that Bhindranwale propounded evoked ready response in the rural areas precisely because it was seen as a kind of crusade against such highly degenerative effects of the green revolution. In the event, it was women and children in rural Sikh families, the worst affected segment of the population, who were in the forefront of his widening support base. This was natural because it was this section that was the worst sufferer of the evils generated by agricultural prosperity in village society. It was only a matter of time before the men too fell in line because they could not hold out indefinitely against children and women, who 'formed a block within the family against the drunken and drug-addicted father/brother/husband. The morally degenerated adult male had no anchor to hold on against this attack from a moral religious posture. The second phase of Sant Bhindranwale's popularity was when male adults also increasingly came to accept the moral hegemony of his preaching'.[4] This was the beginning of a very significant reform movement in the state as far as the Sikh young people were concerned. The latter would increasingly turn to religion for solace and inspiration, abjuring the use of intoxicants and indulgence in other forms of vulgarity. This would coincide with the rising graph of Sant Bhindranwale's popularity and the spread of his cult that would soon transform the rural environment in a major way.

It would thus appear that the first phase of his public life was devoted purely to religious reform, a component of which was to make young Sikh men and women *amritdhari* or baptized Sikhs, strictly observing all the prescribed traditions and practices of their religion. It also involved the initiation of a campaign against casteism and obscurantism, which he deemed to be the outcome of Brahmin cultural intrusion. In this phase of his movement, the Sant would prove to be the most effective of all Sikh reformers in reaching out to scheduled caste Sikhs to get baptized in the Sikh tradition and thus reassert their identity as equal partners in the rural Sikh social hierarchy, customarily dominated by the Jutt Sikhs.

*

In a well-researched study of Sikh militancy in the 1980s, *Violence as Political Discourse*, Dr Birinder Pal Singh of Punjabi University, Patiala, views the Sikh militant movement in the 1980s decade as comprising of four phases. The first phase from 1978 to 1980 coincided with the period when the Akali-BJP coalition was in power in the Punjab and marked the gradual tapering off of Sant Bhindranwale's social reform movement, consequent to the Baisakhi clash between the Sikhs and the Nirankaris at Amritsar. This could be called the gestation phase, when the grievances were piling up and his idiom was growing progressively strident.

The second phase covered the period 1981-1984, starting with the dismissal of the Akali-BJP coalition government by the Centre on return of Indira Gandhi to power in 1980, and ending with the assault on the Golden Temple by the Indian army in Operation Blue Star in June 1984. This phase was marked by growing estrangement between the Akalis and Bhindranwale, although a veneer of unity was maintained for strategic reasons, more so by the former than the latter.

This phase was also marked by a progressive rise in killings by his followers, acquisition of weaponry, militant rhetoric and the transfer of his residence into the Golden Temple complex, first to Guru Nanak Niwas and then to the more secure and sacred Akal Takht, a move considered rather sacrilegious by sections of the community though the feelings of hurt, if any, remained unexpressed; understandably so. A few Hindu-Sikh riots also took place during the period, starting off from Patiala in 1981, which would greatly aggravate mutual hostility between the two communities and lead to the emergence and consolidation of combative Hindu organizations like the Hindu Suraksha Samiti, Hindu Rashtriya Sangthan and Hindu Shiv Sena, particularly active in urban centres of Ludhiana and Patiala, besides the older RSS to confront the Sikh militants. Set up by one Pawan Kumar Sharma in Patiala on 26 September 1982, the *samiti* remained active in many Punjab cities for some time, distributing huge *trishuls* and other weapons to Hindu young men and generally awakening the community to the dangers looming large before them.

The parallel communalization of both Hindus and Sikhs in urban Punjab set off a number of Hindu-Sikh clashes in Ludhiana and its neighbourhood in the run-up to Operation Blue Star, giving a fillip to the emergence of lumpen elements in both the communities. If the Sikh militants were branded as criminal and deviants, the young members of the newly formed Hindu organizations were no less, most of them coming from the class of lumpen urban gangsters. Only their brawn and muscle power was now used for religious rather than personal purposes. The members of these diverse *samitis* were financed and otherwise patronized by rich Hindu traders and businessmen and gained substantially, both in financial terms and in prestige. The Patiala riots of 1981 could also be seen in terms of an economic dimension as a tussle for supremacy in trade and business between the migrant Khatri-Bhapa Sikhs from Pakistan and the older Hindu-*lala* shopkeepers living and doing business in the town for ages. This phase is important as before its end in 1984, the Akali party had been virtually eclipsed by Bhindranwale, who had also more or less annexed the Sikh political and religious space by then. While we will deal with the many controversies surrounding the 1984 army operation in Amritsar in more detail later in this book, let it be mentioned in passing that the Akalis too were involved in playing an active though behind-the-scenes role in promoting the idea of induction of the army for the express purpose of cutting Bhindranwale to size.

The years 1984 and 1985 together would appear to form the third phase, which was marked by state repression of a massive scale and the launching of operations Blue Star and Wood Rose, the assassination of Indira Gandhi in reprisal and the widespread Sikh killings in Delhi and several other Indian cities and towns, possibly to teach the Sikhs a lesson they will not forget in a hurry.

The fourth and last phase embraced the period from 1985 to 1992, during which militant violence would escalate to alarming proportions and, for a time, it looked as if the state had exhausted all its resources and abilities to overcome the militant challenge. The sharp intensification of militant violence in the post-1986 period, for reasons to be gone into later, raised grave doubts about the adequacy of the country's legal and judicial processes to cope with serious eruptions of terrorist violence, inspired by perceived threats to their distinct identities by sundry minority segments in a country of India's monumental diversities. The law-enforcement authorities were hard put to match the ingenuity and novelty of the operational techniques and terrorist hardware employed by militant groups in holding the entire state to ransom by the end of the decade.

It would not be long before a desperate Punjab police, supported by large contingents of central paramilitary forces and the Indian army and, evidently, with the implicit authorization of the state and Union governments, would finally turn its back on even the outward trappings of due process of law in its fight against the mounting wave of terrorist violence. That the political authorities were kept fully in the picture with regard to the extra judicial methods used by the security forces in combating terrorism in Punjab is no longer the best kept secret of the times. The inadequacies of the Indian legal and judicial processes, steeped in mid-nineteenth century concepts and procedures, make it incumbent on law-enforcers to reach outside the boundaries of law to find solutions to uncommon and critical situations of public peace and order. If widespread rumours are to be believed, it seems that by the end of the 1980s decade, the situation in the matter of terrorist killings in almost the whole of Punjab had become so acute that a bewildered police leadership thought it was time to take the highest political authority in Delhi into confidence and seek his approval to resort to what was then referred to as the *capture and kill* strategy to deal with the menace, then being projected as a threat to the unity and integrity of the nation. That the police and central security forces were already practising this stratagem, was another matter. We will revert to the subject at an appropriate time later.

Interestingly, the Akalis figured prominently in the list of four enemies of the panth that Bhindranwale spoke about so frequently, especially after he moved into the Golden Temple complex. The other three were the Nirankaris, whom he called *narakdharis* or denizens of hell, the state and its repressive mechanisms and ideological biases and the Hind Samachar group of newspapers for its communal and anti-Sikh orientation and writings. The Akali leadership came under attack for its failure to safeguard Sikh interests and using *panthic* issues for narrow political and power-seeking purposes. Significantly, while upbraiding the Akalis for their incapacity to take care of the long-time interests of the community in the face of persistent assaults from the Congress-ruled Indian state and other enemies, Bhindranwale was only repeating what the Akali Dal had been clamouring about since before independence. He also became very critical of the Akalis during this phase for their evasive approach towards the Amritsar killings of April 1978, although being in the government, they possessed all the power to take decisive action. While addressing the growing numbers of his followers and admirers in his typical rustic idiom of Punjabi, he now often bracketed the Akalis with other forces, antagonistic to *panthic* unity and self-respect. A recurrent theme in his sermons was to rhetorically invite his audience to identify those who 'having sucked the blood of the martyrs, having beaten the *dug-dugi* (small drum) in the *panth's* name, having addressed the *narakdharis* as father, having used the kesari flag, that one who wants to retain his power, recognize him O Khalsa'.[5]

We have already mentioned that the marginalization of the Akali party as a long-time political voice of the Sikh community was an integral part of the political strategy evolved by Zail Singh and the top Congress leadership in Delhi and it was to be accomplished with the help and support of Bhindranwale. It needs to be added at this stage that soon after attaining a position of some influence within the community, the latter would gradually disengage himself from the Congress and come to pursue an autonomous course, a move that will gather strength as his influence and appeal among the Sikh masses grew while the Akalis lost their supremacy and authority in the community. While the eclipse of the Akali Dal as the chief source of political leadership to the community appeared to serve the Congress objectives for the time being, the emergence of Bhindranwale as an alternative focus of authority was certainly not an unmixed blessing, as that venerable old party would soon discover. In fact, such a development was beset with some very grave consequences in terms of political and administrative stability, not only for the state and the country but also for the South Asian region as a whole.[6]

*

We have already discussed the raison d'être of Sikh militancy in an earlier chapter. A reference to an important attribute of Sikhism will make it easier to recognize the underlying logic of Bhindranwale's exhortations to his followers and why they made such profound sense to them, a process that would play a major role in setting off the decade-long militant movement in north India. Born in an age of ruthless religious persecution and oppression, Sikhism remained engaged in a prolonged fight for survival, for much of its short history, against an all-powerful state, bent upon stifling its very identity. Finding it impossible to defend their followers' freedom of religion through mere passive adherence to a regimen of rites and rituals, most Sikh Gurus were obliged to practise and preach an aggressive blend of religion and politics. The notion of separation of religion and politics—in the sense in which it is generally viewed in modern theories of governance—

is foreign to the Sikh religion. Although the Sikh leadership has often affirmed this reality as an article of faith, it continues to be a much-misunderstood and baffling feature of Sikhism, particularly in the new democratic context, with its special emphasis on secularism.

Thus, faced with a grave threat to its very survival early in its history, Sikhism had to rely on a different set of core concepts to safeguard its integrity and identity in an environment marked by brutal state repression against an enfeebled Hindu clergy, somewhat ineffectively resisting state-supported Islam. It is not as if the new creed was the only one among the major religions of the world to advocate resort to violence to defend itself against repression and injustice. Just as most modern, rationalist-scientific theories have no problem with the use of violence to seek justice for an oppressed class or section of society, most religious belief systems all over the world too support the use of violent means to redress a wrong, when all other modes prove ineffective. 'These philosophies too have a matching and balancing combination of pacifism and radicalism, non-violence and violence. The latter is never invoked in the first instance, be it the just war of radical Christianity, jihad in Islam and *dharamyuddha* in Hinduism and Sikhism. All these religions do preach and practise non-violence, but take to violence only at its extreme to restore order and justice in society'.[7] Where the Sikh faith differs from the conceptual acceptance of violence as the weapon of last resort by other religions is the universality of its invocation at all religious functions and during all the prescribed daily rituals and prayers that constitute the principal schedule of worship and piety in the religion. This notion of justifiable violence as an integral part of an organized and coherent religious structure to the extent of its inclusion in daily rituals and modes of worship is probably unique to Sikhism.

It is not for nothing, therefore, that the appeal of Bhindranwale to the Sikh masses was instant and impassioned. For, both the cultural and religious tradition and practice in Sikhism attributes a positive value to the use of violence to recover lost dignity and honour, and to fight evil. Sikhism also legitimizes the use of violence provided it is rooted in human values, though humanist militancy may also turn into martial militancy, if and when circumstances so warrant.

Though the concepts elaborated above find mention in the writings of most Sikh Gurus, it is the tenth Guru, Gobind Singh, whose numerous literary compositions reveal his fierce belief and support for what would probably be called the doctrine of martial militancy in modern parlance, for securing justice and equity for all oppressed and persecuted peoples, and not for the Sikh *panth* alone. The *Dasam Granth*, an anthology of his writings, contains umpteen references to the concept of just and valid violence and the weaponry, which is an essential prerequisite for fighting injustice and tyranny and guard humanist ideals, the place of honour among these being accorded to the sword. He created the Khalsa in 1699, keeping in mind the pursuit of that specific mission and made the sword an obligatory part of the every day attire of the Khalsa Sikhs. The Khalsa was given a distinctly military appearance, both in form i.e. costume and weaponry and in content or ideology, as enshrined in the *Dasam Granth*. In other words, the Sikhs were given a brand new personality and assigned a new role in keeping with the philosophy of the Gurus.

'Guru Gobind Singh's religion cannot live on this earth without the sparkle of the sword...war is a cruel thing, but what is life when viewed from the standpoint of

Not-god, but an endless cruelty, one crushing the other? So it is the sword that is capable of destroying darkness and this has to be gone through...War is creative of great nobilities; thus, when viewed in the whole scheme of things, it has a purpose. Without passing through it, thrust on them as it was, the Gurus could not have created an ever-inspiring New Order for the Khalsa.'[8] *Shastarmala*, a major treatise on the typology of weapons of violence, used during the war, along with their history and the legends associated with them, forms an important part of the *Dasam Granth*. The daily prayer recited in all Sikh homes and gurudwaras all over the world and at the time of all religious and important political functions comprises of an invocation and homage to *Bhagauti* or the sword. A rough translation in English would read something like 'Contemplate on Guru Nanak, having first evoked the *Bhagauti*.' This Guru extols the virtues of the sword, no doubt understood as a symbol of resistance to oppression and injustice, in many of his compositions included in the *Dasam Granth* such as *Bachitarnatak*, *Chandi di Var* and *Zafarnama*. The latter, meaning an epistle of victory, a long poem in Persian addressed to the Mughal emperor Aurangzeb, contains probably the most explicit statement of his doctrine of martial militancy. The following couplet will illustrate the point more clearly:

> *Choon kar az huma har heelay dar guzasht*
> *Halal ast burden ba shamsheer dast.*

Rendered in English, it would read, 'When all other means have failed and gone unheard, it is righteous to draw the sword out of its scabbard'. Reminding his audience about how heroically the Gurus conducted their many battles against an unjust and invidious system, Bhindranwale found no difficulty in winning over the bulk of the community to his line of thinking. We will conclude this chapter by reproducing here the final stanzas from the Guru's long epic poem *Chandi Di Var*, which are recited in the form of an inspirational prayer not only in Khalsa schools all over the country, but also in the Sikh regiments of the army. It runs as follows:

> Grant me this boon, O Lord;
> May I never turn away from righteous action;
> May I never know fear as I engage in battle with
> The foe, and resolve firmly to win.
> May I ever instruct myself in the passion to utter Thy
>   praises;
> And at the last when the hour of destiny arrives,
> May it be granted me to lay down my life fighting on
>   the field of battle.[9]

3

The Build-up

By the end of the 1970s, the Akalis clearly seemed to be on the defensive in view of the growing popularity and influence that Sant Jarnail Singh Bhindranwale came to acquire among the Sikh masses. The former were now feeling increasingly insecure, both in political and physical terms. Considerable overt and covert support being extended by the top Congress leadership to Bhindranwale had significantly enlarged his support-base in the community, which made it imperative for the Akalis to take a more radical stand in respect of the oft-voiced Sikh demands, in a bid to beat Bhindranwale at his own game.

It was as part of this change of stance that the Akali Dal now set out to more actively stress its commitment to the redressal of so-called Sikh grievances and fulfillment of their long-standing demands. In their attempt to wean away the Sikh masses from Bhindranwale's influence, the Akalis would adopt a two-pronged strategy. One, they would take direct action by launching a series of *morchas*, one after another, to draw pointed attention once more to the various grievances and demands of the community, especially those that could broadly be considered as pertaining to the overall interests of all Punjabis, rather than only the Sikhs. Two, politically engage with the Union government in a series of meetings, spread over several months, in order to pressurize the latter to address issues peacefully, thereby strengthening their standing in the community vis-à-vis Bhindranwale.

However, the prolonged process of negotiations, lasting some two-and-a-half years from 16 October 1981 to 15 February 1984, proved to be an exercise in futility. The failure of the talks, in fact, led to a considerable accretion to Bhindranwale's popularity and appeal within the community and a correspondent diminishing of the Akali influence. Sant Harchand Singh Longowal, the then president of the Akali Dal, led his team during most of such meetings, while the government was represented by bureaucrats and central ministers. Prime Minister Indira Gandhi was present only in three meetings. Nine of these were secret, held either at Delhi or Chandigarh to facilitate the participation of some jailed Akali leaders.

In as many as ten such meetings, political parties other than the principal participants too were invited to take part, ostensibly to achieve what was called a national consensus, though it could have also been a clever device by the Congress to isolate the Akalis and prepare the country for harsher measures in Punjab, such as the involvement of the army in some kind of an operation in Amritsar. As part of their direct action, the Akalis launched four *morchas*, starting with the *Nehar Roko* (or stop the digging of the canal) *morcha* in a village in Patiala district on 24 April 1982. In the initial stages, this *morcha* also had the support of the Communist Party (Marxist), since it was meant to safeguard the interests of farmers, their principal constituency. The Marxists, however, withdrew their support soon after, presumably under pressure from the Communist Party of India, which was known to be following a pro-Congress line under advice from Moscow.

A *Rasta Roko* sit-in was started on 4 April 1983, followed by *Kam Roko* (stop work) and *Rail Roko* agitations on 29 August 1983. Bhindranwale went along with the Akalis in all these agitations, collectively termed as *dharamyudh* or holy war, despite the fact that they were obviously designed to prevent the reins of leadership slipping into the hands of the former. It is another matter that the ongoing marginalization of the Akalis could not be halted, thanks largely to political manipulations on the part of the Congress, the infamous political feud between Zail Singh and Darbara Singh, both of the Congress party, and the clashing ambitions of different Akali leaders, always at each other's throats to access the huge gurudwara funds. Self-seeking by nature and tradition, politicians of whatever persuasion could not care less if, in the process, the state administration was paralyzed and the entire region plunged into a decade-long dance of death and destruction.

By the middle of 1983, Bhindranwale's popularity among the mass of the Sikh people appeared to alarm the Akalis sufficiently for them to think of hardening their position in respect of the *morchas*. Notionally, of course, Longowal continued to be the dictator of the *dharamyudh morchas*, despite tell-tale signs that Bhindranwale was becoming stronger by the day. When asked by the editor of a newsmagazine in August 1983 as to who was leading the *morchas*, Longowal or he, Bhindranwale coolly replied, 'The *morcha* is being led by Sri Guru Granth Sahib. I am

His humble servant. Otherwise there has to be a general in the war. But Sikhs are not jumping into the *morcha* for a particular person but for the protection of their dharam and freedom'[1]. While addressing the Sikh congregations too, he denied any leadership role. 'I am neither a *sant* nor a leader but your humble *das* (servant).' Despite such self-deprecatory gestures, he was well aware that the community had come to repose more faith in his leadership than that of the Akalis.

*

The decision to launch the *dharamyudh* was taken at a World Sikh Conference on 15 July 1981, attended by more than 100,000 Sikhs. Such gatherings, sometimes held as Sarbat Khalsa meetings, had acquired considerable status among Sikh religio-political institutions because of Guru Gobind Singh's decree transferring the responsibility of leading the community after his death to the Sikh *sangat* or congregation and the Granth or the holy book. This became necessary also because there was no living Guru to fulfil that role now.

The tradition took firm root during the troubled times of Muslim persecution after the death of the tenth and last Guru, Gobind Singh. In the period before and after Operation Blue Star, the institution of Sarbat Khalsa would often be utilized by the Akalis and Sikh Congressmen like Zail Singh and Buta Singh for advancing their respective partisan agendas. Later, when the talks with the Union government appeared to be making no headway as the government considered some of the Akali demands unconstitutional, Sant Longowal tried to clear the air by reiterating on 29 November 1983 in an address to his party that the main demands of the party were based on truth and justice and were within the framework of the Indian Constitution.

In another address some time later, he stated that the Akali party had given 'full opportunity to the central government to solve the Punjab and Sikhs' problems through goodwill and negotiations but the Delhi rulers cared a fig for this goodwill by treating it as their weakness...As a last resort, to peacefully face the oppression and highhandedness of the central government rulers, (the Akali Dal) initiated the second phase of its *dharamyudh* at Amritsar for a decisive battle'. Despite the dwindling hold of the Akali leadership on the community, however, their *morchas* proceeded peacefully and non-violently, even in the face of excessively harsh action taken by the state police. In the *Rasta Roko* agitation on 4 April 1983, for example, CRPF contingents opened fire at a number of places, in which some 20 agitators lost their lives. The *Rail Roko* agitation passed off peacefully because all trains passing through the state on that day were cancelled by the government. However, stray killings of Hindus, policemen, informants and followers suspected of disloyalty to Bhindranwale's ideology, had already started, the most prominent of these being the killings of the Nirankari guru at Delhi and Lala Jagat Narain of the Hind Samachar group at Phillaur near Ludhiana. Hindu-Sikh riots too had broken out in Patiala, Phagwara and some other places, giving a sharper edge to a variety of rumours and fears among the people.

The social climate in the state was growing more and more rancorous with each passing day. The developing situation seemed to clearly portend the occurrence of some calamitous event in the not too distant future. We will deal with the state response to these omens later in this chapter. Let us now take a close look at the Sikh demands and grievances.

*

In an earlier chapter, we spoke about the intensely emotive issues of identity and survival that have troubled the small Sikh community during most part of their short history. The complex interplay of diverse social, economic and political forces in post-independence India had fortified their sense of unease and discontent with the new Indian power structure.

The notion that a Sikh homeland alone will resolve all their problems and dilemmas has remained etched deeply in the Sikh psyche for a long time. Khushwant Singh, the noted Sikh scholar, claims in his study of Sikh history that the ideal of a sovereign Sikh state has never been very far from the Sikh mind. 'Ever since the days of Guru Gobind Singh, Sikh congregations have chanted the litany *Raj karey ga Khalsa*—the Khalsa shall rule—as a part of their daily prayer and innumerable Sikhs gave their lives to achieve this ambition. The establishment of the kingdom of Ranjit Singh confirmed the belief of the Sikhs that it was their destiny to rule the Punjab. The fall of the kingdom was considered a temporary setback'.[2] Although the founders of the Indian republic had wisely stuck to the long-time Congress policy of giving to the country a secular constitution, despite quite a few Congress leaders favouring some kind of a Hindu rashtra, the demise of Jawaharlal Nehru in 1964 would mark the beginning of a definite pro-Hindu stance in its polity. The process of Hinduization of the Indian state structures would gather speed after the Congress returned to power in 1980. With a resurgent Hinduism gaining more clout and influence in the polity and an increasing number of Sikhs giving up on religious symbols and rituals, which amounted to a virtual slipping back into Hinduism, the Sikh leadership was faced with a new challenge. Two key components that go into shaping the Sikh consciousness in post-independent India are their fear of being absorbed in Hinduism and the importance of a homeland to guard against such an eventuality.

Khushwant Singh further elaborates the point. 'With the resurgence of Hinduism, the official commitment to secularism is being reduced to a meaningless clause in the Constitution. The emphasis on Sanskrit and Hindi, study of the Aryan classics, insertion of cow-protection as a directive clause in the Constitution, the increase in the number of cow-protection societies, the growth of Hindu political groups such as the Bharatiya Jan Sangh and the militant RSS and the suspicion with which other communities have come to be regarded are but indications of the way the wind is blowing...'[3]

The realization of the vision of a secure and stable homeland, where alone the community could live up to the ideals set by the Gurus and nurture its cultural and religious values to the full, formed the principal thrust of all the charter of demands put forward by the Akali Dal, starting with the memorandum put up to the viceroy in 1931 to the Anandpur Sahib resolutions of 1973 and 1978 and the variety of demands that formed the subject matter of the prolonged negotiations with the Union government in the period immediately preceding Blue Star. It is necessary, therefore, that the Akali *morchas* as well as the decade-long militancy in the Punjab be viewed in a historical context as all Sikh agitations and *morchas* derive their inspiration from the community's past experience.

A large majority of the Sikhs appeared to support the goals of the movement, at least during its initial ideologically driven phase. The activists themselves preferred to be called *kharkus* (militants) and not *attwadis* (extremists) or terrorists, and most Punjab newspapers as well as the official media like Doordarshan and All India Radio went along with their dictates. More discriminating writers varied the use of these terms from time to time, depending on the character of the movement at a particular juncture, sometimes even giving up these terms and using the more expedient expression 'extremist'.

The inability of the Akali leadership to hold out against the rising influence of Bhindranwale was further compounded by squabbles within the party. Axiomatically, the leadership overload, so characteristic of Sikh politics, tends to crowd the limited political space available at the top of the Sikh religio-political realm. This phenomenon makes a sustained political struggle very difficult indeed. Thus, at any given point of time, a number of factions would be contending with each other to appropriate the political space, each faction flush with a profusion of leaders. The trio of Gurcharan Singh Tohra, Harchand Singh Longowal and Parkash Singh Badal dominated the Sikh religio-political landscape during much of the pre-Blue Star period, with many smaller players like Talwandi, Umranangal, Mann and others also coming to the forefront off and on. Tohra was an archetypal Jathedar, well known in the traditional gurudwara culture, with a reputation of being a hardliner in politics and a shrewd operator. He remained the president of the well-endowed Sikh Gurudwara Parbandhak Committee (SGPC), a statutory elected Sikh body for management of Sikh gurudwaras in Punjab, for 13 consecutive years during most part of the 1970s and early 1980s. He was also a member of the Rajya Sabha for long. He is reportedly the first mainstream Akali leader to have claimed in recent times that the 'Sikhs are a nation'.

Sant Harchand Singh Longowal was truly a saintly character and represented the moderate face of the Akalis. He remained president of the Akali Dal for many years during that difficult phase. He entered into a most controversial accord with Prime Minister Rajiv Gandhi in July 1985, allegedly against the advice of his colleagues in the party. He was shot dead in a gurudwara shortly thereafter in somewhat mysterious circumstances.

Badal comes from an affluent land-owning background and is arguably the coolest (in its most modern sense) of the three, having survived all attempts by Congressmen and his Akali colleagues to finish him off politically. Both Tohra and Longowal are no more on the scene, leaving only Badal to claim the political legacy of the original threesome. And although several factions have cropped up to claim Bhindranwale's militant legacy since his death in 1984, Badal retains the maximum influence in the Sikh religio-political arena, controlling both the party and the SGPC. Longowal and Bhindranwale were hardly on speaking terms, the former referring to Bhindranwale as 'Chambal', the notorious dacoity area in Madhya Pradesh, the latter would return the compliment by calling Longowal 'Gandhi Ashram', for obvious reasons. The situation inside the Golden Temple remained severely vitiated by infighting, often marked by exchange of hot words and fisticuffs. Bhindranwale shifted his residence to the Akal Takht towards the end of 1983.

While the Akalis were pursuing *morcha* politics and engaged in never-ending but apparently fruitless talks with the Union government, Bhindranwale had set himself a grueling touring schedule and considerably widened his *amrit prachar* (a Sikh form of baptism) movement in the rural areas, his principal constituency. His sermons were often loaded with religious and political imagery, harking back to the idiom used by the Gurus. He would fervently allude to the dual concepts of *miri* (temporal) and *piri* (spiritual) in the Sikh tradition and their inseparability from each other, especially in times of strife and turmoil for the *panth*, as symbolized by the sixth and the tenth Gurus. The metaphors and similes used by him found a ready response among his audience and, what is more, the political overtones implicit in his sermons were not lost on them, especially as he spoke openly about the current demoralization in the community, brought about as much by the Brahmin-Bania ruling elite in Delhi, as by the decrepit leadership of the Sikh *quom* itself. The frequent references in Sikh folklore to Brahmins as hostile to the Sikhs is rooted in the reported betrayal of the two younger sons of Guru Gobind Singh by his cook, Gangu Brahmin, to the nawab of Sirhind, who had them later bricked alive at Fatehgarh, when they refused to convert to Islam. Or so the story goes.

'One may find a clear direction to the militant movement being given by him in his religious discourses. His finding faults in his own community and suggesting a remedy of "connecting with the guru" implied subordination of *miri* to *piri*, of temporal power to spiritual one. It opened vistas for a struggle on the Khalsa lines'.[4] Huge congregations of Sikhs would listen intently to his lectures at Gurudwara Manji Sahib in the temple complex and carry glowing accounts of his austere bearing and ardent attachment to the values and beliefs advocated by their Gurus back to their villages, thus giving him a larger-than-life persona. Many of his sermons at the time appeared to clearly validate his confrontational approach for the redress of Sikh grievances, a task the Akalis had failed to accomplish for the last half a century after independence. 'It is a sin for a Sikh to keep weapons to hurt an innocent person, to rob anyone's home, to dishonour anyone or to oppose anyone', he would declaim. 'But there is no greater sin for a Sikh than keeping weapons and not using them to protect his faith...and to seek justice.'[5] Despite provocative speeches by Bhindranwale impliedly castigating the Akali leadership for their indifference to the sufferings of the Sikhs, the latter kept their cool as far as he was concerned but tried their best to beat him at his own game by trying to focus more on religious issues. However, Bhindranwale was always a step ahead in his extremist rhetoric and the Akalis soon found themselves fighting a losing battle.

*

The World Sikh Convention held at Amritsar in July 1981 called upon the Akali Dal to work more energetically for the acceptance of the Anandpur Sahib resolutions. Later that year, the Dal submitted a charter of 45 grievances and demands to Prime Minister Indira Gandhi, which would mark the beginning of prolonged but unfruitful talks between the Akalis and the Union government and the diverse *morchas* organized by the party, as already mentioned. Altogether some 200,000 Sikhs courted arrest during these agitations, conducted in a strictly non-violent satyagraha mode, leading to an acute congestion in the state's prisons. When the government in desperation decided to set the detainees free, they refused to be released, forcing the authorities to resort to some rather odd practices to get rid of the prisoners some way or the other, a phenomenon peculiar to this part of the world.

The state police, not given to treating law-breakers, even peaceful non-violent agitators, with kid gloves, would often use excessive force, both at the time of taking the agitators in custody and later when they refused to be set free. This considerably aggravated the already existing anti-police and anti-state sentiment in the countryside and, together with the enormous mass mobilization, created a widespread climate of instability and unrest in the state.

Soon the political and sectarian atmosphere in the region grew so surcharged that every new incident, even remotely suggestive of a sectarian link, would become one more cog in the chain of mutual suspicions and misgivings between Hindus and Sikhs on the one hand and between the Sikhs and the state administration, especially the police, on the other.

An event of considerable import that exacerbated the Hindu-Sikh antagonism occurred in Haryana in November 1982. The Akali Dal decided to hold demonstrations at Delhi during the Asian Games to protest against the non-acceptance of their demands by the Union government. Haryana police went out of their way to harass and maltreat Sikhs travelling to Delhi through Haryana territory. Needless and excessive force was used in a calculated attempt to insult Sikh travellers, including senior retired and serving defence and police officers, and jeer at their religious symbols. A few persons also lost their lives. Chief minister Bhajan Lal appeared to have amply repaid the favours done to him by the Congress top brass a few years ago in the allocation of Punjab's river waters. These incidents would not make the resolution of the emergent situation of conflict and chaos any the easier. Dipanker Gupta, former attorney general of West Bengal and a close observer of the Punjab scene, offers a different view of this episode. He writes: 'But what is perhaps unknown to many is that on the eve of the inauguration of the Asiad in 1982, an agreement was actually arrived at between the Congress (I) and the Akalis, where even H.S. Surjeet of the CPI (M) was involved. While the Akali leaders, such as P.S. Badal, and the Congress (I) mediators were toasting this event and waiting for the official declaration from the cabinet, Indira Gandhi suddenly announced that the agreement was not acceptable to her'.[6]

The Indian Constitution brackets Sikhs with Hindus for certain purposes in respect of some aspects of personal law. The Akali Dal, claiming that the offending Article was violative of the Sikh affirmation of a separate identity, decided to publicly burn copies of Article 25(2)(b) of the Constitution of India, which contained the relevant provisions, in Delhi and in Chandigarh on 25 February 1984, to show that 'Sikhs were not Hindus'. While the police were able to foil the attempt at Chandigarh, Badal succeeded in reaching Delhi, disguised as a truck driver, to carry out the plan in a somewhat furtive manner. The reportage of the event in the media, misconceived as it was, did immense harm to the Sikh cause by aggravating the unease and alarm among large sections of their countrymen, already being fed biased reports by sections of the media, both official and non-official.

Bhindranwale, in the meanwhile, had gained immensely in stature vis-à-vis the weak-kneed Akali leaders because of the disdain and arrogance with which he was reported to have treated his interrogators, including senior CBI officers investigating the murder cases of the Nirankari chief Gurbachan Singh and Lala Jagat Narain. Excerpts from these interrogation reports were being freely circulated in the villages. He had also secured a clean chit from no less a person than the home minister of India, our good friend Zail Singh. 'No relation could be established in

Sant Jarnail Singh Bhindranwale's connection with the murder of the Nirankari chief. Since Sant Jarnail Singh is not guilty, the government harbours no intention to arrest him and he is free to preach in any corner of India'. So stated the Union home minister in reply to a calling attention motion in the Lok Sabha.

At about the same time, Rajiv Gandhi, the only surviving son of Prime Minister Indira Gandhi, himself a future prime minister of the country, too had publicly stated that Bhindranwale was only a religious preacher, not a criminal or a militant. Ironically, that is what the Sant would have remained except for the scheming genius of many well-known Congress leaders. Such manipulative politics at a most critical stage in Punjab's history for narrow ends has often been noted by observers. To quote just one, 'Hindu communalism is no backlash. The raw material of popular Hindu perception was carefully worked upon by the Congress (I) such that in Punjab today one has two completely distinct views, one Sikh and one Hindu, on almost everything.'[7] It was also widely believed that the goons of the Hindu Suraksha Samiti too received furtive support from Congress party leaders.

*

The period 1980–1984 was marked by a steady deterioration of social and political relations between Hindus and Sikhs, not only in the Punjab but also in its neighbouring areas. The states of Haryana and Himachal Pradesh had formed part of the British province of the Punjab for well over a century, right from the time the British annexed the north-western region. Whereas the principal victims of militant attacks in the Punjab were Hindus, the minority Sikh people were at the receiving end in Haryana and Himachal. Apart from the rough treatment meted out to Sikhs travelling through Haryana territory in November 1982 at the time of the Asian Games, the most serious episode was the anti-Sikh riots on 14 February 1983 at the district headquarter town of Panipat in Haryana, located about 50 miles from Delhi on a busy national highway, targeting Sikhs and their places of worship, resulting in much loss of life and property of the Sikhs and extensive damage to a few gurudwaras.

The police remained a mute spectator, as is their wont in such state-sponsored pogroms, as witnessed in umpteen sectarian riots all over the country for the last many decades, two recent and more prominent instances being the Sikh killings in Delhi in November 1984 and in the anti-Muslim carnage in the Western Indian state of Gujarat some two decades later. Indian law enforcers, it may be reiterated, by law and tradition function in a ruler-supportive role rather than in defence of human rights and civil liberties, with the police owing no accountability to the community.

The continuing violence against the Hindus in Punjab and the Sikhs in Haryana and Himachal would considerably strengthen Bhindranwale's logic of militancy and weaken the political platform preferred by the Akali leadership. The former became more vociferous in making fun of the Akali leaders and stressing their ineptitude in the matter of getting the Sikh grievances redressed. 'The Sikh leaders (Akali Dal) may keep hankering after the Centre with begging bowls but would never obtain anything. You would get something only if you are united under one *Kesari* flag... because *kou kisi ko raj na de hai, jo le hai ni bal se le hai*. The Khalsa always fights for his rights but never begs,' he would hold forth quoting the Sikh scriptures, while addressing huge congregations in the Temple complex. At other times he would say, 'It suits the government to publicize me as an extremist, thus making an excuse to frustrate the just cause and the legitimate demands of the entire Sikh community and the Punjab state.'[8]

This phase also coincided with some degree of communalization of the security forces in the two states of Punjab and Haryana. Indian police no longer lived upto its reputation for functional impartiality between different communities as during the British period. In the late 1960s, with most of North and Central India passing under the control of non-Congress governments, comprising of discontented breakaway Congress legislators, administrative proprieties and impartial decision-making suffered a serious set-back. This trend continued to gain momentum in the succeeding years.

With the onset of militancy in Punjab in the early 1980s, the Hindus started feeling uncomfortable with the state police, a predominantly Sikh Jutt constabulary, suspecting it of being pro-Sikh in their dealings. So the central government inducted the Central Reserve Police Force (CRPF), a Union-controlled paramilitary police, to assuage Hindu worries on this score. This move did not go down well with the Sikhs, who suspected the CRPF to be pro-Hindu in its approach, a belief based on the circumstances in which this force was inducted, as also because a vast majority of its personnel were Hindu, which was but natural for a national outfit.

Further, for lack of alternative facilities, more often than not the CRPF had to be lodged in Hindu dharamsalas and temples, which further substantiated the Sikh perceptions about the pro-Hindu character of this force. Hindu neigbourhoods would also provide lavish hospitality to the CRPF staff, wherever deployed on duty. This naturally agitated the Sikhs, who now began to look upon the traditionally oppressive Punjab police as an effective counterpoise to the CRPF. The stress of serving under such nerve-racking conditions could not but adversely affect their morale and discipline, leading to a marked deterioration in relations and even an occasional clash between these two forces of law and order.

Sikh misgivings regarding the CRPF were further strengthened when the latter opened fire at the Harimandir, the Sikh sanctum sanctorum in the Golden Temple complex, in February 1984. Acting on the charge that the Punjab police was pro-Sikh and therefore somewhat indulgent in dealing with the rising tide of Sikh militancy, the Centre imposed a ban on recruitment to the state police. This would seriously impair its competence to adequately meet the twin challenges of mounting Hindu-Sikh discord and the widening base of militant activity. In July 1984, when this writer took over as director general of Punjab police, the force was carrying a huge number of vacancies in its ranks, almost one-fifth of the total. It took a lot of lobbying at the highest government levels in Delhi for me to get the ban lifted, though all fresh recruitments were made exceedingly restrictive and conditional upon adherence to several safeguards.

In due course, all serious functional distortions that led to inter-force conflicts were taken care of through sustained efforts by senior officers of the respective forces and mutual mud-slinging was strongly put down. The CRPF was taken out of Hindu temples and provided independent accommodation. Not long afterwards, the Punjab police would live down its pro-Sikh reputation and emerge as the principal player in counter-militancy operations, especially after the militants went all out to target policemen and their families in the 1990s, when its successes were applauded by the national media and many a Hindu organization all over the country. The then Punjab police chief would become hugely popular, especially outside the Punjab, and an ecstatic national media would henceforth refer to him as the supercop, a unique distinction in Indian police history. He was also showered with umpteen honours and encomiums from a variety of voluntary and other organizations in all parts of the country, such as 'Son of India', 'Saviour of Mother India', 'Rajiv Gandhi Award for Excellence in Secularism', 'Safe Skies Award' etc.

*

The Punjab police responded to the increased militant activity in the only way it knew, mastered over decades of dealing with violent crime. It may be recalled that the policing traditions in north-western India, the last region to become part of the British empire, were somewhat different from those in the rest of the country, which came under occupation earlier. Due to its markedly turbulent history in the initial years of British rule, the local government in Punjab allowed the police considerably more functional latitude than in other provinces. Remnants of such policing policies would persist after independence, both in the Indian Punjab and in Pakistan. The police sought to deal with the mounting incidence of militant crime by routinely rounding up suspects in large numbers, keeping them in illegal custody for prolonged periods of aggressive interrogation and often killing some detainees in staged encounters. Since such lawless activity had the tacit approval of the top brass in the state police, inquiries into complaints by even senior police officials rarely carried credibility with the people. Ordinary citizens had little faith in the state's ability or inclination to deter police high-handedness, so rarely would an aggrieved person approach even senior state officials, except those in the higher judiciary.

However, with Bhindranwale's emergence as a power to reckon with, the police was confronted with an unusual situation—because he would often threaten retaliatory action, of which he was becoming increasingly capable. When the police took some of his men in custody from his jeep near his headquarters in Chowk Mehta for interrogation in connection with some murders, he sent his close associate Bhai Amrik Singh to complain to the Punjab Governor, then visiting Amritsar. The meeting ended in some acrimony and the Governor reportedly expressed his annoyance to the local officers, which the latter considered enough reason to frame Amrik Singh in the Nirankari chief's murder. During his custody, Amrik was presumably given third degree treatment by some policemen, including Deputy Superintendent of Police Giani Bachan Singh. Bhindranwale reacted sharply and held out ominous threats to the concerned police officials, among them Bachan Singh, D.R. Bhatti and A.S. Atwal, the last two belonging to the Indian Police Service.

Earlier, two other Bhindranwale men, Kulwant Singh and Gurmit Singh, had been killed in police encounters. Bhindranwale now started preparing hit-lists of his and the *panth*'s enemies, which to him were no different from each other, and announcing them at his largely-attended *diwans* or religious congregations. Most of those on his hit-lists would send emissaries to plead with him for a reprieve. Soon afterwards, Giani Bachan Singh was killed, followed a little later by Atwal and others in due course. D.R. Bhatti would survive two deadly attacks by the skin of his teeth.

In the struggle for supremacy in Sikh politics, Bhindranwale had clearly acquired the upper hand. His band of heavily armed retainers was becoming bolder by the day, committing murders and bank robberies. With the bulk of the police force feeling demoralized and insecure, the Punjab administration found it very difficult indeed to effectively deal with the worsening law and order situation, and to rein in the growing band of Sikh militants. With Bhindranwale slowly but surely acquiring a clear pre-eminence in the community and reading out his hit-lists every now and then, not many in the state administration would dare stick their necks out. Thus, an era of terror had well and truly taken off in the state.

Bhindranwale also emerged as an alternative centre of power in the state, with all kinds of petitioners approaching him for redress of their grievances. He would routinely issue directions to the offending parties; such writs soon came to acquire almost the force of law. The administration, already in a state of imminent collapse due to intense political rivalry between Zail Singh and Darbara Singh, seemed powerless to curb his growing clout.

The first major incident that exposed the soft underbelly of the state's law and order machinery was the murder of A.S. Atwal, deputy inspector general of police (DIG) Jalandhar range, which covered the major militancy-ridden districts of Amritsar and Gurdaspur. It seems Atwal was a regular visitor to the Golden Temple, probably out of religious conviction, even after his name had twice figured on Bhindranwale's hit-list. He was shot dead by an unidentified assailant near the main gate of the Temple on 25 April 1983 in broad daylight and in full view of magistrates and police officials on duty. An 11-year old boy was injured in the shootout and died later in hospital, while a third person also received bullet injuries. An eyewitness account indicates that Atwal was being followed by his assailant/s right from the time he entered the Temple. He seems to have sensed the imminent danger to his life at an early stage, hurriedly carried out his religious rituals and made for the exit. However, the attackers got him just inside the gate.

The extent of demoralization of the state security set-up can well be imagined from the fact that not only did the police and magistracy fail to rush in to save the DIG, no effort was made for several hours even to retrieve his dead body from the spot where he had been felled. The incident seemed to have pushed the entire state administrative hierarchy into a state of utter paralysis, with the police and civil service top brass looking to the chief minister, the hapless Darbara Singh, and the latter waiting for clearance from the top bosses in Delhi, where the prime minister and her close advisers were locked in indecision or worse. Our good friend Zail Singh must have been playing his own games to weaken his fellow Congressman but bitter rival in the Punjab chief ministerial chair.

A senior Punjab police officer, then posted at the Punjab police headquarters in Chandigarh, believes that Atwal probably did not wish that particular visit to the Temple to be publicized and did not, therefore, communicate his programme to the Amritsar district police. He is also believed to have visited a contact in a posh locality in the city before making for the Temple. Also, a religious ceremony (*akhand path*) was in progress at his house in Jalandhar and he would not normally have left home, except under very pressing circumstances. The mystery of Atwal's visit that day was never fully solved and his murder was duly attributed by the government agencies to Sikh militants, though all factions of Sikh militants as well as Bhindranwale himself vehemently refuted all such imputations and condemned the misdeed in no uncertain terms. The Akali leadership had, of course, already distanced itself from all violent acts of the militants.

Sant Longowal even issued a statement implying Darbara Singh's involvement. When asked by a newsman who could possibly be responsible for the DIG's murder, the Sant said, 'The one who is afraid of losing his seat (of power).'[9] Bhindranwale too condemned the incident, describing it as the 'handiwork of the Punjab government' and 'an attempt to foil the Akali agitation and to malign the Sikhs... We do not believe in violence, particularly around the Golden Temple,'[10] he added for good measure, probably with his tongue firmly in his cheek. Another strong denunciation came from Harminder Singh Sandhu, president of All India Sikh Students Federation (AISSF), a militant organization of young Sikhs, owing allegiance to Bhindranwale. He asserted that Atwal's murder was anti-Sikh, the handiwork of certain elements in the ruling party and demanded a judicial inquiry to uncover the truth.[11]

The dithering in the Punjab government on the question of taking prompt and resolute action after Atwal's murder was attributed by knowledgeable sources to the failure of the prime minister's office (PMO), then presided over by principal secretary P.C. Alexander, to convey the prime minister's views in the matter to chief minister Darbara Singh and the Punjab administration. Does that point to skullduggery in the elimination of a senior DIG of the Punjab police, then embroiled in a grave militancy situation in the state? Politicians are not averse to engineering critical situations in order to deflect looming threats to their position. Some political analysts have gone to the extent of attributing the slaying of DIG Atwal to just such a desperate endeavour by Darbara Singh, because the Congress high command had very nearly decided to replace him, partly for his ineptitude but mainly to satisfy the Akalis, who had asked for the change.

The media carried reports of imminent 'far-reaching political-administrative changes' in Punjab by the Congress leadership, after a lengthy round of talks between Rajiv Gandhi, then a member of Parliament and general secretary of the Congress party, and his party legislators in Punjab in Chandigarh on 19 April 1983.[12] As expected, the immediate fallout of this murder most foul was that all talk of Darbara Singh's removal ceased. Instead, he was given full responsibility to deal with the growing stridency of Sikh militancy and several central paramilitary battalions were placed at his disposal for the purpose. 'In the face of the challenge thrown by the extremists in Punjab, following the murder of a DIG near the Golden Temple, the Centre has given up thinking in terms of replacing the chief minister, Mr Darbara Singh, and has on the contrary given him all powers to put down violence with a heavy hand. It has also reinforced the state's armed strength,' disclosed a report in the *Statesman* New Delhi, dated 26 April 1983.

However, the reprieve for the chief minister proved short-lived, thanks to the manipulative genius of his arch enemy, Zail Singh, sitting pretty in the seat of power at Delhi and enjoying the confidence of the all-powerful prime minister and her close advisers. To be sure, it did not take him long to engineer another hugely awkward situation for Darbara Singh, necessitating the dismissal of his ministry and imposition of central rule in the state. He spent his last years in virtual exile in Delhi as a member of the Rajya Sabha, full of derision and scorn for many of his erstwhile colleagues and fellow Congressmen and women, and died a bitter man. Less than a year later, whenever I called upon him in Delhi, in my capacity as director general of police, Punjab, he used to share his cynical estimation of quite a few Congress bigwigs with me. Such intra-party intrigue is in fact quite common.

The abrupt exit of a chief minister in a seriously problem-ridden state was bound to make a grave situation even more critical. The question that often baffles detached observers is why Delhi chose to act in a manifestly arbitrary manner in this matter, with diverse vital issues of governance crying for special attention.

First let us look at the incident that led to the dismissal of the Darbara Singh ministry and imposition of President's rule in Punjab. On 5 October 1983, six Hindus were pulled out of a Shimla-Delhi bus by some armed miscreants near Dhilwan, a small wayside village in Jalandhar district and shot dead. Being the first incident of the kind, it naturally created widespread alarm in the country and attracted severe condemnation all around, with the mainstream media calling for stringent action by the Centre against whoever was found responsible for the dastardly crime. Although all segments of the Sikh religio-political spectrum too condemned the misdeed in the strongest possible terms, a section of the media in Jalandhar did not desist from making fairly explicit insinuations about the involvement of Sikh militants in the foul deed. A former university teacher and a long-time watcher of the Punjab situation alludes to some very peculiar features of the Dhilwan murders. First, the bus waylaid by the killers was not a scheduled service but diverted from its original route. Second, the six unlucky Hindus belonged to sects and castes not generally found in the area and third, the miscreants just walked away and were never seriously tracked by the police. His conjecture is that the murders could have been authorized by either Zail Singh or Haryana chief minister Bhajan Lal and stage-managed through the Punjab police or some central secret agency. He bases his view on the then political equations in the Congress party and the need to embroil the Akalis and Bhindranwale in the Hindu-Sikh conflict so as to desecularize the Akali platform of claiming to speak for all the Punjabis and not merely the Sikhs. If in the bargain, Zail Singh was able to show the door to his long-time rival Darbara Singh, so much the better. President's rule in the Indian context virtually implies rule by home ministry bureaucrats under the control and direction of the Union home minister, in this case Zail Singh.

The Dhilwan killings were followed by another such incident when four Hindus were pulled out of a bus and shot dead near village Khabi Rajputan on 18 November the same year. Not unexpectedly, these two incidents caused a great deal of insecurity among the Punjab Hindus. The government of India, as well as a major section of the so-called mainstream media, promptly held the Akalis, Bhindranwale and the Sikh extremist elements responsible for the two outrages, although all of them had squarely and unequivocally condemned these and other episodes of violence directed against the Hindus and even demanded a judicial inquiry by a Supreme Court judge into the whole gamut of terrorist violence in the state during the previous few months. Several Sikh leaders, including Longowal and Bhindranwale had also severely deplored the incident of a train derailment, allegedly due to sabotage, on 21 October 1983, resulting in the death of 19 passengers. A deep sense of shock and anguish over the incidents was also voiced in a meeting of Akali legislators

in Chandigarh on 9 October and at a joint meeting of the
party's district presidents, members of parliament and the
Punjab legislative assembly the next day.

The Akali party also called for a state-wide bandh on
7 October and joined the BJP and the RSS in two similar
exercises later in the month. The call for the latter
throughout Punjab, Haryana, Himachal Pradesh and
Chandigarh was given by the Hindu Suraksha Samiti and
supported by the Akalis, BJP, Janata Party, Lok Dal and
diverse social organizations. All these events passed off
peacefully. Notably, the Congress party did not participate
in any of them.

In an editorial on 21 November 1983, the *Tribune*, a
leading English daily of north India, pinpointed certain
'inescapable conclusions as regards the two bus killings.
The first is that such acts of butchery are not sponsored
by the Sikh community as a community, nor even by the
Akali Dal, or (as it seems now) by Sant Jarnail Singh
Bhindranwale, who has condemned the killings as has
Sant Harchand Singh Longowal... The second is that
President's rule has failed to deter them (the extremists
remained unidentified). What is still more noteworthy is
that even the radical Sikh groups, who did not flinch from
claiming responsibility for some other acts of extremist
violence, not only disowned any hand in the bus killings
and desecration of Hindu places of worship, they also
condemned them in no uncertain terms'.

The leading extremist Sikh group at the time, which
had owned responsibility for killing 35 Nirankaris since
1981, was the Babbar Khalsa. It too denied any hand in
the bus killings or indeed in the killing of any Hindus,
bank robberies or religiously provocative acts. For 'our
targets are only those Nirankaris who were involved in
the Baisakhi killings of 1978, and those police officers

who are guilty of torturing and humiliating Sikh youth suspected of having links with the Babbar Khalsa and other extremist groups and their women, relatives and friends'.[13]

Longowal reiterated his plea for a judicial inquiry by a judge of the Supreme Court into all incidents of violence in the state until then, on 20 June 1983 and again on 7 July in an interview with a BBC corespondent.[14] He maintained that if a high level judicial inquiry was held, the connivance of the government would be fully exposed. The Union government, however, did not take the bait. Wisely, perhaps. In any case, the Union government was totally averse to risking a judicial probe at that point of time. Obviously, there were too many skeletons in the cupboard that could not be exposed to such scrutiny.

Desecration of Hindu places of worship and killings of Hindus would continue unhindered for the next few months, but cease abruptly and rather uncannily after the Blue Star operation in June 1984. Could there have been a deeper design and a correlation between the two? Was the spate of terrorist crimes targeting the Hindus, for which the blame could easily and plausibly be passed on to the Sikh religious and political establishment, manipulated by the Indian state, in order to prepare what would later be called a national consensus in favour of the army assault on the Golden temple? There were plenty of insinuations, at the time, of the existence of a 'third agency' in Punjab, charged with carrying out a sinister agenda.

Rajiv K. Bajaj, a Delhi journalist, filed a report in the monthly journal *Surya India* of September 1984, under the title 'Dead men tell no tales', in which he alleged on the authority of what he claimed to be highly placed intelligence sources that 'the total Punjab drama, from the rise of Bhindranwale to the army action, was scripted, enacted and closed by the intelligence agencies, under the directions of the ruling Congress (I),' and that a special intelligence unit under the name of The Third Agency was created 'to aid and abet the murderous activities of Jarnail Singh Bhindranwale and his gang of killers. The Third Agency kept the supply of lethal weapons flowing into the Golden Temple. The Third Agency allowed 47 railway stations to be blown up. The Third Agency incited violence in Punjab.' Further, that 'the whole army action in Punjab was conducted not only to cleanse the Golden Temple, but also to destroy all evidence of The Third Agency's involvement in the whole thing.' It needs to be added, however, that *Surya India* was owned and run by Maneka Gandhi, the estranged daughter-in-law of Indira Gandhi, who had parted company with her mother-in-law amidst a spate of charges and counter-charges.

It is difficult, therefore, to assess the credibility of such reports, though several happenings of a mysterious nature that marked those critical times could not be accounted for otherwise. The assassination of Sant Longowal in August 1985, after he signed a rather debatable accord with Rajiv Gandhi, was one such prominent event. Central rule in the Punjab would remain in force for over a decade, except for a brief period in 1985-86, when a pliable Akali chief minister was installed in office by a shrewd politician-Governor belonging to the Congress party after the elections of August 1985. Central rule allows the central intelligence agencies to have a free run in carrying out their shady operations in a state to advance the interests of the ruling party at the Centre, in this case the Congress.

Killings of Hindus and police informants continued unabated in the new year. According to police records, more than fifty persons lost their lives or received serious injuries in terrorist violence in the period before the army action in Amritsar, some prominent victims being Ramesh Chander, the managing editor of the Hind Samachar group and the son of Lala Jagat Narain, slain earlier, a BJP MLA Harbans Lal Khanna and Giani Bachan Singh, a deputy superintendent of police along with his wife and daughter. There were also some cases of breaches of the Satluj-Jamuna link canal, then under construction. Needless to say, such crimes would considerably damage Hindu-Sikh relations. Expectedly, the dismissal of Darbara Singh's ministry made no difference to the deteriorating situation. While the authorities continued to blame the Akalis and Sikh extremists for the sharp deterioration in the law and order situation, despite the well-entrenched Punjab police tradition of ruthlessly dealing with any such outbreak of violent crime, the Centre steadfastly refused either to institute an inquiry or issue a white paper on the situation, as demanded by the Akalis and opposition parties in Parliament. When, agitated over newspaper reports, opposition MPs asked for action against Bhindranwale, Union home minister P.C. Sethi placed a list of 45 persons, described by him as proclaimed offenders hiding in the Golden Temple complex, on the table of the House on 17 November 1983. Bhindranwale's name did not figure among them. In reply to a query by an MP as to why Bhindranwale's name was not listed, Sethi told him that such proclamations were made by the courts. On being asked whether the government had approached any court for such a proclamation, Sethi remained silent.[15]

Such equivocation on the subject would continue for the next few months, with no one—from the Union home minister to Punjab Inspector General P.S. Bhinder—in a position to clarify the mystery of what action was contemplated against the alleged fountainhead of all militant activity in the Punjab and its periphery, Jarnail Singh Bhindranwale. Until Rajiv Gandhi himself indicated on 29 April 1984 in Chandigarh the shape of the solution, though still in rather vague terms. Asked whether he would prefer to go for a political solution first or deal with the terrorists, he said 'a solution would include resolution of both'.[16] Blue Star would come about just over a month later.

*

Unlike their counterparts in western democracies, Indian police forces enjoy little functional autonomy and, both under law and convention, are bound to comply with all directions from their superior echelons, whether departmental, bureaucratic or political, even when such directions are not strictly covered by law or propriety. Indian Police Act, 1861, which still governs police working in the country, denies any meaningful functional autonomy to the departmental hierarchy. Instead, crucial slots at the district and state levels are assigned to non-professional civilian bureaucracy, the district collector and the home secretary, to whom the district and state police chiefs are respectively accountable for their performance. There is no community accountability worth the name. In the event, since the basic legislation remains unaltered from colonial times, even the minister in charge of police in democratic India continues to discharge his overseeing function through the civilian bureaucracy.

This has induced in the police forces a habit of excessive servility and submissiveness to political and civilian officialdom, and disdain and disregard for the community and public institutions in general. That is why

Indian political classes are forever on the lookout for officials with proven personal allegiance and loyalty rather than merit and efficiency. Further, since statements made to the police in course of investigation are inadmissible in evidence as per the Indian Evidence Act, also of mid-nineteenth century vintage, honest and fair investigation into offences is well-nigh impossible. Even comparatively straightforward police officers are often constrained, therefore, to transgress legal proprieties with a view to securing conviction of accused persons in a court of law. This promotes a culture of deviousness in policing practices, where crime and disorder is sought to be controlled either by concocting evidence or resorting to other short-cut methods, the most common of these being encounters, abductions and disappearances. Most police supervisors now look the other way when their subordinates indulge in such malpractices. Although no Indian police force is above reproach in this matter, some of them seem to have acquired quite a reputation in this dubious sphere.

Punjab police happens to be among the foremost of such forces in the country. So when the Sikh terrorist bands took to killings and other violent crime, the only response the Punjab police and the central security forces could devise was to turn to large-scale lynching of suspected malcontents, their relatives and friends. As if by design, the officer chosen for containing the rising tide of extremist violence in the Punjab was P.S. Bhinder, a Haryana cadre officer, who had made his mark as DIG police in Gurgaon, during the Emergency regime of 1975-77, for liquidating a number of notorious dacoits hailing from neighbouring states of Rajasthan and UP, among them the widely publicized 'encounter death' of dacoit Sunder. When the Janata party came to power after the end of the emergency rule, Bhinder was arrested by the Delhi police and, according to his own account, given third degree treatment by many of his own erstwhile colleagues. When the Congress came back to power in 1980, Bhinder was elevated to the crucial position of police commissioner of Delhi, superceding scores of his colleagues in the Indian Police Service. Later, however, he seems to have fallen foul of the powers that be and was sidelined even during the Congress regime. So his posting to the Punjab as inspector general (law and order) in mid-1983 came as some sort of a challenge to prove his merit, as also his loyalty.

As IG (law and order), he would soon become far more powerful than the state police chief, C.K. Sawhney, notionally his boss. Sawhney would eventually ask for a transfer from the police department, leaving the top position in the state police to Bhinder. Incidentally, B.D. Pande, appointed as Punjab Governor about the same time, too had been elevated to the challenging position to prove himself, having been in some difficulty with the Delhi establishment while serving as Union cabinet secretary.

On the face of it, therefore, it appeared to be an ideal arrangement to deliver the goods in the militancy-ridden state. However, what the Indian state missed out was that the liquidation of dacoits is not exactly in the same league as dealing with religious and political militancy.

The spate of terrorist crimes was sought to be tackled by routinely rounding up a large number of suspects after a terrorist crime took place and killing some of them in staged encounters, mostly in a rather crude manner. Far from leading to normalization of the situation, such ham-handed operational techniques would further inflame passions in the community, give a fillip to militant activity and promote a sense of revulsion among the mass of the people. Not only Bhindranwale, but the entire Sikh leadership as well as the Communists would show solidarity with the victims of police *zulum* (atrocity) and high-handedness.

It may be in order to describe one such encounter to make the point more cogently. According to a report in the *Tribune*, Chandigarh, on 2 October 1983, four bank robbers, all of them Sikhs, were shot dead in an encounter near Jalandhar on the previous day. None of the dead bodies could be identified, nor was any booty recovered from the spot of the encounter. This was sought to be explained away on the presumption that the criminals might have burnt all the currency notes before they started firing on the police parties sent to apprehend them. Another report in the same newspaper four days later provided more gruesome details of the episode. 'The four youths ... might have shot themselves', it stated 'This impression is drawn from the post-mortem reports of the bodies. Reliable sources say there were holes on both sides of the skulls, meaning that the bullets had pierced through the skulls. The holes were three centimeters in diameter. This proved that the shots had been fired from close range. Had they died from police bullets there would have been no holes on both sides of the skulls. The post-mortem reports reveal that none of the bodies had any other bullet injury.'

Unfortunately, this mode of coping with any large-scale outbreak of crime is fairly common in most Indian police forces, though the Punjab police can any day claim 'distinction' in this dubious area. Except for a brief period, when some ex-cadre police chiefs strove to resolutely deter such manifest misuse of power by police subordinates, encounters, abductions and disappearances would continue to be the preferred option in the state in the name of anti-terrorist operations throughout the decade of militancy and later.

Killing of Sikh young men suspected of being involved in terrorist crime ceased for a brief period when the militants too started getting at some of the better known encounter experts in the police. It may be a mere coincidence that the Dhilwan outrage near Jalandhar, the first incident of slaying of Hindu bus passengers in the Punjab, took place just four days after the encounter of October 1983, but there was no dearth of people who tried to find some linkages. It is not that the lynchings and encounter deaths were not public knowledge, every one in the media and the administration, both in Delhi and in Chandigarh, were aware of what was happening in the troubled state and with what dismal results. Only no one in authority had the courage or the foresight to call a halt to police lawlessness, nor presumably did they have a clue as to what other technique to adopt. In the meanwhile, media reports continued to highlight militant activity together with the police strategy of *encounter* executions.

Finally, it was Governor B.D. Pande who seemed to have realized the futility of encounters and thought of other options. A report in the *Tribune* of 10 April 1984, disclosed: 'After assessing the Punjab situation, B.D. Pande came to the conclusion that a policy of reconciliation rather than confrontation would prove rewarding, but the prerequisite was a satisfactory settlement of the outstanding socio-economic, religious and political issues. It is for this reason that the *Governor directed the police to stop the practice of eliminating the terrorists.*' This is the furthest that any head of a state could ever go in openly and so casually speaking of his police being in the habit of routinely transgressing the law. According to reports, however, encounters did not cease. As we shall see later in this study, this particular anti-terrorist strategy would be honed to perfection in the following years and would, in fact, enjoy the endorsement and approbation of the highest political and bureaucratic authorities in the land.

Throughout this period, the Delhi establishment continued to insinuate that it was the Sikh terrorists, emboldened by Akali agitations and closely linked to that party's political activity, who were principally to blame for all extremist crime including bank robberies, though clinching evidence in support of the accusation was difficult to come by. On the other hand, an occasional statement by top officials of the Punjab police seemed to indicate otherwise. A special report published in the *Indian Express*, New Delhi on 2 October 1983, for example, quoted the police chief of Ludhiana, Sube Singh, as claiming that 'Sikh extremists are not involved in the recent bank robberies committed in Punjab during the past few months....Mr Sube Singh told ENS here on Friday that some gangs of robbers from Delhi and other states which had links in Punjab, committed bank robberies as the police had been busy in dealing with the Akali agitation and other acts of violence.'

A few months later, Inspector General P.S. Bhinder told newspersons in Amritsar in January 1984 that 40 extremists had been arrested after the imposition of central rule in the state on 6 October 1983 and that they were all being interrogated for their possible participation in terrorist crimes. 'When asked if any clues pointed towards any political party, he replied in the negative' (the *Tribune*, 2 January 1984). A common enough subterfuge that many Indian police forces, faced with an abnormal rise in crime, would resort to is to shift the blame even for normal crime on whatever special category of criminals are then operating, in this case Sikh extremists. This happens all the time in dacoit-infested states like Madhya Pradesh and Rajasthan, where dacoit gangs are held responsible for all criminal activity or in cities like Mumbai, where mafia gangs are made to take the blame for all rise in crime figures. A report filed by a two-member team of senior journalists, B.G. Verghese and K.C. Kulish, deputed by the Editors Guild of India, after their visit to the state in February 1984, deplored the tendency in no uncertain terms, 'Objection is taken in Punjab to the tendency to ascribe all crime to Sikh extremists. The press must be wary of such stereotypes. Many crimes, robberies and murders have little to do with the current political scene.'

It is not as if the so-called extremist elements were entirely blameless in the matter. It is not unusual for political parties to whip up popular passions to the extreme for the fulfillment of their own self-centered agendas, often of a parochial nature, and manipulate the resulting mass upsurge for making their agitations and movements for redress of grievances more effective. Obviously, the Akalis could not have been any different in this respect from their counterparts in other Indian political formations.

The most popular perception about the Punjab militancy was and continues to be that it was an exclusively Sikh phenomenon. Yet there were a number of non-Sikh members of the militant groups, arrested or shot dead by the police in encounters. This is an area which hardly ever engaged the attention of even close observers of the Punjab scene. The left-wing magazine *Link* offers an interesting low-down on one Roshan Lal Bairagi, the first Punjabi Hindu-turned-Sikh terrorist in its issue of 22 March 1987. 'Bairagis are a Hindu Brahmin sect. This particular Hindu sect has closest links with Sikhism. They are generally poor. Some villages in Amritsar district have one or more Bairagi family each. Traditionally, they earn their living by doing daily labour, occasionally (also) begging and performing religious ceremonies, including in Sikh families.' There were quite a few other Hindus and an occasional Christian among the militant ranks. *India Today* mentions ten such individuals and the British Punjabi weekly *Des Pardes* about six more. Surely there must have been many more. Surprisingly enough, the subject has not attracted appropriate attention and, as stated earlier, remains largely a matter of surmise.

*

Lastly, a word about the so-called arsenal of deadly weapons stashed away by militants inside the Golden Temple complex, allegedly with the help of certain foreign agencies or governments, which not only amounted to a grave violation of Indian sovereignty and became a source of deep concern for the Indian people, but would also provide justification of the army action of June 1984. If indeed there was such a foreign hand actively involved in arming and encouraging Bhindranwale and the Akalis to take to violence and terrorism, thereby causing widespread unrest and turmoil in the state, the case for army intervention would acquire immense support and legitimacy.

While we will deal with the subject in more detail in the next chapter, we would like to end this narrative with the views expressed by Lt-General J.S. Aurora, a highly-regarded Indian army general, who led the country's forces in the 1971 Indo-Pakistan war in the eastern sector, leading to the birth of a new nation, Bangladesh, on the Indian subcontinent. 'The first thing to remember is that in a war weapons get lost! In both the wars with Pakistan in 1965 and 1971, a large number of weapons were picked up and never accounted for. With the large-scale smuggling going on across the Punjab-Pakistan border, some gun-running must have taken place. Since 1960, the government has been issuing arms to certain reliable persons living close to the border for security purposes. So there have been a lot of unaccounted weapons in circulation in Punjab, used often in family feuds, property disputes and dacoity. Their buying and selling has been a lucrative trade. Another point to note is that of the weapons seized inside the Temple, only 60 self-loading rifles have foreign markings. The rest are all of Indian origin. Further, there were no medium machine guns or mortars. There were, however, a large number of light machine guns. Ammunition for both the light and medium machine guns is the same, but a medium machine gun has a higher and more sustained rate of fire. There were two rocket launchers with the terrorists but only one was used. It is obvious, therefore, that there were not so many sophisticated weapons. Quite a lot, yes, but the impression that has been built up in the public mind of foreign governments deliberately arming the terrorists with a view to overthrowing the government is grossly overdone.'[17]

How did all those weapons find their way into the Temple, considering that all the entry points into the place were supposed to be under 24-hour surveillance by security guards drawn from the central paramilitary forces, Punjab police not being regarded as reliable enough? Lots of stories were doing the rounds at the time, including the part allegedly played by some serving and retired Sikh army officers close to Bhindranwale, in arranging the supply of arms from defence sources. All such surmises, however, suffered from inconsistencies and discrepancies of various kinds, and media reports discounted the probability of most such allegations. A popular theory was that the weapons reached the militants concealed beneath building material being carried to the Temple in *kar sewa* trucks, though the security guards were under strict orders to subject all such vehicles to rigid and thorough checks.

A rather curious but generally disregarded episode of this period needs to be mentioned in this connection. In the words of a Punjab cadre IAS officer, who held several top posts, including that of state chief secretary during those difficult years, Inspector General Bhinder is believed to have got a comparatively junior officer, Ajay Pal Singh Mann, posted to the crucial position of the senior superintendent of Amritsar district, 'without the knowledge of Governor Pande, the chief secretary and the home secretary by getting the approval of Jagatpati, adviser to the Governor, Punjab. It is believed that he (Ajay Pal Singh) was conniving at the free flow of arms into the Golden Temple. The fact that Mann was not recalled by Pande would show that Bhinder had the Central government's approval'.

Bhinder, however, held a different view in the matter, as reflected in an interview he gave to two correspondents of the *Statesman*, New Delhi and published in its issue of 8 July 1984, within a week of his removal from the Punjab scene, when he discovered that along with P.C. Sethi and B.D. Pande, he was to suffer the ignominy of being made a scapegoat for the Punjab fiasco. He stated that the government did have correct information from intelligence sources about the supply of weapons and that arms and ammunition were being carried inside the Harimandir Sahib complex in *kar sewa* trucks, meant to carry food and construction material, but nothing was done to check it. 'They were not intercepted because there were oral instructions from the top until two months ago, not to check any of the *kar sewa* trucks.' Another report in the same newspaper the previous day had noted, 'The arrival of light machine guns and sophisticated self-loading rifles had been taken note of by the various agencies. The information received was so detailed that even the make and the country of origin of the weapons was known...The authorities had some idea of the source of these weapons, mainly smuggled from Pakistan and obtained through thefts and robberies and leakage from Indian ordnance units.'

There were also rumours that large consignments of such weaponry were procured by intelligence agencies through regular channels and against dollar payments. Although all the murky details of such undercover operations can never see the light of day, in the present case we have before us a lucid account of the gun-running activities of his organization during those heady days by top intelligence officer M.K. Dhar, as given in his recent book *Open Secrets*. We will talk about this matter in greater detail later in this book. Mann was duly dismissed from service, under an emergency provision of the Constitution, which empowers the government to terminate the services of any state official without framing specific charges and holding formal disciplinary proceedings, allegedly for complicity in the smuggling of weapons into the Golden Temple complex. Whether this was a ploy to hide something more sinister on the part of the authorities may never be known. Not even the Akalis shed any tears at Mann's dismissal.

An interesting sidelight on this subject is provided by Bhindranwale himself. He would often revert to the issue in his discourse: 'People come to me and ask: from where we get the SLRs? I tell them: gun factories are right at your doorsteps. That is, snatch rifles from the CRPF personnel on duty in your street,' he would proclaim in chaste Punjabi.

4

The Conflict

As late as 29 April 1984, i.e., just about a month before Operation Blue Star, Rajiv Gandhi, then the general secretary of the Congress party and undoubtedly the most influential of party leaders, described Bhindranwale as a religious leader and added that the latter had shown no inclination towards politics[1], thus bestowing respectability on the presumed principal fountainhead of Sikh militancy. In the meanwhile, the growing rift between Hindus and Sikhs all over urban Punjab was on public display every other day. The Hindu Suraksha Samiti, allegedly supported by the Congress, was in the forefront in this dubious contest. When the Akalis organized a procession in Amritsar asking for a ban on the use of tobacco and meat products in the vicinity of the Golden Temple, the Samiti staged a demonstration in favour of tobacco etc. the very next day. When some bomb blasts took place in Hindu places of worship or dead cows or calves were discovered there, all the Sikh religious and political formations, including Bhindranwale, lost no time in severely condemning the misdeeds and calling for high-level inquiries.

On its part, the Congress high command was doing all it could to portray the Akali agitation as just a religion-based stir, rather than a composite movement for redress of diverse political, economic and territorial issues, affecting the interests of all Punjabis, though with a few religious concerns of the Sikh community also thrown in.

As the year 1984 advanced into its second quarter, the political environment was thick with uneasy portents, as if some special event was about to happen. There was an occasional exchange of fire between the militants holed up in the Temple and a CRPF post atop the Brahm Buta Akhara, overlooking the Temple premises. Some army and IB officers were spotted circumambulating the Golden Temple and covertly surveying the area. No one, however, appeared to have the ghost of an idea as to the nature or timing of the likely event.

To quote Rajiv Gandhi again, he stated even on 23 March 1984, 'I think we should not enter the Golden Temple. The police can enter the temples, but it is a question of what is good balance. Today, as we see it, it is not as if Sikhs are against the Hindus, and we should not do anything that separates them.'[2] While the statement indicated that some type of military action had clearly emerged as a possible answer to the worsening law and order situation in the state, it also implied that the precise contours of any such possible action had yet to be specifically delineated.

The ruling party was apparently looking for a strategy that would not only do away with the presumed principal source of turmoil in Punjab but also yield the maximum possible benefits to the Congress party in political terms all over the country. The timing too was important, again for obvious reasons. As for frequent references at the time to the close relationship between Bhindranwale and some top Congress leaders, we may recall what an eminent historian and long-time observer of the developments in the region, Prof. J.S. Grewal, had to say on the subject.

Why the Akalis did not always keep a politically respectable distance from Sant Jarnail Singh Bhindranwale is a relevant question. According to Mark Tully and Satish Jacob, Giani Zail Singh enabled Sanjay Gandhi to discover Sant Jarnail Singh for breaking the Akali Dal after its electoral success in 1977. They also looked for a cause, which could be both religious and political. For this, they identified the Nirankaris. The Dal Khalsa, floated by them some time later, was also anti-Nirankari. After the death of twelve Sikhs at the hands of the Nirankaris on Baisakhi day of 1978 at Amritsar, anti-Nirankari agitations were encouraged, not by the Akalis but by the local committee in charge of gurudwaras in Delhi controlled by the Congress party. The Dal Khalsa as well as Sant Jarnail Singh contested elections for the SGPC in 1979 against the Akali candidates. In 1980, Sant Jarnail Singh campaigned for Congress candidates, including R.L. Bhatia. He is believed to have shared a platform with Indira Gandhi. In any case, she admitted that he had supported a Congress candidate.

After the murder of Baba Gurbachan Singh, the Nirankari Guru in April 1980, Giani Zail Singh told parliament that Bhindranwale had nothing to do with the murder. After the murder of Lala Jagat Narain in September 1981, the chief minister of the Punjab wanted to get Bhindranwale arrested as a suspect. He was in a Haryana village at that time. Giani Zail Singh rang up Bhajan Lal government not to arrest him. In October, Giani Zail Singh told Parliament that there was no evidence of his involvement in the murder. He was released. 'The government has done more for me in one week,' he (Bhindranwale) remarked, 'than I could have achieved in years'.

After the murder of Santokh Singh at Delhi in December 1981, his memorial service was attended by Sant Jarnail Singh as well as Giani Zail Singh and Rajiv Gandhi. The Akalis may not have known all this, but they knew that Sant Jarnail Singh was being supported and protected by the Congress to undermine the Akalis. They, in turn, were tempted to use Sant Jarnail Singh against the Congress, if and when they could. When the Akali leaders met Indira Gandhi in October 1981 for the first time, they told her that Sant Jarnail Singh was being backed by the Congress. If some of the Akali leaders maintained their contact with him until the end, so did some of the Congress leaders. The Sant had fallen out with the Congress by the end of 1981 but the Congress did not fall out with him. Indira Gandhi continued to consult Giani Zail Singh when he became the President of India. It was possibly due to his influence that Sant Jarnail Singh was not arrested after the murder of DIG Atwal in April 1983. When the government of Darbara Singh was suspended and President's rule was imposed in the Punjab after the cold-blooded murder of some Hindu passengers in the first week of October 1983, a senior colleague of Darbara Singh claimed that President Zail Singh was in daily contact with Sant Jarnail Singh. The implication was that Darbara Singh's downfall had been brought about through the Sant's instrumentality.

Indira Gandhi maintained contact with Sant Jarnail Singh through R.L. Bhatia, who remained in regular contact with Bhai Amrik Singh until April 1984. Even if the idea of the president and the prime minister of India was to use Sant Jarnail Singh for their purposes, the knowledge of his connection with them added much to his prestige and influence. The Akalis had to contend with him, his prestige, and his influence.'

(Prof. J.S. Grewal, *Sikh Identity, the Akalis and Khalistan; Punjab in Prosperity and Violence*, Chandigarh, 1998, pp.83-85.)

*

By the first quarter of the year 1984, an ominous climate of fear and foreboding appeared to have seized the people of the region in a vice-like grip, with law and order situation fast slipping out of control. A string of shocking incidents of terrorist violence and communal clashes had generated a collective fear psychosis among the people. Terrorist crime was growing fast, both in intensity and range, militant groups now striking freely even in the national capital. Bomb explosions had taken place in underground Palika Bazar and inter-state bus terminal in Delhi, a temple in Yamuna Nagar in Haryana and, of course in Punjab. Senior Congress, BJP and Akali leaders were shot at and killed or gravely wounded in Delhi, Haryana and Punjab. The Centre had succeeded to a large extent in pushing the Akalis into assuming an extremist position in their public statements so as not to lose out completely to Bhindranwale. Even then, they did not give up their efforts to prevent their *morchas* and protests from being taken over by extremist elements and to keep them within the limits of moderation, despite clear indications that the talks were making no worthwhile progress and the Centre seemed to be only playing for time.

The marked eagerness of the mainstream Akali leadership to engage in the talks, even in the face of obduracy on the part of the government to address their principal concerns in the matter of river waters and territorial disputes, was possibly construed by the Delhi establishment as a sign of weakness. Every single terrorist act by the militants weakened the Akalis' position—while strengthening that of Bhindranwale. The end result was a serious deterioration in Hindu-Sikh relations and more riots, killings, vandalization of places of worship and other ugly incidents. The Punjab police was proving increasingly inept and clumsy in handling the growing spread and sweep of militancy and terrorist violence. Their brutal and oppressive operational techniques were fomenting further restlessness and extremism. The Central Reserve Police Force (CRPF), too was unable to deliver optimally, partly due to lack of local knowledge but mainly because of inadequate backing from the district administration. So, far from showing any signs of improvement, the law and order situation continued to get worse by the day.

This was a state of affairs tailor-made for central intervention in a major way, perhaps just the kind of exigency the Centre desired. Although, the administrative chaos and confusion prevailing in the state was chiefly the outcome of inept handling of a critical situation by the government itself, Delhi lost no time in shifting the entire blame to the Akali leadership for its failure to resolve the problem due to its intransigence and lack of vision. This could only be directed at winning over the entire national political spectrum and to forge a national consensus in favour of a strong enough strike against what were projected as forces of separatism, supported by a hostile neighbour. All these various moves were probably also intended to create suitably disquieting conditions in the state so that army action would appear to be the sole option to bring the state back to normalcy, a job that the police would find beyond its capacity because of its overly complex nature and the high risks involved.

*

Several political analysts and security experts believe that Sant Jarnail Singh Bhindranwale and his followers could easily have been dealt with through a determined police or paramilitary operation, without causing much loss of life and avoidable hurt to collective Sikh psyche. Viewed in that light, the deployment of the army in Amritsar does appear debatable on many counts. However, such a notion would seem to fly in the face of many otherwise inexplicable contemporaneous developments such as propping up Bhindranwale with a view obviously to marginalising the Akali party, escalating Hindu-Sikh tensions, emasculation of the Punjab administration and persistent efforts to forge a national consensus against the Akalis and Bhindranwale. Could all this have been part of a grand design—to pave the way for an army operation? Once a clear design had emerged, only the precise timing remained to be set, which must also correspond with the total subjugation of the Akalis by militants, fundamentalists, anti-nationals, secessionists etc., as set out in the white paper by the Union government soon after the army operation.

Military forces rarely launch a major operation without thorough reconnaissance, briefings and rehearsals. An important element of their action plans is surprise. It is safe to assume, therefore, that even after the political decision to deploy the army against Bhindranwale's men was taken, the D-day for the action must have been left to the military top brass. That can be the only logic behind launching the operation on the martyrdom day of the fifth Sikh Guru, when thousands of Sikh men, women and children had gathered in the Golden Temple to observe the day of mourning as per tradition, unaware of the death and destruction lying in wait for them. One tends to fondly assume that if the D-day were to be determined by a civilian authority, it could not have been so fixed as to coincide with a *gurupurab* (sacred day). Surely, the purpose of the army action was to neutralize the terrorist gangs, led by Bhindranwale, not the slaying of large numbers of civilians in cold blood. While a proper assessment of the gains, if any, in eradicating militancy and terrorism from Punjab will be attempted a little later in this book, let it be mentioned at this stage that the adverse impact of the operation and the way it was conducted left a lasting legacy of antagonism between the Indian state and the Sikh community. In the event, militant sentiment would spread throughout the community and extremist violence grow manifold, impelling even such a pro-establishment writer as Khushwant Singh to relinquish state honours.

In his recent book *Through the Corridors of Power* (2004), Dr P.C. Alexander, then principal secretary to the prime minister and inarguably the most powerful of her advisers at the time, provides a graphic account of the many gruesome happenings of the time in an apparent effort to justify the deployment of the army. 'The basic flaw in the Akali agitation', he states, 'was that the triumvirate who started it completely lost control over its tempo and found themselves sidelined by the militants. In the early stages, the Akali leaders thought that they could use the militants in order to pressurize the government, but this stage lasted only for a year or so. The militants contemptuously ignored the Akali leaders as "toothless tigers" irrelevant to their scheme of things. The fundamental error committed by the Akali leaders was that even after they realized that they had been displaced, they insisted on maintaining the charade of being in charge of the *dharam yudh*. Eventually, the Akali leaders became too weak and too insecure in their position to accept a settlement even when they were convinced about its overall merits.'[3] In his attempt to explain away the many shortcomings in the handling of the Punjab problem in its initial more manageable phases, he has taken recourse to generous doses of spin, a favourite bureaucratic device.

At another place, while lamenting the inability of the local administration to apprehend the killers of DIG Atwal in April 1983 from the Golden Temple complex, he fails to mention the severe condemnation of the misdeed by the Akalis as well as Bhindranwale. More importantly, he avoids referring to the state of near collapse of the Punjab administration because of the extensive turf battles going on between Union home minister Zail Singh and Punjab chief minister Darbara Singh, a feud which the Congress high command could easily have aborted. We have discussed this matter in some detail in an earlier chapter.

After the 1975-77 emergency regime, personal loyalties and factional allegiances play a key role in the transaction of government business. Thus, most high officials in Punjab, as in other states and Union ministries, were only too eager to secure the goodwill of Zail Singh, since the Union home minister wielded immense power in career advancement of IAS and IPS officers. Atwal's murder was indeed a major challenge to the state of Punjab, and there is no reason why the chief minister should not have reacted firmly and speedily, or prevented the police and the magistracy from pursuing the killers in a determined and professional manner.

In actual fact, however, it was the prime minister's office (PMO), then presided over by Alexander himself, which is reported to have stalled police entry into the Temple complex. We have it on the authority of some senior police officials, then holding crucial position in the state, that Darbara Singh was unable to get a clearance from the PMO despite repeated calls to Dr Alexander. The failure of the state administration to grab the initiative would cause incalculable damage to police morale and discipline, already in a stage of collapse. Equally clear is the immense boost it would have given to militant gangs indulging in extremist violence all over the region, extending even to Delhi and UP towns. Alexander admits that the decision taken 'at a fairly high political level that the police need not enter Guru Nanak Niwas to make the arrests'[4] was a mistake, but underplays his part in it. He also wrongly states that Longowal did not condemn the murder. Not only he but even Bhindranwale did so in no uncertain terms.

*

By this time, a battle of sorts seemed to have erupted between Bhindranwale and the Akali leaders, marked increasingly by squabbles and clashes, both sides obviously locked in a power struggle of the classical type. Slogan-shouting, taunts, derisory heckling and frequent skirmishes among their respective supporters were now a common enough occurrence. It may be recalled that Bhindranwale had temporarily shifted base from his headquarters in Chowk Mehta to Guru Nanak Niwas, a rest house adjacent to the Golden Temple for housing visiting pilgrims. A firm tradition had been established during British rule that the police would not enter the Temple premises, then thought to comprise of the Harimandir and Akal Takht, for the purpose of making arrests—not that there was any legal bar for the police to do so. This convention had generally been honoured after independence, except once. Sensing that he may not be quite safe from police action while staying in Guru Nanak Niwas, Bhindranwale shifted base to the Akal Takht towards the end of 1983, as the latter was definitely more secure, being next only to the Harimandir in sanctity. Akali leaders and priests did raise some feeble objections against this patently sacrilegious move, but Bhindranwale had by then acquired a commanding position in the community and was virtually beyond the control of the party or the Sikh clergy. By taking residence in the holy Akal Takht, built and sanctified by the sixth Sikh Guru, Hargobind, as the Sikh supreme seat of temporal power, Bhindranwale captured the imagination of the Sikh masses in a significant manner. They looked up to him as their only hope against an uncaring government and an oppressive police. The process that had commenced in 1980 with Bhindranwale being promoted by some top Congress leaders as a counterweight to the Akalis had come full circle, Tohra favoured Bhindranwale, Badal was an indifferent onlooker and Longowal completely out of depth. Events in the Golden Temple complex on 27 January 1984, as reported in the *Tribune*, Chandigarh, the next day, provide good insights.

When Sant Longowal announced the Akali Dal plan to burn copies of an article of the Indian Constitution that equated Sikhs with Hindus for certain specific purposes, and sought to reaffirm his command of the *morcha*, 'abusive and sarcastic remarks' were freely made by non-Akali Sikhs against the Akali leaders. 'No sooner was the Akali decision made public than a large number of Sikh youths gathered outside Teja Singh Samundari hall and demonstrated for over two hours raising slogans against Sant Harchand Singh…The demonstrators, who carried firearms, swords and lathis, tried to forcibly enter the hall but their move was frustrated by equally well-armed followers of the Akali Dal chief, who raised pro-Longowal slogans…For over an hour, it appeared that a bloodbath was inevitable.'

Two days later, Longowal pointedly reiterated his 'fundamental differences' on policy matters with Bhindranwale, while clearly denouncing and disowning the militant stand of the latter. He also took this opportunity to once again clarify the Akali Dal position on the controversial issue of Khalistan. While terming the 14-page Khalistan constitution, released by Balbir Singh Sandhu, the self-styled secretary general of the council of Khalistan, on 26 January 1984 in Amritsar as just a 'stunt', Longowal went on to remark, 'How many times do we have to clarify our stand on the issue? The Akali Dal's policy is clear and open. Does it contain any references to Khalistan?'

The Akalis and Bhindranwale factions did not desist even from killing each other's supporters. The murder of Surinder Singh Sodhi, a close associate of Bhindranwale, on 14 April 1984, was promptly avenged by the other camp by torturing and slaying the suspected killer. All this immensely embittered relations between the Longowal and Bhindranwale camps, and created deep ruptures in the Sikh religio-political establishment, an eminently exploitable situation for Delhi. At some stage, the Akali leaders seem to have become so exasperated that they would not mind even a determined police assault to neutralize Bhindranwale. Some reports even implied that the army action too was cleared by the Akalis. As for Bhindranwale, he had by now grown into a veritable icon among the Sikh masses, attracting quite a few adherents even from the academia and the professions. In the true tradition of Indian idolization, his taped sermons and speeches could now be heard all over rural Punjab. Anyone with a first-hand experience of the atmospherics in the Punjab generally and Amritsar and Gurdaspur districts in particular in those extraordinary times would testify to the sense of foreboding that enveloped the area. As reported by Tavleen Singh, an intrepid journalist, 'The state seemed to have come to a grinding halt and slowly the security forces started closing in on the Temple. Paramilitary pickets were now visible from the Golden Temple itself and once or twice they got close enough to provoke exchange of fire...Fortifications started coming up at strategic places and an iron fencing was erected around the main entrance to the Golden Temple. The preparations for war had begun.'[5]

*

A unique feature of Akali party agitations is the participation of Sikh ex-servicemen. Several senior Sikh defence service officers have from time to time been associated with the organization. This is attributable partly to historical reasons but mainly to the innate sense of religiosity that governs the daily life of the members of the

Sikh community. It may be recalled that sizeable sections of Maharaja Ranjit Singh's army were drafted into the British Indian army after the annexation of the Punjab in 1839. Such units, later to constitute the Indian army's Sikh regiments, continued to adhere to the traditions and religious symbolism of the Khalsa army, including the Sikh war cry of *Bole So Nihal*, when going into battle. The initiation ceremony and oath-taking of Sikh troops was carried out before *Guru Granth Sahib*, the Sikh holy book, in the unit gurudwara. It was not unusual, therefore, for the Akali leaders to tap this resource to strengthen their movements and boost their credibility while engaging in agitational activities. Ex-servicemen from rural areas had traditionally been participating in Akali *morchas* on an individual basis as members of an integrated village community, while a few former officers had often remained associated with the party either as advisers or as part of its organizational set-up. A few of them would later transfer their support to Bhindranwale after the Akalis appeared to have lost the battle of wits against the powers that be in Delhi.

For example, Major General (retired) Shabeg Singh, an acclaimed expert in weapon systems and anti-insurgency techniques and the key organizer of the Mukti Bahini in the Indo-Pakistan war of 1971, who had courted arrest during the Akali agitation, would later join Bhindranwale as a sort of chief of staff. He was mainly responsible for training, equipping and deploying the militants to face the Indian army in Operation Blue Star, in which he also met his end. What now alarmed the authorities was the repeated calls given by Longowal and Bhindranwale to ex-servicemen and officers to join the *dharamyudh morchas* in large numbers. In a letter sent out to retired Sikh officers and men of the armed forces in December 1982,

Longowal asked them to rise to the occasion as 'the *panth* requires your services as it is facing a crisis.'[6] The proposed meeting took place at Guru Ram Das Bhawan on 23 December and, according to media reports, attracted some 5,000-9,000 persons, including about 200 officers, among them at least five major generals. Resolutions passed at the gathering promised unqualified support to the movement for the fulfillment of demands contained in the Anandpur Sahib resolutions. The ex-servicemen also affirmed that they would support these demands with '*tan, man, dhan* i.e. physically, emotionally and financially'[7].

After the success of the ex-servicemen's convention, another such high profile meeting was held in Amritsar on 9 January 1983, this time attended by doctors, lawyers, journalists, university teachers, writers and retired bureaucrats and civil servants.

*

All through 1983 and the first half of 1984, while the talks between the Centre and the Akalis were going on in a somewhat desultory fashion, along with several agitations and *morchas* organized by the latter, Bhindranwale's rhetorical flourishes too were gaining strength and attracting a growing number of adherents. The response of the police and security forces, faced with increasing terrorist activity, was on expected lines i.e., illegal confinement of suspects and their family members, torture and encounter killings. Expectedly, this did not help in either controlling extremist violence or lessening the appeal of militancy, thus swelling the ranks of militant groups. With the prime minister's office in the driver's seat and calling the shots, the state government appeared to be fast losing touch with its field units and, consequently, with the situation on the ground. On their part, the district magistrates and police superintendents were functioning either on their own or as per directions of Union home ministry officers. In the event, they would either over-react to the rising tide of militancy or fail to respond at all.

In other words, the state administration was fast moving towards a state of collapse and the Governor was required to fly to Delhi almost on a daily basis, sometimes even twice a day, to seek directions from the PMO in all administrative and operational matters. Indian bureaucracies are apt to repose too much faith in the efficacy of unending meetings to throw up solutions to crisis situation. As the charade of Centre-Akali talks entered its third year and the people in Punjab and, indeed, all over the country watched helplessly, militant violence soared by the day. Even at that late stage, however, many well-meaning persons of high social and intellectual standing seemed not to have given up hopes of persuading the powers that be in Delhi to recognize the gravity of the situation and come to an understanding with the Akalis, which was necessary to weaken the forces of extremism, both Hindu and Sikh.

On 22 January 1984, a large number of Delhi citizens, among them former civilian and military top brass, authors, artists, journalists, doctors, lawyers and other professionals, who called themselves Punjab's silent majority and whom the *Tribune* of Chandigarh described as representing the country's top intelligentsia, asked the Union government in a public statement to give up its policy of drift and apathy towards the Akali demands. 'It is imperative that the demands voiced in Punjab be demarcated as demands not of a particular community but of a region as a whole.

This is the context in which they must be seen and pressed....On the face of it, none of these demands seems to be insuperable. It is the Centre's inaction, its disquieting lack of will to take decisions, that has allowed the frenetic play of extremist forces to flourish and grow...There has been enough talk and discussion. Agreements have been reached on several occasions. They have not been honoured or implemented. The Union government owes the Indian people an explanation for its inaction and drift.'[8] The statement was signed by some 150 persons with impeccable credentials, among them Hindus, Sikhs and Christians. Some of these men and women would continue their efforts to bring about a rapprochement between the contending parties right until the end, under the name of the Punjabi lobby, one of its members would later become the country's prime minister for a few months.

Although there was noticeable uneasiness and anxiety among the mass of the people and an air of deep apprehension pervaded the state, with rumours about a possible army strike flying thick and fast as the deadlock in the Akali-Centre talks remained unresolved, there was no clear indication as to the nature and timing of the action, which made the wait even more taxing. The earliest demands for army intervention, couched in such terms as martial law, army rule, army take-over, imposition of emergency etc., were made by Hindu organizations like the RSS, Hindu Suraksha Samiti and the BJP. Later, other national and professedly secular parties also joined the Congress in asking for determined action. The clamour for such action became more strident after the Centre succeeded in building up what was called a national consensus favouring a hard-hitting policy towards the elements gathered around Bhindranwale and allegedly egged on in their activities by the Akali leadership. This is apparently what the top Congress leadership had been working for during the previous few years.

The first indication of such a consensus was available in a lead article titled 'Perils of Akali extremism: a disaster awaits us all' by noted journalist Girilal Jain, at the time considered close to Rajiv Gandhi, in the *Times of India*, New Delhi on 27 March 1984. 'To be candid, I do not have much sympathy for the Akali agitation, which has gone on and on and in the process acquired extremist, violent and openly communal overtones. I sincerely believe that the agitation is misconceived because Sikhs cannot, in my opinion, have any genuine grievances', he asserted. A few days later on 4 April, the *Hindustan Times*, New Delhi, went even further in an editorial, titled 'Get the killers' when it stated, 'The extremists have taken over the bogus agitation in that state for objectives that are not known to any one, including the agitationists. It is imperative that the forces of law and order make their presence felt...They (the Akalis) are deliberately making the whole thing communal just as the Muslim League did in pre-partition India.'

On 24 April, BJP president L.K. Advani asked for the maintenance of law and order to be handed over to the army. The Punjab Shiv Sena demanded the imposition of martial law on 1 May to protect the Hindus. Three days later, while addressing a largely attended rally at New Delhi's boat club, Charan Singh and Atal Bihari Vajpayee of the National Democratic Alliance 'urged the Centre not to hesitate in sending forces inside the gurudwaras in Punjab with a view to flushing out terrorists taking shelter there'. On 30 May, a delegation of the Arya Samaj called on the prime minister to suggest that either Punjab be put under army control or an emergency declared there.

As is apparent from the tone of statements made by

P.C. Alexander about the Akali leaders and their alleged persistent 'intransigence' as against the 'mature and balanced' approach adopted by the Union government, in his above-mentioned book, none of the PM's political or bureaucratic advisers entertained any doubts as to the accuracy of her diagnosis of the malady afflicting the Punjab and the course of action adopted by the government for restoration of normalcy in the troubled region. Indian bureaucrats had, in any case, long abdicated their right to inform, advise, and caution the ruling political establishment.

There were a few dissenting notes, though, where a discerning writer or political analyst voiced grave misgivings about the policies adopted by the Union government and where they were likely to lead the country in the not too distant future, voices of sanity that remained unheard at the time but were to prove only too true in the light of events following the army assault on the holiest Sikh shrine. Pran Chopra, who served as editor of many national dailies in his long career, wrote in the *Indian Express*, New Delhi, on 23 April 1984. 'No political party should be so stupid as to thrust its executive arm into such a hopeless situation. Yet that is precisely what New Delhi is doing. One would have thought that the *government that works* would have at least understood politics if it cannot understand government....What is needed is not change of the tools of law and order but a change of methods and intentions at the political level....There are rumours in New Delhi that the army might be brought in. That would be the gravest blunder politically and severely harmful to the army itself. It would be the worst form of changing tools. The army cannot do more, and in the given circumstances can probably do much less than the present four agencies after the initial shot of confidence artificially induced by an army show runs out....The third temptation to be avoided is to make a rush at the Golden Temple. There is nothing to be gained by it and much to be lost...The extremists are now operating from many locations, which are widely scattered outside and where they quite freely roam. If the intention is to cut them off from those inside the Temple, it is better to employ *naka bandi*, the practice of controlling and regulating all traffic into and out of the Temple.' However, the full import of what Mr Chopra was trying to convey was lost on the Indian establishment, intent upon playing a different kind of game altogether.

With its earlier plank of socio-economic agenda severely dented, the political and electoral gains to the Congress party in winning over the Hindu majority in preparation for the coming general elections were finally to score over the long-term national interests. Prem Bhatia, another perceptive journalist, then editor of the *Tribune*, sounded a similar note of warning in his editorial comment on 3 May: 'Seeking a paramilitary solution to the Punjab tangle can have disastrous consequences.' Satindra Singh of the same newspaper filed a report from New Delhi on 20 May that 'latest intelligence reports are said to have assured the central leadership that an average Hindu in Punjab would whole-heartedly support any move at rapprochement with the Akalis because it is felt that any other course would grievously undermine national unity, communal harmony and, ultimately, territorial integrity.'

S. Sahay, then editor of the *Statesman*, New Delhi and noted writer and social activist Rajni Kothari were among other such voices in the wilderness that continued to caution the authorities against any precipitate action that might result in alienating an important minority as the Sikhs, with their proud history of sacrifices during India's long freedom struggle and later. However, by this time the top Congress leadership seemed to have already chosen the mode of seeking their own version of a solution to the problem of the minorities, growing fidgety by the day in an India getting increasingly Hindu-ised, as the ruling Congress party sought to consolidate its vote bank among the majority Hindus for electoral gains. Rajni Kothari was to observe afterwards, '...And let us not forget the crucial role of violence perpetrated by the state and its agents on innocent people—in Punjab, then in Delhi—in establishing the dominion of the majority community and raising the desperate banner of threats to unity. It was under this intimidating environment that the nation was taken for a ride, which we politely call a wave'.[9] In the meanwhile, the *Statesman*, New Delhi, reported on 2 June that heavy movements of armed forces were taking place in various parts of the Punjab 'during the last few days'.

*

By leading India to freedom from colonial rule, the Indian National Congress had firmly established itself as the principal party of governance and retained that position for several years after independence, with Jawaharlal Nehru and his contemporaries in firm control of the polity. In the general elections of 1967, however, its supremacy as a pan-Indian party came under serious threat, when sundry ragtag coalitions, led by defectors from the Congress, took office all over north India. Mrs Gandhi, by then an undisputed heir to Nehru's legacy of power, though not so much to his secular vision and political skills, perceived that the earlier policy of addressing grievances and demands of the many minority segments no longer ensured continued Congress rule, resorted to political and socio-economic gimmicks to retain power. The imposition of Emergency in 1975, evidently to ward off the consequences of a judicial verdict that should normally have led to her resignation, in effect, led to a huge loss of credibility for both her party and herself, and dwarfed her stature as a stateswoman. Henceforth, she would have to rely more and more on her advisers, not all of them blessed with qualities required for management of intricate political equations and to devise winning electoral strategies. After her economic and social slogans lost their efficacy, she set about cultivating the massive Hindu vote bank, often in a style that lacked finesse and subtlety. She also started paying frequent and well-publicized visits to Hindu places of worship and pilgrimage centres and trying to fashion a distinctly Hindu identity for herself so as to enhance her acceptability among the Hindus. This would create, in due course, a fear psychosis among the minorities, each proud of its distinct identity and determined to retain it.

The problem of harmonizing separate identities with an overarching Indian nationhood had been part of the Indian dilemma from the very beginning. Nehru sought to resolve it by developing his 'unity in diversity' approach, which appeared to work well during the initial years. Its usefulness, however, diminished as the political scene became more complex and fragmented. In the event, the state was increasingly confronted with delicate policy choices to resolve the many contradictions inherent in India's unique religio-political and cultural-ethnic situation. The so-called national question, thus, became the foremost and the most crucial of the many challenges facing the ruling entities, especially after the end of Mrs Gandhi's emergency regime. Political analysts have spoken of the many difficulties involved in forging an inclusive national identity that would over-ride all separate identities in a multicultural, multi-religious, multiethnic and multilingual society like India's. Was the mode of handling the post-independence Sikh unrest an offshoot of the Indian state's, and therefore the Congress party's, primary dilemma of squaring the circle of sub-national and regional identities? Both the mainstream parties, the Congress and the BJP, strove to devise measures to bring the minority segments into what they believed to be the national mainstream. Because of historical and other reasons, minority discontent was much more pervasive in the country's border regions than in central states.

In the words of Dr Attar Singh, chairman of the department of Punjabi studies at Punjab University, Chandigarh,

> The crisis of Punjab is embedded in the as yet unresolved national question of India in more senses than one. Either the Indian national forces were never strong enough to draw in all the various strands of social, cultural and religious diversities, or they never got the sort of committed leadership, which could wage a struggle for their victory... Thus the contradiction of Hindu nationalism and Sikh nationalism, though quite substantial, remained dormant till the issue of Muslim nationalism was ultimately resolved through the creation of Pakistan... (when) the forces of Hindu revivalism...provided the real *élan vital* of the new Indian state.[10]

Earlier, Pran Chopra had made another pertinent observation in an article in the *Illustrated Weekly of India*, Bombay, dated 11 December 1983, to the effect that 'Mrs Gandhi has lost the art of the politics of accommodation or, more likely, has lost interest in it. Therefore, she does not want to, or no longer knows how to, weave group identities into a national whole. She breaks such identities as she can...But what she cannot break, she merely alienates. This is the real cause of the Punjab problem'.

Operation Blue Star thus falls into place as another attempt by the state, now clearly inspired and defined by the majority Hindu view of Indian nationhood, to steamroll all minority reservations in respect of what the majority Hindus considered a most desirable goal of bringing them into the mainstream of Indian ethos. That the operation was destined to fail in its ultimate goal would become evident in just a few months after the action.

*

As the Punjab police chief during those difficult days, I enjoyed a comparatively easy access to the top echelons of the Union government, including the prime minister and President Zail Singh. Since I happened to belong to the same district in Punjab as the President, he was extraordinarily frank in expressing his views on the subject. In his many conversations with me, he came across as a deeply troubled man, unable to resolve the crisis of confidence set off by the profound conflict between his deep religious convictions and the army assault on his community's holiest shrine, carried out in his name. 'Why should all this have happened when I was the President?'[11] he lamented on 27 September 1984, sitting cross-legged on the floor along with a small congregation in front of the Akal Takht, where the five high priests were engaged in a conclave to ascertain the nature and extent of his responsibility for Operation Blue Star and the nature of punishment that would adequately atone for the highly blasphemous act committed by the army in his name. While he waited patiently for the verdict from the Akal

Takht, as any devout Sikh would, amplifiers were relaying a verse of Bhai Gurdas[12], a revered figure in Sikh history, from the Harimandir, which rendered in English would go something like 'Give a dog a kingdom, it will still lick the grindstone for flour'. Whether the selection of the stanza was accidental or deliberate, the profound symbolism of the parable and the occasion would not have been lost on the Sikh President and other members of the congregation. Providentially, the priestly conclave accepted his plea and took no further action.

He would often revert to the topic in the subsequent period, whenever I called on him in Delhi or Chandigarh. Perhaps, it was this sense of anguish that would later lead to the strained relations between him and Rajiv Gandhi, who succeeded Indira Gandhi after her assassination.

*

It was also important that popular perceptions about the developments in Punjab must correspond to those of the Indian establishment. All this was achieved through deft media management by political manipulators, available in plenty in the ruling party. 'Besides projecting the Punjab problem as communal, the media, official and non-official, branded the Sikhs as 'communal', 'terrorists', 'separatists' and disintegrationists', as 'those who want expulsion of the Hindus from Punjab' and 'want India's dismemberment at the instance of its enemy Pakistan' etc. to mention a few popular perceptions. Such image building was not the handiwork of certain communal organizations but of the state itself. These projections legitimized the use of force and state repression to settle the problem in Punjab'.[13]

The state response to Sikh militancy consisted mainly of two components—political management and upgradation of law and order machinery. The first of these was primarily geared to marginalizing the moderate political voice of the Sikhs, the Akali Dal, and promoting extremist elements led by Bhindranwale at one level, and distorting the character of the Akali movement for the redress of mostly regional grievances into a manifestly religious agitation at another. In other words, what the Centre was trying to achieve in Punjab was the desecularization of an essentially regional secular movement. According to Dipanker Gupta, while the Indian state could easily manage the fallout from nativist movements and those for linguistic states, 'With regional and secularist movements, the ruling party at the Centre, more particularly the Congress (I), was for the first time faced with a political formation that was hostile to it...And the Centre struck back ethnically. It ethnicized secular issues in order to marginalize its opponents, one by one, from the national mainstream'.[14] Political management of the Punjab problem was, thus, entrusted to some of the arch political manipulators in the party, both before and after the climactic events of operations Blue Star and Wood Rose.

The upgradation of the state's law and order machinery was somewhat more complex. As mentioned earlier, because of its predominantly Sikh composition, the Punjab police came under some suspicion early enough for its alleged pro-militant leanings from sections of Hindus, although such fears would soon prove to be misplaced. However, to placate the Hindus, central paramilitary forces were inducted into the state in sizeable numbers. Such forces, however, could not be entrusted with basic police tasks, which had still to be handled by the state police and its allied agencies. A discussion paper, presumably prepared at a senior level in the government of India, just after the conclusion of Operation Blue Star, held the Punjab police largely responsible for the steep deterioration in the law and order situation in the state, because of its low morale, poor intelligence collection, mounting levels of corruption and indiscriminate growth of money-spinning rackets under police protection. The paper also alleged that there was a deliberate distortion in recruitment policies resulting in serious communal imbalance, with the Sikhs forming an overwhelming majority in the constabulary, which then comprised of 73 per cent Jutt Sikhs, 21 per cent scheduled caste Sikhs and only 5 per cent Hindus.

Such a force, the study held, was hardly likely to inspire respect and confidence in society as a whole. It further found fault with the leadership of the force as the appointment of the police chiefs was more often than not determined not by merit but extraneous factors, such as political convenience and caste proximity. In addition, political parties regularly made efforts to infiltrate politically-motivated individuals in the force, a course of action that would over a period of time fashion a police force, guided not by constitutional imperatives but by the diktats of their political mentors. The force was also indicted for lack of discipline and other professional drawbacks. In sum, the state police was adjudged to be grossly unequal to the task of managing the vastly increased levels of militant violence that was likely to seize the state after Blue Star. Clearly, except for the communal imbalance, which can easily be explained as incidental to the occupational preferences of Punjabi Hindus and Jutt Sikhs, the study findings would apply equally to all state police forces and not to Punjab police alone.

The paper suggested a number of remedial measures to offset the operational and other deficiencies as identified by the study. Among them were some obviously naïve suggestions like transfer of the Punjab armed police battalions to other states and their replacement with central paramilitary forces on a permanent basis, and staffing of police stations with personnel drawn from other police forces, preferably from the Hindi-speaking states. It also suggested that those Punjab cadre IPS officers who had come to adverse notice should be permanently drafted into other state cadres. Similar action was proposed for deputy superintendents of police, which was, of course, impermissible under the existing rules. The paper also made some interesting points regarding the low performance levels of the civil service and magistracy. While a more judicious reorganization of the Punjab police would have to await the setting up of a more broad-based high level committee, efforts to strengthen its repressive capacity were already under way, such as the provision of additional and more deadly weapons and logistical resources like vehicles, communication equipment and additional financial grants. Several new laws were enacted to give more teeth to anti-terrorist strategies. However, for the time being, the police and the central forces continued to operate in the same age-old manner, indulging in indiscriminate killings in staged encounters and other such lawless activities, thus adding to discontent in the community. The repression let loose in the rural areas by an increasingly lawless police vastly aggravated the hiatus between the Indian state and the Sikh community. Hard interrogation of suspected militants in newly opened centres like the one in Laddha Kothi near Sangrur left many young Sikhs maimed for life, if they survived the torture, that is.

Punjab police was to be thoroughly reorganized after Blue Star, which we will discuss in greater detail at an appropriate juncture. Now, we must move on to probably the most significant event of the decade of militancy that would critically impact the relations between the Sikh community and the Indian state for many years to come.

5

The Climax

Genuine democracies do not deploy their armies for handling internal security problems. All tasks of an internal security nature are to be entrusted to the civil police forces, duly supplemented by armed components, when necessary. In case the civil police cannot cope with an internal security situation, as in Northern Ireland, the authorities would promptly address the causes and inadequacies with a view to improving police competence through legal, logistical or physical reinforcement.

Post-colonial South Asian regimes, on the other hand, routinely resort to deployment of their armed forces to suppress regional or religious dissent. In the Indian context, the armed forces of the Union include, besides the defence forces, several central paramilitary forces raised after independence and working directly under the control of the Union government. While it is not uncommon for the latter to be called out in strength during sectarian conflicts and other civil disturbances, army units are regularly pressed into action in situations of terrorist and extremist violence as in Jammu & Kashmir and the north-east currently, and in Punjab during the decade of militancy. Occasionally, the army may also be called upon to handle communal riots, when the state police and the paramilitary prove partisan or incompetent in controlling the situation, as in the Delhi carnage of 1984, Mumbai riots of 1993 and the Gujarat killings of 2002, where the police and bureaucracy were found to be acting in collusion with the miscreants, in league with the ruling party.

The Indian Constitution contains no provision for martial law. The only way Union armed forces can be deputed in an internal security situation is to deploy them in aid to civil power, at the request of the state authorities, empowered under the law to seek such assistance. Such deployment, however, does not lead to the abrogation of the jurisdiction and authority of the civilian administration. The Constitution remains the supreme repository of all political and administrative authority under all circumstances and no other administrative arrangement can ever be stipulated nor has such a situation ever been witnessed in India, though almost all of its neighbouring countries have from time to time been governed under military decree, either because there was no constitution or it had been abrogated or suspended. Even when external or internal emergency is formally declared during the periods when the nation is in grave danger due to external aggression or grave internal disorder, only a few Constitutional provisions, relating mainly to human rights and fundamental freedoms are suspended for the time emergency remains in force. Internal Emergency imposed by Indira Gandhi in June 1975 was the only instance when internal security situation was cited as the justification. The normal law and order machinery, i.e., the police and the magistracy do not cease to function as such and retain their full powers under the law, despite such an emergency regime being in force.

In theory, all the various actions that the army undertook in Amritsar and other Punjab towns during the course of operations Blue Star and Wood Rose too derived their legitimacy and authorization under the omnibus expression 'military aid to civil power'. But in the initial stages at least, neither the police superintendent nor the district magistrate of Amritsar were taken into confidence. By training and tradition, the army brass is known generally to hold the police in some contempt and the manner in which they excluded the Punjab police from all important decision-making at that point of time was not unexpected. But to prevent the district magistrate from fulfilling the obligations of his office was most unusual, to say the least. More of that later.

*

Although the air was thick with rumours about the imminence of some sort of military action in Punjab in general and Amritsar in particular right from the beginning of the year 1984, the nature and magnitude of the operation was still unclear. Talks between the Akali Dal and the government of India seemed to run into rough ground time and again. Tentative agreements that looked promising one day would be disowned or refuted the next day, either by the Akalis or the government. While the latter seemed to be pussy-footing, probably to gain time for the so-called national consensus to emerge before deciding on the final strike, Bhindranwale and his followers were getting stronger by the day and winning over more and more young Sikhs to their viewpoint, helped immensely also by the reign of terror let loose by a frustrated and demoralized police force. In sheer desperation, the Akali Dal gave a call for 'Rail roko' (stop the trains) early that year, which passed off peacefully because the government cancelled all the trains passing through Punjab. The Akali Dal then upped the ante by calling for the 'Grain roko morcha'.

By this time, almost the entire mainstream media and political establishment had come to largely accept the government position on the Punjab situation. Hindu political outfits had, of course, for long been clamouring for a major army intervention. In other words, a national consensus had clearly evolved. However, even at this late stage, Punjab Governor B.D. Pande was reported to have stressed the need for a political settlement with the extremists, citing 'present improved atmosphere' in a meeting with Mrs Gandhi (Indian Express, New Delhi, 8 April 1984.) This was in keeping with his consistent view that a political solution was the only realistic alternative in the situation then obtaining in the state. Two months earlier, Mr Pande was reportedly of the view that 'the situation in the Golden Temple complex had crystallized as a result of which it is now possible to identify the extremists and their leaders. The Akali leadership has tried to disassociate itself from the extremists, which it has been avoiding recently'.[1]

Is it possible that the Punjab Governor, the most important state functionary at the time, was not privy to the larger purpose that the central establishment seemed to have in mind, while fine-tuning its Punjab strategies and was being used as a sounding board or, what is worse, as a red herring? In Punjab, both Governor Pande and Inspector General P.S. Bhinder had to take the blame for a botched situation, although it was the Union government that was handling the crisis all through, with the local administration allowed little initiative. At the Union level, it was home minister P.C. Sethi, reputedly one of the more honest politicians of his generation, who had to be sacrificed for what was described as the continuing 'drift' in the Union's Punjab policy. It must be said, though, to Mrs Gandhi's credit, that Sethi was allowed to stay on in the posh ministerial bungalow in close proximity to where she lived. As to his responsibility for the so-called drift in the Punjab policy, far from being consulted on policy matters, Sethi was not even kept in the picture with regard to top level postings and transfers. When I went to call on him in early July 1984 after being appointed director general of police, Punjab, he told me disarmingly that he had read about it in the newspapers. In normal circumstances, it would be inconceivable for the Union home minister not to be in the picture with regard to such a crucial posting in a disturbed state. This is not a matter about which top politicians would like to share their thoughts with civil servants. Perhaps, he could talk to me frankly because he had known me when he was the chief minister of Madhya Pradesh.

Not that Sethi was the only top Congress politician to be sidelined in key decision-making processes. During the decade of militancy in Punjab, Governors and police chiefs were changed literally at the drop of a hat, just as in other militancy-ridden states.

*

Finally, an army operation, code-named Blue Star, was launched by the army in Amritsar on 3 June 1984, on the directions of the government of India. Its stated and specific objective was to flush out Sikh terrorists, who had turned the holiest of Sikh shrines, the Golden Temple, into a veritable fortress. According to P.C. Alexander,

> It was the proverbial last straw. The Akalis declared on 23 May 1984 their intention of intensifying the agitation by calling for stoppage of movement of food grains out of Punjab as well as a refusal to pay taxes and other charges from 3 June. This call was a virtual invitation to anarchy, which the state police would have found impossible to handle in addition to having to cope with the daily (heavy) quota of killing, destruction of government properties, looting of banks and other crimes. It was immediately after this call by Longowal, on 25 May to be precise...that Indira Gandhi finally made up her mind to summon the Army. She sent for General AS Vaidya and asked him to keep the Army on alert as the civilian authorities may require its help to deal with the situation in Punjab...Her expectation was that the very presence of the Army and the demonstration of its strength through flag marches would, by themselves, act as deterrents. Consequently, she felt that there would not be any need for use of excess force by the Army.[2]

Alexander conveniently overlooks the many roadblocks periodically set up by the government itself in various ways, that would virtually sabotage any prospect of success in the talks by inducting third parties into the process, such as chief ministers and leaders of the opposition from neighbouring states or converting bilateral talks into multilateral ones at crucial stages in the course of negotiations. Whether such a course was adopted by design or otherwise is immaterial from the long-term perspective. He also fails to mention that at many crucial junctures during the talks, Longowal continued to defer the dates fixed for the commencement of any fresh agitational programmes so as not to precipitate a situation that could lead to the final breakdown of talks with the government as, for instance, in the case of submission of resignations by Akali legislators and parliamentarians and the cancellation of the observance of '*Azad panth* week' on 1 April 1984, in response to a statement by Union home minister P.C. Sethi that the government was prepared to amend 'the relevant portions of Article 25 of the Constitution to remove doubts expressed by the Akali Dal'. If the government had agreed to do this earlier, even though as a strategic political ploy, the course of events might have taken a different and happier turn.

There were many other gestures, probably born out of desperation on the part of the Akali leaders as they saw the initiative pass out of their hands into those of the militants, as it seems now, to do all that was possible so as not to allow the situation to reach a point of no return. Instead of supporting Longowal in his efforts to keep the militants at bay by preventing Bhindranwale's ascendancy in the *morcha* agitations, the authorities were clearly accelerating the process. The registration of a case of sedition against Longowal on 20 April 1984 on the charge that he had written an article four months earlier, simultaneously with outlawing the All India Sikh Students Federation, closely allied to Bhindranwale, virtually placed the moderate Sant Longowal in the same league as the other Sant, well known by now for his violent outbursts, as far as popular perception was concerned. According to the *Hindu* dated 22 March 1984, the government 'has a penchant for complicating issues by introducing fresh irritants...(the moves) against the top leader of the Opposition in the Punjab...are counterproductive'. When some MPs questioned the propriety of the case of sedition against Longowal, the Union home minister described it as 'merely a technical matter, implying that no action was contemplated against him' and indeed no action was ever taken in the matter.

Expectedly, factional battles within the Sikh leadership were now at their peak and exchange of hot words and physical assaults were a daily occurrence. *The Tribune* of 14 April 1984 carried a report from its Amritsar correspondent that 'the division between Sant Harchand Singh and Sant Jarnail Singh is obviously complete now'. A week later, the *Hindustan Times* quoted Longowal as expressing fears about his personal safety to a group of foreign visitors. 'Very soon, even I and my supporters may be on the (extremist) hit list, if we are not already on it', he said.

Alexander's version of the events just before Blue Star is obviously designed to put a convenient gloss on the deeper aims and objectives sought to be accomplished by the central leadership through the PMO, over which he presided. It is a different matter that the kind of political management of the nationality question that the authorities were attempting would prove calamitous, leading, to aggravation of the problem, not only in Punjab but also in Kashmir, the north-east and some other parts of the country.

Operation Blue Star, for all the sound and fury it was to generate and the disastrous effect it was to have on the future course of the militant movement, derived its title from a light-hearted talk between a major general, then holding a key position in the army headquarters and his deputy. The general, now living in semi-retirement, told me in an informal chat over coffee how an inquisitive junior colleague, while driving home with him, asked if such an operation in Amritsar was indeed on the cards and if so what would it be called. They were at the time passing by a large hoarding singing the praises of Blue Star air conditioners. How ironical that an army operation that was to prove so catastrophic should be christened after an air conditioner!

*

In a late night address on 2 June over the electronic media, the prime minister dwelt at great length on the grim situation then obtaining in Punjab, holding the Akali leaders responsible for the failure of the long series of talks with the government and offering to 'sit around a table to find a solution through discussions' even at that late stage. She went on to remind her 'Sikh brothers and sisters' about their heritage of love and tolerance and exhorted them not to let 'a miniscule minority among Sikhs be allowed to trample under foot civilized norms for which Sikhism is well known and to tarnish the image of a brave and patriotic community'. In conclusion, she said 'To all sections of Punjabis I appeal: *Don't shed blood, shed hatred.*'[3] Evidently, it was too late in the day to reverse the course of events and the army had already been placed in full charge of the situation. As far as the Akali leaders were concerned, the prime minister's address could not have brought any comfort as they had already been confined within the precincts of the Temple complex, with the entire state being placed under army control and curfew orders.

An earlier chapter takes account of the protracted pattern of talks between the Akalis and the government, marked by frequent one-upmanship and policy shifts on the part of the latter in a climate of growing clout of

Bhindranwale and the weakening hold of the Akalis among the Sikh masses, largely flowing from the many acts of omission and commission by the state. The Akalis could obviously not become a party to a settlement with the government, which would be seen by the bulk of the community as a sell-out, especially when Bhindranwale was seen to be moving to occupy centrestage in the Sikh religio-political sphere with his militant rhetoric. Nor was the government keen to bail them out of the dilemma that they were faced with as the 1980s decade unfolded.

How else to read the actions and motives of the central establishment that allowed the situation to deteriorate to a stage where the army call-out would remain the only option to sort out a mess, largely of their own making due to lack of decisive action at the appropriate time and in a well thought-out manner, except by lending credence to the theory that the whole thing was crafted to finally put the many developing minority insurgencies out of the way, once for all? In other words, to seek to resolve the still unsettled national question of India, not through the time-tested Nehruvian dictum of unity in diversity but through subjugation of diverse and distinct minority identities in pursuit of an elusive homogeneity, based primarily in the ethos and culture of the central Indian Hindi-speaking and Hindu majority states. That the army action in Punjab failed to accomplish any of the goals it had set out to do is another matter. We will deal with the post-Blue Star situation in some detail a little later in this study.

Unsurprisingly, authentic data about the number of deaths and injuries was hard to come by although there were plenty of rumours floating around, which remained unverified. It was also not possible to ascertain as to how many of the dead were militants and how many noncombatants in the army lingo. The white paper on the Punjab situation, published by the government of India about a month later, put the figures at 554 civilians/ terrorists killed and 121 injured in the Golden Temple area and other religious places or for curfew violations and during cordon and search operations in other areas. On the army side a total of 4 officers, 4 JCOs and 84 other ranks died, while 15 officers, 19 JCOs and 253 other ranks sustained injuries in the course of the entire operation in the state. In addition, a total of 4,712 civilian/terrorists were apprehended—1,592 from the Golden Temple, 796 from other religious places and 2,324 in operations in the rest of Punjab.[4] Non-official sources, of course, put the number of casualties at a much larger figure. The grouping of civilians and terrorists indicates that the army commanders failed to carry out a proper identification of the dead bodies as required by the very elementary legal provisions, either because they did not sufficiently appreciate the importance of the same or were engaged in deliberate prevarication, for obvious reasons. It is clear, though, that the pilgrim-victims of the army action had no escape route, because even if some warnings were issued over loud speakers for the inmates to leave, as claimed by the authorities, the panic, uncertainty and acute alarm prevailing in the Temple and the city would have made it impossible, except if the army had taken the help of the Akali leaders, also trapped inside the Temple.

Apart from the damage inflicted in terms of lives lost, the troops also allegedly set fire to the Sikh memorial library, well-stocked with precious manuscripts and memorabilia of great historical value, some dating back to the Guru period. There were also reports of executions by firing squads of groups of people with hands tied behind their back.[5] Indian law makes it incumbent upon the authorities to account for all deaths in such circumstances and also arrange to get post-mortem examination conducted as soon as possible. This requirement too appears to have been dispensed with, otherwise all such speculation could have been effectively laid to rest. The overall gains of the operation, measured in terms of containment of terrorism and violence, were hardly worth the game. The bulk of the militants, reportedly hiding in the Temple, in fact, made good their escape through the many lanes and by-lanes around the Temple, which remained unwatched and unsecured, obviously due to reconnaissance inadequacies. The confusion and chaos of the operation and its aftermath could have been handled better if the government had only allowed the normal channels of information to function openly, at least, after the whole messy affair was over. With the army taking over control of the entire state apparatus in the beginning of the month, all accredited correspondents and newsmen, both Indian and foreign, were asked to leave. Only one exceptionally enterprising and intrepid youngster stayed on and went to make history with his dispatches to a foreign newspaper. All that the police could do was to register case after case against him under various sections of the Indian Penal Code and looked for him everywhere but to no avail. He remained elusive for a long time to surface only after the things had settled down. In due course of time, he would mature into one of India's finest English language columnists.

*

The government's explanation as to why the army action could not have been delayed beyond 3 June, which happened to be the *shaheedi gurupurab* (martyrdom day) of the fifth Sikh Guru and was expected to draw thousands of pilgrims to the Temple, was that the calls given by the Akali leaders for blocking the movement of grain outside Punjab and the exhortation to the people not to pay any government dues was likely to create a situation of extreme chaos and anarchy in the state, an intolerable situation for any administration. Also that the spate of killings, robberies and other unlawful activities let loose in the state by terrorists made it imperative for the authorities to act urgently and effectively. There were also reports that a *hukumnama* (a religious edict) was likely to be issued soon from the Akal Takht, commanding all Sikhs to congregate at the Temple for its defence against an imminent attack by the army.

It is true that the moderate Akali leadership was, indeed, faced with a very difficult situation at the time, trying to guard its turf from repeated forays by the extremist group within its own fold, led by the likes of Jagdev Singh Talwandi, as well as Bhindranwale and his growing band of ruthless and reckless followers, while at the same time striving to keep some kind of a dialogue going with the government, which resolutely refused to give them any opening to regain their diminishing credibility among the Sikh masses. All actions of the government, on the other hand, tended to strengthen Bhindranwale's hands. We have to leave it to history to judge whether by pursuing such a course, the government was trying to attain some sinister goals of its own or was doing so to serve what it considered to be the best interests of the people. In any case, the stand of the authorities that the latest Akali *morchas* would lead to immense turmoil and lawlessness in the area would appear to be unfounded in the light of their previous *morchas* as well as the readiness with which Longowal had agreed to postpone his programmes in the past. Except during the *Rasta roko morcha* on 4 April 1983, when 21 persons died in police firing, all their agitations had been peaceful, involving no physical confrontation between the protesters and the law enforcers.

Then why this sudden apprehension that the 3 June movement would be any different from the previous ones? According to a report in the *Tribune*, Chandigarh, dated 24 May 1984, filed by its Delhi correspondent Satindra Singh, official observers in Delhi were not too perturbed over the likely fallout of the non-cooperation call given by the Akali Dal, as they believed that the agitation would neither affect the collection of land revenue nor the purchase or movement of wheat by government agencies. Their optimism was based on sound common sense and historical experience. By withholding the payment of land revenue, the farmers will be putting their title to the land in jeopardy, a risk they will never take. This tactic did not succeed even during the freedom movement. As far as the procurement and movement of food grains outside the state was concerned, 90 per cent of the surplus wheat would already have been procured by the deadline of 3 June and as for the rest, the farmers would find it extremely difficult to find adequate storage space through the coming rainy season, especially in view of the bumper crop that year. As regards the apprehension that Sikhs in their thousands would converge upon the Temple, surely the vast resources at the disposal of the civil administration plus the newly deployed army battalions could have easily met the threat posed by mostly unarmed mobs, if the report proved true at all, that is. Only a few days earlier, a potentially explosive situation in the main gurudwara in the sub-divisional town of Moga, had been contained by the police and the paramilitary forces without any avoidable loss of life. As it turned out, only a few hundred Sikhs from nearby villages set out for Amritsar on hearing of the army assault. As expected, the security forces found no difficulty in summarily disposing of any threat they may have posed.

*

How well prepared and fortified were the militants inside the Temple? Contemporary media reports and the white paper issued by the Union government, soon after Blue Star, gave the impression that the Golden Temple had been conversed into a veritable fortress by the militants and nothing but a formidable army action could crush their resistance and dislodge them from their stronghold. But is it possible that the reality was somewhat different and the strength and defensive capacity of the militants had been grossly overstated? An eyewitness account would have us believe that the spent ammunition found in the Temple after the army operation was over was sought to be greatly exaggerated by the authorities, probably in an effort to justify the use of heavy armour.

Let us turn to what Lt-General J.S. Aurora, a veteran of many battles and a national icon at the time of the 1971 Indo-Pakistan War, had to say on the subject (he died in May 2005). To be fair to him, while making his assessment, he did not hide the deep sense of personal hurt felt by him and, indeed, by all Sikhs to whichever section of society they belonged, at the macabre turn of events. 'It is not easy to rationalize when your deepest sentiments are injured,'[6] he ruefully stated and went on to describe the situation within the Temple at the time:

Much has been said about the quantum of weapons and preparation of defences by the extremists. When I visited the Golden Temple with my wife in December 1983, and spent two hours one evening and two the following morning, I could see no defences of any description. As a devotee, I visited various parts of the temple as well as Baba Atal Gurudwara. There were no signs of any defensive preparations anywhere. Bhindranwale was living in Guru Nanak Niwas at that time. I next visited the Golden Temple on 24 February 1984, by which time he had moved into the Akal Takht building. I saw people carrying weapons in the *parikrama* area. But there were no fortifications. The top of the *langar* (a community meal in Sikh tradition) building had been fortified with sandbags: I was told there was periodic firing from the CRPF and the sandbags had been put up for protection. The defences did not appear very formidable, as anything on top of a building can be knocked off quite easily. When I visited the Temple again on 6 July, exactly a month after the operation, I saw some of the defences, which might have been built over, but a large number had been left to show to the people what the terrorists had built. It was obvious that in the period of three months—between March and June—much had been done and the defences had been well sited. I know Major General Shabeg Singh, who had served under me during the Bangladesh operations. He had not lost his professional touch.[7]

Evidently, the stockpiling of weapons and raising of fortifications must have occurred during March-June 1984, a period that coincided with the hardening of the government stand and the peaking of its attempts at building up a national consensus on the need to give a bloody nose, as the army lingo goes, to the sundry groups of terrorists and extremists taking shelter in the Temple and the Akalis, who were allegedly encouraging them to draw political mileage out of the rising tide of terrorism. This supposition would tie up rather nicely with the premise that the entire chain of events and the long protracted process of negotiations with the Akali leadership for the previous three years was geared to achieve but one purpose, i.e., the resolution of the long-standing nationality question. If true, this could well amount to a most sinister goal on the agenda of a federal democratic polity.

General Aurora also pooh-poohed the general impression that the militants were in possession of highly sophisticated weaponry. Based on the official disclosures about the recovery of arms and ammunition from the Temple after the operation, he opined, 'The use and stocking of firearms inside the Golden Temple is reprehensible and inexcusable. I make no excuse for Bhindranwale and his followers for preaching and practising violence as this is against the tenets of Sikhism. There is, however, the need to correct the picture that has been painted by the media that sophisticated weapons were found inside the Temple...It is obvious, therefore, that there were not so many sophisticated weapons.'[8] To add insult to injury, official handouts after the conclusion of the operation referred to the surrender of Sant Longowal and other Akali leaders to the authorities, though some newspapers ascribed the expression to a bureaucratic gaffe.

However, the white paper issued after a month also used the same language on page 49: 'At 0100 hours on June 6, Sant Harchand Singh Longowal and Shri G.S. Tohra surrendered near the Guru Nanak Niwas with about 350 people.' Was it necessary to further humiliate and defame the Sikh political leadership in the eyes of their own people and damage their capacity to rein in the extremist elements in the post-Blue Star phase? As for Bhindranwale, however important he may have been when alive to serve the political agendas of the Delhi establishment, a dead Bhindranwale could not have been of much use, so he too was summarily cast aside. All India Radio and other official media reported that no one came forward to claim his dead body, a natural enough event under the circumstances, one would think. But the news was given out as if he had been sort of disowned by the community. An intrepid political analyst, on the other hand, claims that a number of Sikh individuals and institutions had approached the authorities for the custody and cremation of his dead body.[9] He was finally cremated in the presence of the district magistrate of Amritsar and a Punjab criminal investigation department (CID) officer.

*

We must turn at this stage to Dr Alexander for a ringside view of the developments at that crucial juncture and why the army commanders were unable to keep their word to the prime minister that there would be no damage to the gurudwaras, especially the Golden Temple, except minimally. He states,

> I would like to state here categorically that the military operations that the prime minister authorized on 25 May 1984 and which Vaidya (the army chief) discussed with us on 27 May were confined to the siege and flushing out operations in the identified gurudwaras in different places and in the Golden Temple at Amritsar. Till that point of time there was no reference to any plan except for an effective siege

of the buildings, involving cutting off telephones, electricity, water, food and inflow of men and weapons...Vaidya after a quick visit to Punjab and after consultations with his senior colleagues in the Army, sought an urgent meeting with the prime minister on 29 May to inform her about some important changes in the plan. He met Indira Gandhi at her South Block office on 29 May and explained to her the revised plan and the reasons for the change. R.N. Kao (security advisor to the PM) and I were present at the meeting...Vaidya told the PM that he had discussed the plan of the siege with Lt General Sunderji and other senior officers directly in charge of the operations and it was now their considered view that while the plan of siege could be followed in respect of all smaller *gurudwaras*, then under the control of the extremists, it would not be practical to follow the plan in case of the Golden Temple. Instead, he said, there would be a quick seizure of the hideouts of the terrorists inside the temple, using minimum force. The seizure, he said, would entail a commando operation inside the Golden Temple, which would be conducted with such swiftness and surprise that it would not result in any damage to the temple buildings.[10]

The PM was reported to have felt 'quite perturbed' at the suggestion for the use of force inside the temple and asked Vaidya several questions seeking clarifications, on a number of points as to how long would it take to subdue the terrorists in case they put up stiff resistance, particularly if they took refuge in the Harimandir where Guru Granth Sahib was placed. Also, why it became necessary for the army chief to change a plan he had himself suggested just four days ago. And finally, what will be its fallout on the

Sikh troops in the armed forces. Vaidya explained that the
earlier plan had to be recast as suggested by his senior
colleagues, probably referring to the charismatic Sunderji,
then the western army commander at Shimla, of whom
many contemporaries seemed to be in awe because of his
impressive service record, handsome personality, intellectual
arrogance and, of course, an exaggerated sense of self-
importance and swagger. Alexander elaborated further,
'Vaidya spoke with such confidence and calmness that the
new plan he was proposing appeared to be virtually the
only option open to the Army. He said that the other
option was fraught with dangerous consequences and
hundreds of innocent people may fall victim to firing
along the roads leading to Amritsar and in the vicinity of
the Golden Temple. He noted that Army casualties could
also be heavy as the siege may last several days in view of
the reaction to be expected from the frenzied mobs. On
the other hand, he emphasized that the new plan would
be executed so quickly that everything would be over by
the time the people come to realize what was happening.
On the question of damage to the temple, Vaidya asserted
that strict instructions would be given to the Army to
ensure that no damage was caused to the temple buildings
under any circumstances.'[11] In short, the new plan put
forward by the army chief received the PM's approval,
though not without some reservations on her part, as
Alexander goes to great lengths to emphasize.

*

Dr P.C. Alexander defines Blue Star simply in terms of
'freeing 35 gurudwaras in the state as also the Golden
Temple in Amritsar, from the control of the terrorists'.
And that while operational goals were achieved quite

easily in the case of all minor gurudwaras, except the one in Patiala, the action at the Golden Temple turned out to be rather awkward. Lt General K.S. Brar, the force commander at Amritsar, presented his, and presumably the army's, version of the events in *Operation Blue Star: The True Story* published in 1993, a few years after his retirement from the army. 'Operation Blue Star was, in my opinion, one of the most extraordinary and sensitive operations ever undertaken by any army in the world...I am convinced that it was the Indian soldier, who through an act of supererogation, finally gave his life, defended his honour, and in so doing, averted a major cataclysm in cotemporary Indian history.' This is how the good general sums up the Operation, while paying rich tributes to his men and officers all through the book, as a true-blue general must.

However, contrary to his assessment, far from averting a major cataclysm in Indian history, Blue Star would actually precipitate a much more deadly phase in the Sikh militant movement.

As became apparent soon after the operation began, the army brass had not cared to collect even the bare minimum details about the strengths and weaknesses of the enemy the troops were to confront before rushing into the Temple for the action. The general's description would have gained in authenticity and effect, if he had gone deeper into the logistical and tactical failures of his enterprise and given a more equable and balanced account of the botched operation. It is now quite obvious that what actually happened, and which has now been confirmed by the accounts given by Alexander, was vastly different from the sanitized version given by Brar. Also, it is now possible with the benefit of hindsight and on the basis of revelations made by police and gurudwara officials, who happened to be present inside the premises at the time, to arrive at a reasonable assessment of the situation. Evidently, things did not quite work out as planned.

Let us first turn to what Alexander has to say on the subject.

> Finding that the militants were not in a mood to surrender, the Army proceeded to the next stage of the operations, namely, entering the temple through a commando operation. Most unexpectedly, the commandos came under heavy fire. It was *only then* that the Army commanders realized that they were up against an enemy well entrenched in secure positions within various unapproachable labyrinthine passages inside the building and very well equipped with machine guns and other heavy weapons...the Army found itself suddenly faced with a situation that it had not anticipated and for which, therefore, it had not been prepared. It was obvious that the information that the commanders had gathered about the weapons and men inside the temple was grossly inadequate and they had started the operations on the basis of insufficient data...The entire strategy and tactics had to be changed quickly...Eventually, armoured personnel carriers and tanks had to be brought in to tackle the new situation that confronted the Army. At that point they realized that there was no possibility of ensuring the surrender of the militants without causing damage to the buildings.[12]

At about that point of time, both the civilian bureaucracy, monitoring the action in Delhi and Chandigarh and the army brass appears to have lost control over the situation in the Temple, the former secure in the belief that they had done all that they could and now it was for the professionals in the army to handle the problem. On his part, the army chief must have been content to leave all crucial decisions to Lt-General Sunderji, the western army commander, in whose jurisdiction the whole action was taking place. Dr Alexander, of course, goes to great lengths to prove Mrs Gandhi's bona fides in the entire affair, throwing all the blame for the death and destruction within the Temple onto the army commanders, especially Gen Vaidya, then chief of the army staff.

The army as well as the government went out of their way to explain that it became necessary to use excessive force within the Temple premises due to unexpectedly heavy armed resistance from the militants holed inside, which they ascribed to the lack of intelligence from the police and the CID, the most convenient whipping boys of the Indian establishment. It is simply not true that there was dearth of intelligence, as the Punjab CID had set up a sizeable presence in the city as well as inside the Temple and was operating a number of very reliable sources. An intelligence officer of the rank of a police superintendent practically lived and worked inside the premises all through that fateful period and was regularly feeding relevant information to the CID headquarters in Chandigarh through written and telephonic reports on the critical developments taking place there. By virtue of his long stint in Amritsar and the nature of his duties, he enjoyed an excellent but discreet rapport with many senior leaders both in the Akali party and the Congress as well as among the militant groups. If the army chose to launch an operation of such magnitude on the basis of inadequate data, as mentioned by Alexander, it was not because of paucity of information but because they must have deliberately disregarded police reports due to their customary disdain and contempt for the organization. In any case, what prevented them from carrying out thorough surveys and reconnaissance before finalizing their plans, as is incumbent upon the armed forces in all situations? It was possibly the famous Sunderji swagger and audacity that must have played a major role in selling the far from perfect operational plan, as was to become only too evident later, to a trusting Vaidya and a skeptical but somewhat over-awed prime minister. It could also be that the latter, not very well-served by advisers even at the best of times, could now afford to sit back and watch the turf battles between the Akalis and Bhindranwale boil over and the possible resolution of the national question of India.

General Sunderji's claim to fame rested on his vast intellectual capacity to propound newer and eye-catching doctrines of regional supremacy through military prowess and what he called a forward foreign policy. In the case of Blue Star, he was probably able to overrule an accommodating Vaidya through sheer brilliance and the proverbial gift of the gab and, of course, by establishing direct rapport with the PM and outlining a plan of operation which provoked little opposition, precisely because of its incredible simplicity. The plan revolved around the deployment of army commandos to swiftly seize Bhindranwale and his close associates and neutralize the militants in the thick of the night, without causing any damage to the buildings. The operation was to start after the *Guru Granth Sahib* was taken to Manji Sahib for the night, as per tradition (*maryada*), and would be over before it was reinstalled in the Harimandir the next morning. Any tell-tale signs like bloodstains would have been cleaned up before the devotees started gathering the next day. No one would even know that any abnormal event had occurred.

Evidently, either Sunderji had placed too much confidence in his commandos or had grossly underestimated the strength and dedication of the militants. In both cases, it was indicative of poor leadership and inadequate appreciation of the situation.

Not unexpectedly, the operation was to prove a disaster in more senses than one. Not only did it fail in its immediate task of apprehending or eliminating a sizeable number of militants hiding in the Temple, the operation actually triggered a high degree of discontent and consternation in the community that would lead soon afterwards to a major intensification of militancy and terrorism in the region. Even the more enlightened sections among the Sikhs felt betrayed and outraged at the turn of events. It was at this point that Khushwant Singh, a nominated member of parliament and commonly perceived until then to be firmly pro-establishment, surrendered a high state honour and wrote bitterly about the army action and the desecration of the holiest of Sikh shrines. Bhindranwale and his militant rhetoric, which had earlier left the bulk of the Sikh community somewhat unamused, would acquire considerable credibility and acceptability after his death in the operation. A surprisingly large number of ordinary Sikhs would refuse to believe that he was indeed no more. Myths and legends would soon grow around him, and it would take many years before his ghost could be exorcised.

*

Who was responsible for the botched operation? Dr Alexander finds it expedient to pass off the whole blame onto the army commanders, possibly in an attempt to shake off any blame being ascribed to his boss. He faults the generals on three counts. First, why did they have to change the original plan, approved by the PM after an extended discussion? Second, why did they embark on an operation without being armed with sufficient intelligence? Third, why did the commanders of the Sikh regiments not take necessary precautionary measures to forestall the unrest among the troops on hearing of the action in the Temple that triggered mutinous conduct in their units?

He also claims that the timing of the action was left entirely to the army commanders and if they wanted more time to collect information and to prepare for any change in perspective, there would have been no problem on that score. While his misgivings about the army commanders are not without some substance in the limited sense of the failed operation, he mostly steers clear of the larger issues involved, such as why the government allowed the situation to deteriorate to an extent that an army operation became necessary in the first place, and who was responsible for it. In fact, his entire line of reasoning is evidently structured to finding alibis for the political establishment in this whole murky affair. Could this be due to his zeal to deflect any criticism that may fasten to the late prime minister and, by implication, also to him as her most trusted advisor at the time? It is easy to shift the blame onto the generals because men in uniform are by tradition reticent in boldly expressing their views on such sensitive matters. Besides, both Vaidya and Sunderji are no more, the former killed by Sikh militants in Pune, where he had settled down after retirement, and the latter dying of natural causes in an army hospital in Delhi, unrepentant and unapologetic until the last.

The only major achievement, if it could be so termed, of the action was the killing of Bhindranwale, Shabeg Singh, Amrik Singh and a few other close associates of the former. At a different level, however, the cynical and high-handed conduct of the troops during the operation, not unusual in army manoeuvres, would influence the subsequent course of Sikh militancy most critically. Besides, the deep hurt caused to the Sikh psyche on account of the vindictive manner in which the army conducted itself during operations Blue Star and Wood Rose, the latter would also generate a chain of disastrous events, primarily in Punjab but also in many other parts of the country— Mrs Gandhi's assassination being probably the most tragic and significant of them. It also radically redefined the nature of the relationship between the Sikh people and the Indian state by seriously undermining their intrinsic faith in governmental institutions to dispense even-handed justice and be fair-minded in assuring them a place of honour and dignity in the polity.

*

Blue Star was accompanied by a parallel operation in the countryside, code-named Wood Rose, aimed at clearing the rural areas of terrorist and extremist elements. This action proved to be even more counter-productive in meeting its objectives because the area of operations was much more extensive and the command structure more diffuse than in Blue Star. Wood Rose involved a string of siege and search operations in the villages in which the troops would lay siege to the target village early in the morning to stop all movements out of the village and confine the residents within their houses, preparatory to conducting house-to-house searches for possible militant presence. Indian villagers commonly depend on the open fields for their excretory functions, which are mostly performed in the early mornings. Also, most work relating to village life entails morning activity. Siege and search operations, which blocked all movements during a most important part of the day, therefore, caused immense distress to the villagers and were, thus, deeply resented.

Often the troops would return to a particular village again and again for similar manoeuvres, acting on some motivated information. Also, since the most likely targets of such searches were the young people, they would often try to hide or run away to escape the army teams. Later, many of them would go across the border into Pakistan. In the beginning, the Pakistani authorities put all such trespassers behind bars. However, it wasn't long before they realised the immense potential of the situation as the resentment and distress among these young men could be easily exploited for subversion and worse. Many of these young Sikhs would later return to India, indoctrinated, armed, trained and motivated by the Pakistani authorities, to set off a most deadly phase of terrorist violence in the country. The brutal and insensitive behaviour of the troops, even towards old and infirm Sikh men and women during Wood Rose, which is not uncommon in such operations, reinforced the impression that the army was indeed engaged in a deliberate and systematic suppression of a minuscule minority.

What is worse, the troops did not spare even old soldiers with distinguished careers in the armed forces behind them and many a battle-scarred veteran. It may be mentioned that Sikh ex-servicemen form a sizeable fraction of Punjab's rural population, estimated to be close to half a million at any given time. Expectedly, the countryside was flush with rumours that the Indian state and its army were out to finish off the younger generation of the Sikh community.

A climate of fear and suspicion continued to pervade

the Punjab countryside for several months, even after Operation Wood Rose was formally called off and army units withdrew from active duty, as the Sikh people continued to be at the mercy of an authoritarian and suppressive state apparatus and the mistreatment of old soldiers did not cease. The *Tribune*, Chandigarh, carried a report on 15 June 1985 about a meeting of the executive committee of the Punjab unit of the Indian Ex-services League, presided over by retired Lt-General G.S. Buch, which expressed regret over the incidents of 'harassment and humiliation' of former soldiers by the security forces all over the state. Also that 'In a resolution, the meeting called upon the government to ensure the dignity and honour of ex-servicemen'. The police and central security forces that had replaced the troops were following much the same strongarm tactics as the army in the conduct of their counter-terrorist operations. After the initial patriotic zeal had worn off, both operations Blue Star and Wood Rose were to receive unfavorable media coverage, both in India and abroad. Serious doubts about the goals and conduct of the operations, the quantum and kind of armour employed, their timing and the exact nature of the tasks accomplished, continued to cause concern in large sections of the Indian people for several months. Neither the army nor the governments in Delhi and Chandigarh were able to clear the air in a manner that carried conviction.

In the event, a deep sense of disgruntlement and distress seized the Sikh community, which was to last a long time. This would later become a significant factor in precipitating one of the most lethal militant movements in the world, taking a toll of thousands of lives, severely damaging the institutions of civilized governance and the alienation of a whole generation of Sikhs. One of the more serious allegations floating around at the time related to the burning down of the Sikh memorial library and the commission of some other acts of unnecessary vandalism by troops during the operation. A section of the Sikh community even believed that the uncalled for excesses and destruction by the army were tantamount to an attempt by the Indian state to destroy the cultural and spiritual heritage of the community.

In the event, the June 1984 army operations in Punjab and the way they were conducted would gravely fracture Hindu-Sikhs relations, placing the two communities firmly on opposite sides of the fence for several years. Barring rare exceptions, Hindus were generally prone to justify the assault on the Golden Temple, while the Sikhs collectively viewed the action as an outrageous and blasphemous act, intended to destroy the self-respect and integrity of the *panth*. The operations were widely hailed by Hindus in Punjab and Delhi amid widespread rejoicing and distribution of sweets, an unsavoury gesture to express triumph and happiness, an act that some sections of the Sikhs would reciprocate in equal measure a few months later when Indira Gandhi was assassinated by her two Sikh security guards. This writer was an uneasy witness to open expression of glee and jubilation at a dinner in a posh New Delhi colony, where all the guests except one were Punjabi Hindus, on the day Bhindranwale was killed in Operation Blue Star. The intriguing love-hate relationship between the Sikhs and Punjabi Hindus has often baffled third party observers and needs to be studied by social scientists and psychologists.

*

What were the overall gains of the army operations in Punjab and how far did they go in stemming the rising tide of terrorist violence in the region? This writer took over as director general of police of the state about three weeks after the end of Operation Blue Star, though Wood Rose was still in full swing. Apart from the deep distress in the community due to the manner in which the army conducted the two operations, the sheer enormity of brutal and offensive behaviour by the army and the police during the period of army occupation made ordinary Sikhs feel severely vulnerable and defenceless and left the community seething with collective anger and frustration. This would soon turn into extensive support and endorsement for the ideology advanced by the militant leadership under Bhindranwale. Now that the latter was no more and the entire Akali leadership was in detention, the field was wide open for many new entrants to step into the dangerous arena of militancy and terrorism.

Ideological scaffolding would come from newer sources of inspiration such as Dr Sohan Singh, a former director of health services in Punjab, reportedly a frequent visitor to Pakistan like several other militant leaders, who would set up the first *panthic* committee to guide the disparate groups of militants. More such committees will come into being later, but Sohan Singh's committee continued to enjoy a position of primacy among them. We will speak about these committees in more detail later. Even in purely strategic terms, the operational gains were somewhat limited, as an alarmingly large number of militants, holed up in the Temple, were able to make good their escape. This happened because several exit points out of the Temple premises remained unsecured, possibly due to inadequate appraisal of the ground situation, which signifies poor planning and execution of a most sensitive manoeuvre in the sacred precincts of a universally respected religious place. The elimination of Bhindranwale and his close associates could hardly be termed as a major enough gain, as later events would reveal, although at the material time it did look like a considerable achievement.

Shortly after taking over, I advised the government that the army be relieved of its civil commitments to make way for the bureaucracy and the police, which I thought would help restore a sense of normalcy in the state as the civil organs of administration are normally better equipped to handle such situations. So although the army's presence was still very much palpable, with the corps commander at Jalandhar looking after the departments of home and internal security, as adviser to the state Governor, the process of restoration of civilian administration had commenced in right earnest. A few brigadiers and colonels would take a few more weeks to withdraw fully from district commands, but it was only a matter of time before they departed.

*

Operation Blue Star finally concluded on 6 June with the death of Sant Bhindranwale, Shabeg Singh and a few others in the assault on the Akal Takht, where they had been living for several months. In the process, the building of the Akal Takht, the most sacred of the five Sikh *takhts* or centres of temporal power, was razed to the ground and its many holy relics destroyed. The sanctum sanctorum of the Harimandir too received numerous bullet marks. This was perhaps inevitable in an operation of the kind the army launched in the Golden Temple, although there is reason to believe that a more circumspect and better planned action after a thorough assessment of the possible options, before finalizing the operational details, would have been more successful without causing so much needless loss of life and destruction to the holiest of Sikh shrines. In his frequent briefings to the media, Sunderji used to claim that the troops went into action in the Temple 'with humility in their hearts and prayers on their lips' and that 'we in the Army hold all places of religion in equal reverence'. While, all this may well be the case, the overall effect of the two operations and the alleged conduct of some sections of troops during the manoeuvres do not appear to fully uphold Sundarji's assertions. The full impact of the damage caused to the Golden Temple and the boorish behaviour with rural population on the collective Sikh psyche during the two operations, was not adequately realized by the authorities until it was too late to send out reassuring signals to the community. More than any other factor, this was the most persuasive argument the militants employed to win over the community to their point of view.

The *Times of India*, New Delhi was later to carry a rather poignant account of the extent of damage caused during Blue Star in its issue of 5 June 1993 under the caption 'Unforgotten scars of temple'. An abridged version of the report is reproduced below:

> Even after nine years, the scraps left by Operation Blue Star on the Golden Temple are distinctly fresh. Bullet-riddled manuscripts, soot-laden roofs of Teja Singh Samundari Hall, pock-marked towering *bungas* (defensive watch towers) bring alive the telling story of the operation which is likely to go down as one of the most momentous events in the Sikh history. The milling crowds that visit the Golden Temple every day curiously watch these marks, which are left unrepaired, reviving memories of the strife-torn period. Photographs of Sant Jarnail Singh Bhindranwale, and his lieutenants Shahbeg Singh and Amrik Singh, are still displayed prominently in some parts of the temple premises, including the temple museum where, of course, Sant Bhindranwale's picture is conspicuously absent for he is still believed to be alive...The most

gory fallout of the operation was the irreparable loss to the Sikh reference library and museum, where age-old rare manuscripts and paintings were preserved. The Sikh reference library, which was the repository of rare and ancient works, most of them compiled by the scholars by hand, was virtually reduced to ashes. According to the library staff, at least 13,000 books and manuscripts vanished from the shelves, which were later set afire by the army. The SGPC has been corresponding with the Centre asking for the return of the books, which are supposedly still in the possession of the Army...The Army is believed to have dumped the books in more than 150 gunny bags, though until recently it has not been officially admitted by the Centre that the books were removed from the library before the operation. The SGPC officials believe that the stock is lying in Meerut under the possession of the Army. In the library, one can still find albums and manuscripts pierced by bullets. Some of the racks too bear the bullet marks at a place of research and learning. In the museum, 103 paintings were reduced to ashes or damaged beyond repair, besides *gadari pothi* and *khanda*, which were priceless treasures. The 'scars and injuries' inflicted by the operation would remain deeply ingrained in the Sikh psyche because we feel that the community was befooled by the Centre, said an SGPG official. It was not only that the sanctity of the sanctum sanctorum was grievously violated but it inflicted injuries on the minds of the Sikhs and these bullet marks would just symbolize that, he added.

Another account of the operation as given by Prof. J.S. Grewal, a renowned authority on mediaeval India and the Sikhs, in his book *The Sikhs of the Punjab*, written in 1994, for the *New Cambridge History of India* series may also be of interest:

On June 3, the Punjab was cut off from the rest of the country and movement within the state was made impossible by the presence of troops everywhere. The supply of water and electricity to the Golden Temple complex was stopped. On June 4, the army opened exploratory fire. On June 5, the commandos and CS gas proved ineffective. On the morning of June 6, tanks were used against 'the enemy' in the Akal Takht. Meanwhile tanks and helicopters were used, among other things, to deter the thousands of agitated villagers from converging upon Amritsar, and several other gurudwaras in the state, taken over by the army. The crucial action in the Golden Temple complex was over before the nightfall of June 6. A large number of pilgrims including women and children died in cross firing. The infuriated troops shot some young men dead with their hands tied behind their backs with their own turbans. Some died of suffocation in the 'prisoners camp' set up in a room of Guru Nanak Niwas. According to one estimate, the total casualties of officers and men were about 700 and of civilians about 5,000. The Sikhs were outraged at the attack in the Golden Temple complex and the destruction of the Akal Takht. All sections of Sikh opinion, from the urban sophisticates sipping scotch in their bungalows in Delhi to the peasants in the fields were horrified at what had happened. Even those who had never condoned secession could not get themselves to justify the army action...Operation Blue Star revived the memories of Ahmed Shah Abdali in Sikh imagination.

The destruction of the Akal Takht, which occupies a unique position in Sikh history and tradition, was a most distressing event for the community. For, it was here that the sixth Sikh Guru first raised an army to fight the tyrannical rule of the Mughal emperors and their viceroys in the Punjab. Over the centuries, the place had become a symbol of resistance by armed force, if necessary, to injustice and oppression, providing a focal point to the community to meet and choose an appropriate course of action when faced with adversity that could come in various forms in an environment of insecurity and fear at the hands of an autocratic and brutal state structure. Operation Blue Star was undoubtedly the worst disaster to befall the Akal Takht in over two hundred years—the last time it happened was in 1764, when Afghan raider Ahmed Shah Abdali had had it razed to the ground. As a rallying point for a community in distress with its identity and self-esteem under grave threat, the Akal Takht has served in the brief history of the community, both as an inspiration and an opportunity to reorganize and prepare to fight for their rights another day. Such a process of resurgence was accomplished through community congregations, called Sarbat Khalsa, whenever the community was under attack. These congregations were marked by a process of democratic decision-making, such decisions being described as *Gurmatas* or the Guru's injunctions. It is important to understand the correct connotation and significance of these terms as they figured frequently in contemporary writings on the subject and were often used to put a different gloss on the events, either out of ignorance or deliberate misinterpretation by the authorities.

Khushwant Singh wrote in *Gentleman*, a Bombay magazine, on 15 July 1994:

> What I protested against, by returning the Padma Bhushan, was that my warnings to the government, through my speeches in Parliament, had been ignored. I had said repeatedly that after having, through

administrative neglect, allowed people like Bhindranwale and his followers to smuggle arms in large quantities into the Harmander complex, any action to expel them by force could result in bloodshed, which, in turn, would hurt and alienate the Sikh community, a large number of whom are not concerned with the politics of Bhindranwale or any one else... Barring a handful, almost all Sikhs are outraged and I can say that this includes the President of India...Another reason I opposed a crackdown was that a bloodbath would create a fertile ground for Khalistan. I think by this action, the government has sown the seeds for Khalistan. It will now be very hard for moderate Sikhs to combat this movement, which I know will be suicidal for the interests of the Sikhs and, needless to say, will do irreparable damage to the integrity of the country. For there is no doubt that this action has provided the Khalistanis their first martyr in Bhindranwale and their focal point of resentment against India. Also, they can now point to what a Hindu government did to a Sikh shrine and use that as the focal point for their resentment.

Khushwant Singh was not alone in questioning the dubious gains of the army operations, although, as a Sikh and a historian, his perception of and perspective on the entire course of events in the Punjab was indeed more succinct. Kuldip Nayar, a long-time Punjab watcher and an avid supporter of the Punjabi ethos or Punjabiyat, referred to the widening gulf between Hindus and Sikhs in mid-July 1984, that is, after the army action in Amritsar. He wrote,

The two communities are polarized to the last child. Even the rumours that affect them are different. As I travelled through the state for three days, I could feel this sense of separateness...The feeling of hurt among the Sikhs is deep, even five weeks after the army action. Many among them, though outraged by the actions of Sant Jarnail Singh and his men outside the Golden Temple, seem to have been swept off their feet by the tide of emotion...In fact during my travels and talks I found that the anger of the Sikhs was not directed only against Mrs Gandhi but against the Hindu community...The general feeling among the Sikhs that they have a separate identity has increased after the army action...I have returned sad and disturbed from Punjab because I find the Punjab ethos nearly dead.[13]

Several other civil society groups, sections of the intelligentsia, social scientists and political analysts would gradually come to realize the many shocking features of Operation Blue Star and its long-range impact, foreseen and unforeseen, on the Sikh psyche and the Punjab situation. The CPI (M), a party to the 'national consensus' painstakingly built by the Delhi establishment not long ago, was the first of the major political parties to recognize the full implications of the army assault on the Sikh shrine in Amritsar, in terms of a deeply hurt and indignant Sikh community and the fractured unity in the crucial border state of Punjab. Both Jyoti Basu, the CPM chief minister of West Bengal and party general secretary E.M.S. Namboodripad termed it as 'unfortunate and avoidable'. Harkishan Singh Surjeet, the veteran Communist leader from Punjab with long-standing links with grassroots politics of the state, who would acquire immense political importance in Delhi in an era of unstable coalitional politics in the country in the 1990s and later, stated in an extended interview carried by the *Illustrated Weekly of India*, Bombay in its issue of 29 July 1984, under the title 'Khalistan has *now* become a reality...' that:

Secularism has become the worst victim in this country. The total reaction among the Hindus has been dismaying. They do not demarcate between the extremists and common Sikhs and look upon the Sikhs as if they were all responsible. This is having an adverse effect on the minds of the Sikhs, who are being further alienated. This is very harmful for the country...Earlier, there was microscopic scope for Khalistan. But today, the situation is such that anybody can be misled. The feelings of separatism are growing... And it is imperative that the government takes serious note of this and fights it. By political measures. By a process of reconciliation. Once the situation in Punjab calms down, once feelings are assuaged, healthy elements will slowly prevail. But, *today*, Khalistan has become a reality.

Granted that politicians are for ever seeking to advance their special political prospects in whatever crisis situation the nation may be faced with at any given time, Blue Star evoked widespread censure across the nation, except, of course, in the rightist Hindu media and official handouts. Several Sikh Congressmen and women too were critical but chose to either keep quiet or prevaricate, another evidence of the growing Hindu-Sikh divide. Of course, the healthy elements, in which Surjeet appeared to repose a great deal of faith, were in detention and would not be set free for months to come. The internment of the entire Akali leadership had created a political vacuum in the community at a most vulnerable time in its history, a situation tailor-made for the extremist elements to assert their authority and occupy the vacant political space for their own ends. This is exactly what would happen in the post-Blue Star period. Sikh militancy would grow exponentially.

6

The Fallout

Apart from fuelling the flames of militancy in the region, Operation Blue Star set off a grave situation in the army, with several Sikh regiments being confronted with acts of indiscipline and mutinous conduct by hundreds of troops. With its record of loyalty and discipline, it seemed inconceivable that the Sikh soldiery would indulge in such aberrant conduct. However, accounts of the assault on their most cherished religious structure, sometimes also overstated, that reached them in the distant cantonments, could not but cause a deep sense of outrage, which would have assumed even graver dimensions due to a possible failure of regimental leadership to sustain the requisite level of mutual trust between the officers and the men. We have referred earlier to the unique history of the Sikh regiments of the British Indian army. Although quite a few units in eastern and western India showed substantial signs of unrest, the cantonments of Ganganagar in

Rajasthan and Ramgarh in Bihar were the worst affected. On 7 June, some 500 soldiers of the 9th battalion of the Sikh regiment stationed at Ganganagar seized unit vehicles and drove through the town, shouting anti-government slogans, some of them even crossing the border into Pakistan. Soon similar incidents, many of a graver nature, flared up in places such as Alwar, Jammu, Thane and Pune.

In the Sikh regimental centre in Ramgarh, Bihar, large groups of Sikh recruits under training broke open the armoury, carried away big caches of weapons, shot dead brigade commander S.C. Puri, and headed towards Amritsar in seized army vehicles, shouting slogans against the government. Notably, the bulk of the men who took part in these activities comprised of impressionable young other ranks (ORs) or recruits. Not that Sikh officers did not share the resentment and frustration of the more impressionable cadres, but the benchmarks of discipline were obviously higher at those levels. Command and control failures too must have played their part in provoking mutinous conduct among the soldiers. In Ramgarh, 'as many as 20 out of 23 officers left their positions in the Sikh regimental centre and sought refuge with their families elsewhere. It was only after the officers left their posts and their troops leaderless that mass anxiety gripped the soldiers.'[1]

The 9th battalion would later be demobilized. Predictably, the authorities failed to provide any authentic information about the number of desertions and mutinous conduct by Sikh soldiers, but well-informed sources put the figure at around 10,000, of which some 5,000 approached the SGPC and the Akali Dal for rehabilitation. After the containment of the turmoil, internal inquiries were set in motion to take disciplinary action against them under the Army Act and severe punishments were handed out to all those found guilty. The rehabilitation of Sikh soldiers, dismissed for such misconduct, would later become one of the principal demands of the Akalis and form part of the Rajiv-Longowal accord, to be signed in July 1985.

Lt-General (retired) Harbakhsh Singh, the colonel commandant of the Sikh regiment for a record twenty years (1951-71) and an illustrious army commander, reacted strongly to the dismissal of Sikh soldiers for desertion in protest against the storming of the Golden Temple. He defended the spontaneous and natural reaction of the soldiers against what he called 'a case of unprecedented and extreme religious provocation to the Sikh soldiers'. In the course of an interview carried by the *Telegraph*, Calcutta, on 7 September 1984, under the title 'Sikhs Provoked to Desert Army', he specifically alluded to the continued employment of Sikh religious rituals and practices for the purpose of infusing the requisite martial spirit of the Khalsa into Sikh regiments in the army.

> I consider it my moral duty to apprise the general public that the Sikh soldier...is nurtured, of old, on his religious tenets and traditions, which have been fully approved and supported by the Army and the government of independent India for the last 37 years. The Sikh soldier draws inspiration from the Khalsa of Guru Gobind Singh and the Khalsa army of Maharaja Ranjit Singh. Before being inducted into the army as a trained soldier, he takes the oath of allegiance at a ceremonial parade by physically touching with both hands the *Guru Granth Sahib*, which is displayed on parade for the purpose...Thereafter, he is led to the regimental war memorial (which again, in this case, embodies the

chakra and the *khanda*—coat of arms of the Khalsa) and ceremonially repeats and adopts as his own, the vow taken by Guru Gobind Singh at the time of taking up the sword of righteousness against Mughal oppression. The official motto of the regiment—*Nische kar apni jeet karon*—is taken out of this vow. And it is enjoined on every soldier and officer (whatever the latter's religion) of the regiment to memorize this vow and act upon it. The war cry of the Sikh soldier—*Bole so nihal...sat sri Akal*—is a legacy from the Khalsa of Guru Gobind Singh. The chakra of the Khalsa coat of arms is part of the regimental badge and is embossed on the letterhead of the regiment. A full-size chakra adorns the turban of the Sikh soldier in his ceremonial dress. A gurudwara in the barracks, which is built by the men by *kar sewa* (voluntary labour), is a must for a Sikh battalion, where kirtan and prayers are held regularly and *gurupurabs* (religious days) celebrated by the men with great enthusiasm. And what may be known to very few, the *Guru Granth Sahib* accompanies the battalions of the Sikh regiment into the operational area. The martyrdom of Guru Arjan Dev, which fell on June 3, being the epitome of supreme sacrifice in the face of extreme persecution, has a special significance for Sikh soldiers...Unfortunately, this also happened to be the day of the Army action in Harmandir Sahib.

The point that the general was trying to make was not that mutinous conduct in the army should be overlooked but that there was failure of command and control functions of their commanders. If they failed to anticipate the reactions among the men and to preempt their rebellious conduct by timely briefings and other precautionary measures, it was a grave lapse on their part.

For, not only did they allow a most disciplined and valiant regiment of the Indian army to take to the streets to ventilate its anguish and indignation and, in the process, completely disintegrate, they also sowed the seeds of disaffection and disgruntlement in many other regiments, which did not openly revolt but did not remain unaffected altogether. What, if any, preventive and remedial steps have been initiated by the army and the government to ensure that such situations are avoided in future is unclear. Sikh regiments still abide by the same rituals and traditions as before.

*

Significantly, far from putting a stop to extremist violence, killings and terrorist acts, Blue Star, in fact, led to a marked escalation in extremist and terrorist offences within weeks of the brief period of shock and uneasy calm in the state. P.C. Alexander concedes as much on page 311 of his book *Through The Corridors Of Power*.

> No appreciable abatement of violence occurred despite the large-scale operations by the Army and the arrest of many extremists and other suspected to be their supporters. The government was facing more or less the same situation as it existed before the Army action,' he states. Obviously, what the army had accomplished by their high-sounding rhetoric and grossly inept handling of their mandate was a big zero, apart from the fact that the operations had spread the discontent and anger over a much larger segment of the community. On 5 July 1984, an Indian airlines flight from Srinagar to Mumbai via Delhi was hijacked by about ten Sikh militants and taken to Lahore. They wanted the release of all

detained members of All India Sikh Students Federation (AISSF) and a ransom of $20 million in cash. Later, they surrendered unconditionally to Pakistan authorities and were granted asylum by the latter. On 24 August the same year, Sikh militants hijacked another Indian Airlines flight from Chandigarh and forced it to fly to Lahore. They demanded to be flown to the United States, but ultimately landed at Dubai via Karachi, where they gave in. They were finally brought to India on 2 September to face prosecution. Once again, Alexander felt that 'it appeared as if the extremists could again strike at will as in the days before the Army action.

The rumblings of discontent and anger were visible all around, and although the protests were noticeably low key, they were much more widespread than in the pre-Blue Star phase. The younger Sikhs in the cities and villages, in colleges and schools as well as in the professions, were more zealous in this regard. Saffron turbans and *dupattas* had become common wear for the younger Sikh men and women. The obvious and profound symbolism of the act could not have been lost on the state authorities, as the colour saffron is associated with defiant sacrifice in the Hindu and Sikh tradition. Tapes of Bhindranwale's speeches and many other forms of *panthic* texts were in wide circulation in the state, though, of course, mostly covertly. Barring the general run of Punjabi Hindus and rightist Hindu parties, a major segment of Indian intelligentsia perceived the military action as an electoral attention-grabber to impress upon the predominantly Hindu (83 per cent) population of the country the extent to which the ruling party would go to guard the nation's integrity against alleged Sikh separatism. Terrorist acts included mass as well as selective killings, arson, sabotage, blowing up of railway tracks, roads, bridges and irrigation canals, looting of banks, bombing of public places and public transport, assassinations and hijacking of aircraft and buses.

The response of the Punjab administration continued to be inept, harsh and clumsy. The scars left by Blue Star and Wood Rose on the collective Sikh psyche were still too tender and the continued incarceration of hundreds of men and women, even children, picked up from the Golden Temple and the countryside, did not improve matters very much. As is their wont, the authorities now proceeded to deal with the increasingly critical situation in the border state in the by now familiar and time-worn manner. Both the Governor and the police chief were shifted out, a committee was set up to suggest reforms in the state police and a white paper was issued to explain the rationale of the army action and seek to justify it. The only typical ingredient missing in the state response to the death and destruction caused by the two botched operations was that the government did not appoint a commission of inquiry to fix responsibility. Not that ample grounds did not exist for doing so or there were no demands for the same. In fact, a national debate would rage around these aspects for a long time, until some more crucial events in subsequent months would pose even bigger dangers to peace and harmony in the region and, at another level, even to national integrity.

Also, people would have come to terms with the tragedy of Blue Star sooner or later, except that several scheming politicians would now come to occupy centrestage and indulge in a series of manipulative acts, supposedly to manage the fast deteriorating situation but actually making it worse. There was also a lot of talk about the need to apply a healing touch to the hurt Sikh psyche, which would soon become a big joke, because nothing would really come out of it. The so-called white paper, which came to be termed in many circles a white paper on black deeds, was itself a virtual travesty of a healing touch, as far as the Sikhs were concerned.

*

I was appointed as the director general of police, Punjab, in the post-Blue Star change of guard to succeed a rather bitter Inspector General P.S. Bhinder, after the post was upgraded in keeping with my seniority. K.T. Satarawala succeeded the other fall guy, B.D. Pande. My selection to the top police post in the deeply troubled state came to me as something of a surprise. Although I had served in some very important positions in the police department, I was hardly the kind of policeman likely to be the preferred choice of most contemporary politicians, well known as I was for being a strictly apolitical person, most unwilling to bend the rules or act against the requirements of law and propriety to please the political establishment. My personal and official relations with them had never been anything but correct and proper. However, within the limits of legitimacy, propriety and decorum, I was able to foster and maintain excellent relationship with many well-meaning and decent politicians. Among those with whom I shared a mutually respectful relationship were P.C. Sethi and S.C. Shukla, two very fair and understanding chief ministers of my state of Madhya Pradesh, with whom I had the privilege to serve.

My appointment to Punjab must have been approved after assessment at many tiers in the Union government. Perhaps J.S. Bawa, the CBI chief with whom I worked then as joint director, might have floated my name.

Surely, the redoubtable K.N. Rao, the then security adviser to the PM and an old intelligence bureau (IB) hand, must have gone into my record with a microscope. I am not certain, though, if the other top bosses, cabinet secretary Krishnaswamy Rao Saheb and the prime minister's principal secretary P.C. Alexander had a major role to play.

I had to sit through two rigorous sessions with the prime minister though, designed presumably to judge my aptitude and credentials for the top police job in the troubled state, in the course of which she also gave me an all-inclusive briefing on the intricacies of the job that I was expected to handle. She appeared fairly satisfied with the outcome of our meetings, then and later. The media hype accompanying my posting to Punjab created some kind of an impression that I was selected for the crucial assignment by the prime minister herself and thus enjoyed a measure of proximity to her. Such a build-up by the media is not uncommon in India, and though I had free access to her whenever it became necessary for me to seek her guidance, I met her simply as a police chief of a heavily disturbed state would approach the prime minister of the country for guidance and direction.

All the same, the notion that I was specially selected by the prime minister for the top job persisted for several months. Some Akali leaders and *jathedars* would often approach me to intercede with the PM on their behalf. A somewhat junior Akali leader, who had been on the run for some time, fearing that the police might nab him, came to me late one evening with a request that I arrange a meeting for him with the PM. The more I protested my inability to oblige him in the matter, the more insistent he became in his plea. It is a measure of the state of demoralization that had gripped the Akalis in the wake of the unmitigated state terror that my visitor refused even to occupy a chair and preferred to sit on the floor. A few months later, he secured an appointment as a member of the national minorities commission, no doubt flaunting his nationalistic credentials.

I took up my new assignment with a clear idea of the precise nature of my mandate, which seemed to me to be fourfold. Namely, to contain the ongoing violence as early as possible, to examine the causes of the failure of the Punjab police to effectively deal with militancy in its formative stages for initiating remedial action, to address the immediate causes for growing militant sentiment in the Sikh community, such as police atrocities and fake killings, and to minimize the fear and panic among the Hindus, many of whom were fleeing the countryside to find safety in cities. I also realized that it was a formidable undertaking and a constructive approach would be my best option, for which I needed to take the force with me, especially at the middle and cutting edge levels in the district police and armed battalions. I also realized that both these tiers would not take kindly to a DGP from another state cadre (Madhya Pradesh) and were likely to take some time before shedding their suspicions and misgivings about an imported chief.

As for the larger issues involved in sorting out the mess resulting from the two army operations and the restoration of normal functioning of political and administrative institutions, I had no doubt in my mind that it was for the politicians to find political solutions to highly complex problems of governance. For far too long, the Indian state has been in the habit of treating issues of minority dissent and discontent as mere law and order problems, seeking to address them through the use of sheer force, often turning into state terror. I thought it was possible to reverse the course of events in Punjab by adopting an affirmative and positive approach. This and a few other of my assumptions, however, would turn out to be seriously misplaced in the light of some later developments. I will revert to the subject a little later.

*

I proceeded to Chandigarh on 3 July 1984 to take up my new assignment. It is a measure of the scale of attention that Blue Star and the assault on the Golden Temple and some other related events had drawn that almost the entire world media covered the news of the administrative changes in the Punjab. It was not unusual for TV and radio correspondents from obscure networks and countries to accost me on all possible occasions to seek my views on various key issues and request for special interview sessions. It was difficult to accommodate all of them because of sheer lack of time. Naturally, my first priority was to work out a time-bound and viable agenda for reforms in the state police. This became easier since the government of India simultaneously set up a high-level committee of experts to suggest a framework of such reforms in a time frame of six months at the maximum. Presided over by a senior civilian, R.V. Subramaniam, a former adviser to the Governor of Assam, the committee consisted of some very senior and capable police leaders, with this writer as the member-secretary. The Punjab police, one of the country's leading forces not long ago, had been subjected for years to rampant politicization all along its hierarchical spread from the chief of police to the lowest rungs, and other corrupting influences. There had also been a serious crisis of leadership for some time due to various reasons such as a depleted IPS cadre, distortions in promotion policies and a general trend to sideline direct recruits in district postings in favour of state service officers. The bulk of IPS officers simply did not have the benefit of enough space to grow, professionally and personally. The unending feuds to gain political ascendancy among top level politicians critically distorted the basic prerequisites of neutrality and detachment in law enforcement. Starting with Partap Singh Kairon, every chief minister of the state seemed to be intent upon outdoing his predecessor in destroying the established systems and institutions of governance. The administrative decay that had set in from the 1970s would reach its zenith in the following decade, when an effete, enfeebled, politicized and brutalized law and order machinery would suddenly find itself in the eye of a storm and prove woefully inept in facing the militant onslaught. Matters were not helped much by backseat driving from Delhi, where sundry politicians and home ministry and PMO bureaucrats tried to rule by remote control, a classic case of exercising power without responsibility.

The R.V. Subramaniam committee approached its task with remarkable ingenuity and dexterity, coming up with a very useful set of recommendations in a short span of three months. The Punjab government now formed an empowered committee with Subramaniam, who had in the meanwhile joined as senior adviser to the Governor, as chairman and the principal secretaries of home and finance departments as members, with this writer as member-secretary, to implement the committee's proposals. We were thus able to implement the bulk of the proposals on the ground in another three months. The undertaking involved immense hard work and quality input, backed by first-rate secretarial support, provided by the new DIG administration, Chaman Lal, posted to the state on deputation on my request. The exercise entailed preparation of detailed agenda for each weekly meeting of the committee, recording of minutes and mutation of the decisions taken into office notes and orders in files for execution on the ground. Police reform and reorganization is a highly complex task, involving as it does the reconciliation of a number of conflicting claims and imperatives.

Unlike most western police forces, the Indian police enjoys little functional autonomy, its basic structure still being governed by the Indian Police Act of 1861, which vests its control and supervision in a non-professional magistrate at the district level and a civilian home secretary at the state level. Substantial reforms in the Indian police have failed to take off because neither the civilian bureaucracy nor the politicians are ready to give up their control on this powerful instrument of the state. In our exercise, all such issues had to be approached very carefully to preclude service loyalties of the committee members to derail the whole process. This meant that the exercise was directed chiefly at strengthening merely the hardware ingredients of the system rather than its software components like police sub-culture and tactics.

By the end of 1984, we had a fairly competent set-up at the police headquarters in Chandigarh, with a refurbished and expanded intelligence network with enough capacity fall-back at the headquarters and in the district to process, collate and dispense actionable intelligence to field level staff, adequate crime and investigation wings and a logistics division, apart from a reinforced administration division. All these reforms were vital in order to invigorate the district and *thana* police to effectively cope with the newer and more complex challenges from the militants and assorted criminal elements, not only in Amritsar and Gurdaspur, but also all over the state and beyond. The reorganization schemes at lower levels would take some more time, because these involved several district and sub-district units, which were, in a way, even more central to grassroots policing. The initiative had to be seized from lawless elements to re-establish a measure of peace and order in the state. It was necessary to recount the story of Punjab police reforms at some length, because they would prove immensely invaluable at a later stage in coming to grips with the alarming militancy situation that arose after 1986, though in the confusion and chaos that marked the handling of terrorist violence towards the end, many commentators would fail to see the close links between the performance of the Punjab police and the post-Blue Star reforms. Chaman would later distinguish himself as an inspector General in the Border Security Force (BSF), Punjab, for his humane and positive handling of a most complex situation during a period of heightened militant activity, in the process becoming a familiar figure in the militancy-ridden border districts. Punjab villagers would long remember him for his firm but compassionate approach in tackling the menace of terrorist violence and would shower anyone associated with him with plentiful hospitality and rustic charm. Regrettably, he had to quit the area in disgust due to irreconcilable differences with the then police chief on the mode of dealing with the militants.

*

In the meanwhile, hundreds of Sikh detainees picked up by the army and the security forces during the army operations and otherwise, were being leisurely screened by joint teams of the army, intelligence bureau and the Punjab CID, sometimes also including officers from central paramilitary forces. The screening process involved elaborate scrutiny of dossiers on the detained men, women and children (some babes in arms) prepared by the different organizations represented on the teams. After a thorough scrutiny, individuals were classified into three categories: white, grey and black. The 'whites' were assessed to be least likely to be hazardous to the state if set free, while the 'blacks' were rated most dangerous and unlikely to be considered for release in the foreseeable future. The 'greys' needed to be vetted again after a few months. The whole process would take many months, causing avoidable and unjustifiable suffering, misery and anguish to (and discontent amongst) even those detainees and their families, who were to be later placed in the whites category, not that a mere placement in the whites category was any assurance of an automatic release from custody. The way the detainees were treated while in custody would add considerably to the sullenness in an already embittered community due to the destruction of the Akal Takht and defiling of the Harimandir.

Despite clear enough indications that the two army operations in the Punjab had been misconceived from the very beginning and grossly mismanaged in execution and had utterly failed to achieve their objectives, the government persisted in sustaining the myth that the operations had indeed succeeded in breaking the back of militancy in the state, a reading simply not borne out by the reality on the ground. The colonial era belief in the sovereign immunity of the state continued to be an article of faith with post-colonial South Asian states decades after independence, even though the erstwhile colonial powers had long ago discarded the concept. The white paper issued by the government within weeks of the end of Operation Blue Star was part of the same design.

The reality was that the Sikh people all over the world were seething with resentment and helpless anger at what had happened to their most sacred religious sites. To community leaders, this was a time of profound introspection and stock-taking, a time to provide enlightened guidance to their people, to transform their collective resentment into an opportunity for renaissance. This phase 'was an agitated phase for almost every Sikh everywhere. The professionals, the litterateurs, the bureaucrats, the academia, the youth, the folk singers and *ragis* (reciters of *Granth Sahib* with musical accompaniments) played an important role in jolting the political consciousness of the Sikhs. Their emotions of reverence for the defiled sacred complex, and compassion for the members of the community massacred in Delhi and other parts of India got blended with anger and desperation.'[2] We will deal with the Sikh killings in a little while. To adapt the famous Churchillian *bon mot* to the Punjab situation, one could say that never in history was so much violence caused to so many on account of the cynicism and insensitivity of so few.

*

Despite its many limitations, what makes the South Asian police force different from its western counterparts is a highly regimented system of training and orientation, which makes them highly responsive to the subtle signals emanating from the force leadership. Thus, a well-meaning and forthright chief will typically draw a similar set of men and officers around him to carry out his programmes and agendas. So although being an ex-cadre chief in the Punjab police was a considerable drawback in the beginning, my acceptability quotient with the district and police station staff soon attained a fairly satisfactory level. There were still quite a few pockets of resistance, especially among senior officers, which did not matter too much in view of the critical situation we were faced with and the complete support of the ruling establishment, both in Delhi and Chandigarh, including the local army top brass, that I then enjoyed.

I was not happy, though, with some of the ex-cadre officers, who had been deputed to the state, shortly after my appointment, to replace Punjab cadre officers, sent out of the state on suspicion of collusion with militants or allegations of inaction and inefficiency. Since all these reassignments had been effected without credible and open inquiry procedures, the affected officers felt greatly resentful and wronged, understandably so. While I could not do much to alter decisions arrived at before my appointment, I took a firm stand against any more transfers of Punjab officers unwilling to be posted outside the state. I also did not take kindly to any uncalled-for disparagement of local officers at the hands of the deputationists. This helped me greatly in dealing with many difficult problems peculiar to the Punjab police as the local officers were most forthcoming in briefing me about them. Clearly, it was incorrect to foist the entire blame for whatever had gone wrong in the Punjab over the last two decades onto the police leadership, though the standards of policing and law-enforcement had indeed significantly fallen.

We have already discussed some of the salient causes of the failure of the state administration to effectively deal with the many law and order problems arising in the state in the late 1970s, finally peaking in the outbreak of militancy in the 1980s. Within a couple of weeks after I assumed charge of the new post, I came to deeply value the advice and counsel that I received from the Punjab cadre officers on some very sensitive matters, and I made no secret of it during my weekly meetings with the inspectors general. I found no difficulty, therefore, in carrying the Punjab cadre officers with me in some of the very critical situations that we faced during the time. Unfortunately, I could not say the same about those on deputation from other cadres. Among the priorities that I had set before myself, the foremost was to make the Punjab police a highly motivated, efficient and effective force capable of successfully meeting the grim challenges confronting the state but without losing its sense of proportion and fair play, especially when dealing with ordinary citizens. For this purpose, I interacted intensively with all ranks of the force under my command through frequent visits to police stations, police lines, training schools, housing colonies, sports grounds and recreation centres. Inspection and supervision schedules, for long neglected by senior officers on the pretext of excessive preoccupation with law and order and militancy, were strictly enforced, leading to improved rapport between officers and men.

Politicization of state organs, especially those dealing with law enforcement, was a common enough malady all over the country, but the Punjab police had established itself as something of a pioneer in this dubious category. It had been subjected to dangerous levels of politicization over the years with the appointment of successive police chiefs, who themselves were close favourites of one or the other political leader. These links were more difficult to address, but it helped that the state was then under president's rule.

*

However, it was not enough to talk only to the police. The public too had to be sensitized to the perils of the dangerous drift into anarchy into which the current environment in the state was leading. For this purpose, I visited various affected areas of the state and spoke at length to members of village panchayats, school and college students, *mandi* (grain market) committees and indeed wherever I found a suitable forum to generate robust public opinion against the lawlessness and turbulence then threatening the region. There was simply too much to do and too little time available for it. Much of what I had set out to accomplish, however, lost its focus after some time, as I realized that the Indian state was not particularly interested in looking at peaceful and constructive solutions to the untidy mess it had so deftly created.

There occur moments in the life of a nation when the state itself takes to promoting violence and terrorism to serve its own sinister ends. Apparently, the Indian state too was engaged in just such a pursuit at that moment in history. So a mere police chief could not be allowed to undermine the hidden political motives and agendas of an all-powerful establishment in Delhi. In any case, in the Indian scheme of things, police chiefs do not normally form part of the inner circle of advisers around the head of government, involved in devising strategies in pursuit of the state's security functions. Functional autonomy in the police being at a heavy discount, it is not surprising that almost all eruptions of militancy remain unsubdued for decades.

Anyway, we were doing whatever was possible to stem the tide of intensified terrorist violence, triggered by growing disillusionment and frustration in the Sikh community after Blue Star. The Akali leaders being still in detention, the mantle of putting up some degree of opposition to government moves and calling for restoration of Sikh control over the Temple and its management had fallen upon the Sikh high priests. The Akal Takht was being rebuilt by Baba Santa Singh Nihang of the Buddha Dal, traditionally not on the best of terms with the mainstream Sikh priestly class, but with huge government support and financial backing conveyed through Mrs Gandhi's senior cabinet colleague Buta Singh, a dalit Sikh and, consequently not exactly a hot favourite with the Jutt political leadership or the militants. Senior adviser R.V. Subramaniam was Delhi's pointsman for negotiations with the high priests for the withdrawal of the army from the Golden Temple and restoration of SGPC control over gurudwara administration. Though a hard-nosed negotiator in his own right, Subramaniam had still to contend with a powerful Alexander, sitting in the PMO and professing to be the prime minister's conscience keeper, looking into every little detail of the process of decision-making. In the event, the process itself would prove to be time-consuming and cumbersome. At another level, even Santa Singh was growing a bit too big for his shoes and had started running a sort of protection racket of his own, sending out missives to police stations and district officers allegedly for pecuniary considerations, and seriously disrupting the chain of command.

*

Gory tales of atrocities on Sikhs during the two army operations and by the police and central security forces afterwards were being constantly publicized in Punjab villages and towns by folk singers, *ragis* and *dhadhis* (balladeers), and during *kirtans* and religious functions in gurudwaras, often clothed in compelling emotional vocabulary and evoking searing memories of many historical wrongs suffered by the community in the past. These recitations and exhortations would mark the start of a process of a subtle kind of indoctrination of the Sikh people by relating current events to similar incidents in Sikh history and tradition. Out of several such groups going round the countryside and spreading the message was a band of young women called *Nabhe walian bibian* or women from Nabha town, who were especially popular at the time. Veena Das accounts the evolution of the contemporary Sikh militant discourse thus:

> By imputing an identity of events and return of certain key constellations in the history of the Sikhs, a contemporaneity is established between non-contemporaneous events. The function of language here is to create an optical illusion of the contemporaneity of the non-contemporaneous, which comes to be encapsulated in the use of words. Language thus functions more to *produce* a particular reality rather than to *represent* it...At one level the *you* of the oral discourse is directly present to the speaker, which gives it the character of a performance, and allows the use of many kinds of rhetorical strategies by the use of voice and body...At another level, the oral discourse also addresses certain absent others in which the people present become an audience to an imaginary conversation between the speaker and the presumed addresses. This is especially true when the state is sought to be addressed.[3]

In the process, she identifies four main characteristics of the militant discourse, viz., the use of rigorous dualisms to define self and the other, the creation of contemporariness between non-contemporaneous events, the weaving of individual biography into social text through the use of local knowledge and the justification of violence with reference to both mythological motifs and contemporary political processes. These arguments sounded even more convincing in the post-Blue Star situation, except that by then they had acquired a more ready appeal, especially in the context of *bhog* (last rites) ceremonies of the slain militants, which would considerably strengthen the militant movement by widening the recruitment base to its ranks.[4] It would not be long before the Sikh clergy's efforts to keep alive the spirit of resistance and defiance in the community through evocation of historical struggles against oppression and injustice by an all-powerful but insensitive state would produce the first organized militant group, the Khalistan Commando Force (KCF) of 'general' Hari Singh in late 1984. Wassan Singh Zafarwal, who succeeded Hari Singh and was often suspected of maintaining political links with some prominent politicians, was to state in an interview that during his travels in the border areas immediately after Blue Star, he heard numerous tales of torture and killings by the police, 'mothers and sisters raped, then taken outside the village boundaries and stripped naked, the houses searched...We could accept our humiliations but not the humiliation of our women. I clearly saw that we'd have to mobilize for an armed struggle. At first, I thought, let's be peaceful and don't return bullet for bullet...'[5] Zafarwal would later resurface in the Punjab and re-establish his political links. Distributed in penny packets, the KCF carried out isolated and uncoordinated attacks on central security forces in the border districts.

One could regard this phase as a comparatively quieter period as only 63 militant crimes were reported. Militant activity would greatly intensify after 1986 and would peak in the later 1980s for reasons that we will examine in the following chapters.

*

The Union government entrusted the task of rebuilding the Akal Takht, destroyed during Operation Blue Star, to Buta Singh, a senior Sikh cabinet minister, in the belief that being a Sikh himself, he would carry credibility with the community. By reposing their faith in Buta Singh, the Delhi establishment was obviously barking up the wrong tree. Buta Singh arrived on the site armed with official authority and promises of enormous financial resources in money and gold to be provided by the Indian government. This was like adding insult to injury, as Sikh tradition does not allow for such external bounties but favours building or rebuilding religious structures by self-help and *kar sewa*. Moreover, being part of the oppressive state structure, he was least acceptable, his being a Sikh was immaterial. His unacceptability was further compounded when he sought the help of Baba Santa Singh, the chief of a Nihang faction, not on particularly good terms with the Sikh clergy at the time for various reasons, in arranging *kar sewa* by his followers. Facing strong opposition from the Sikh high priests, who were holding the fort in the absence of Sikh leaders then under detention, Buta Singh called a Sarbat Khalsa in Amritsar on 11 August 1984, to approve *kar sewa* for rebuilding the Akal Takht through Santa Singh.

This convention also passed resolutions excommunicating SGPC chief Gurcharan Singh Tohra, holding him responsible for the desecration and destruction of Sikh shrines and severely censuring the Akali leadership and its policies. Obviously a state-managed show, the

convention did not evoke much enthusiasm among the
Sikhs, although Buta Singh contrived to bring the head of
a major Sikh seat at far-away Patna in Bihar to the
convention. A couple of months later, the high priests too
proceeded to hold a rival convention at another historic
gurudwara in Amritsar, because the government would
not permit one in the Golden Temple, and called it the
World Sikh Conference. Notably, while the police and
magistracy were under instructions to ensure maximum
attendance at Buta Singh's convention, which enjoyed
Union government's patronage, they were directed to do
everything possible to discourage participation in the
conference organized by the high priests. The government
media too were asked to inflate the attendance figures at
Buta Singh's convention while playing down the success
of the one organized by the Sikh high priests. Buta Singh
was able to secure the necessary approval for his project
and promptly started the reconstruction with ample
financial and other resources.

However, all the money spent in the venture was
destined to go down the drain when the reconstructed
Akal Takht was pulled down and rebuilt with the help of
donations and voluntary labour by members of the
community under the supervision of Baba Thakar Singh
of the Damdami Taksal, the same seminary of which
Bhindranwale was the head, thus, in a way, linking the
reconstruction of the demolished Takht with the now
dead Bhindranwale. It is another matter, though, that vast
sections of rural Sikhs continued to distrust the official
handout that he was indeed no more. Instead, a dead
Bhindranwale would prove to be even more dangerous
than when alive as legends and myths grew around him,
according him the status of *sant-sipahi* (saint-soldier), a
hallowed concept in Sikh tradition, sometimes used in

relation to the tenth Guru. Bhindranwale would, thus, acquire an image much larger than that of the Akali leaders, a situation that would oblige them to adopt some of his vocabulary, even though for the sake of expediency. All this would seriously impact the course of events in Punjab for many years to come

As for Santa Singh, he was asked to leave soon after the completion of the work entrusted to him, though his final departure did not come about without some avoidable unpleasantness. The process of handing over the control of the Temple premises to the high priests proved to be quite difficult and time-consuming, because the government wanted a written undertaking from them that they would not let the militants reoccupy the Temple again. This the priests were obviously not in a position to do. Finally, some deft handling by R.V. Subramaniam led to an agreement, and the premises were handed over to the clergy on 9 October 1984. The army too left shortly thereafter, thus putting an end to a most unfortunate episode in the history of the Indian army and its relationship with the Sikh people.

That the army action had failed to accomplish its mission was proved once again when some 200 extremists in a show of defiance started shouting Khalistan slogans and making intemperate speeches on 1 October. The police had to be deployed inside the Temple to control the situation. It would later come to light that this incident was actually inspired by some manipulative masterminds among disgruntled Akali factions, duly supported by their mentors in the Congress party, a phenomenon that will be on display time and again in the decade-long history of militancy in the state. By an odd coincidence, at least three of the main actors involved in the above scenario, namely Sant Bhindranwale, Gen K.S. Brar and Baba Santa

Singh belonged to the sub-divisional town of Moga, which also happens to be my home town.

*

Indira Gandhi, the then prime minister of India, was shot down by her two Sikh security guards on 31 October 1984, apparently due to anger at the destruction of the Akal Takht and damage caused to other holy places during Blue Star, although the authorities tried their best to link the act to some deep conspiracy. The assassination set off an orgy of widespread killings, plunder and arson directed against the Sikhs in Delhi and several other Indian cities and towns. The violence was unusually savage, merciless and seemingly well-planned, with many senior Congressmen leading the rampaging mobs and targeting Sikh colonies and houses with the help of electoral rolls, not unlike Nazis going after Jews. Thousands of innocent Sikh men, women and children were done to death and many more rendered homeless. The carnage was carried out with meticulous planning, with even the Sikh police disarmed and taken off duty in Delhi. According to reports, the police had even cajoled Sikh residents in some places to deposit their licensed arms with the nearest police station, on the plea that this was necessary in view of the inflamed passions among sections of the Hindus. The official media in its reports on the assassination, it may be noted, appeared to be playing up the fact that the foul deed had been done by Sikh policemen. Even the first information report (FIR) lodged at the Tughlaq Road police station highlighted the fact that the murderers were Sikh. Whether all this was the result of individual initiative by some high-strung but short-sighted functionaries at local levels or suggested a deeper and more sinister design remains unclear, though the many inflammatory slogans being raised at Teen Murti House ('*Khoon ka badla khoon*', 'Hindu *ekta zindabad*' etc.) where the dead body of the slain PM had been placed for public viewing, clearly audible in the live telecast of the tragic event and the tell-tale gesticulations by senior leaders, seemed to suggest the involvement of some people, at least, belonging to the higher rungs of Congress leadership.

A rather injudicious remark attributed to Rajiv Gandhi, the new prime minister, at a public meeting a few days later— 'When a great tree falls, the ground shakes'— seemed to invest the carnage with official authentication. Consistent with the ubiquitous political culture of obsequiousness, this must have appeared to Delhi Congress leadership as a well-earned pat on the back from the high command for having taught the Sikhs a lesson. This was obviously the genesis of the well-organized massacre of thousands of Sikhs in Delhi and several other towns and cities all over north and west India, especially in the states ruled by the Congress party, just because they shared their faith with the killers of Indira Gandhi. For the next three days, the police vanished from the scene, except to help the mobsters in carrying out their murderous plans, much in the same way as the Gujarat police would do some 18 years later in facilitating the slaughter of Muslims by goons belonging to the ruling party in that state. The Indian police force has been getting more and more politicized and communalized since then.

Noted journalist and writer William Dalrymple painted a most disturbing picture of the anti-Sikh carnage in Delhi in a dispatch to the *Sunday Times*, London, in March 1999 with these words:

> On October 31, 1984, Mrs Gandhi was assassinated by two of her Sikh security guards. In the three days

that followed, Congress party mobs, many of them led by senior MPs, knifed, lynched, murdered and incinerated around 2,150 innocent Sikh civilians in Delhi, while many more were attacked and killed in cities across Northern India...For three days, Rajiv Gandhi, the new elected prime minister of India, refused to call in the army, remarking only that 'When a great tree falls, the ground shakes.' In Delhi, most of the killings took place in the impoverished 'resettlement colonies' in East Delhi, well away from the prying eyes of journalists, diplomats and the middle classes. When the first journalists arrived— inevitably several hours after the massacres had finished—dogs were fighting over piles of purple human entrails, while charred and roasted bodies lay in great heaps in the gullies. Piles of hair, cut from Sikhs before they were burnt alive, lay on the verandas. Yet, this was not some boondocks town in a banana republic; this was the capital city of the great country of Mahatma Gandhi. I don't think I will ever forget interviewing a man who, from his hidden place, saw his two sons have rubber tyres placed around their necks, saw them doused in petrol, then let alight. He described the entire attack in chilling detail; how the Sikhs had got together to form self-defence units; how they had been disarmed by the police and told to keep to their houses; how the police had then stood by as the mob went from house to house pouring kerosene over, then burning alive, any Sikh they found. The mob had been personally directed by a prominent Congress MP, who came armed with voter lists to help identify the houses belonging to the Sikhs. The MP went on to become a cabinet minister. To this day, not one of the Congress party leaders responsible for the massacres has been brought to justice.

Dalrymple's account gains credibility from many other sources; among them the reports prepared by citizens' committees, and commissions of inquiry, presided over in one case by a former chief justice of India. These killings would later form the key component of a process that would provoke deep anger and resentment among the Sikhs, converting the pre-Blue Star militant movement into one of the world's deadliest types of terrorism, especially in its more intense post-1986 phase. Union home minister Narasimha Rao remained unavailable during the crisis, as was his wont during such situations. He simply refused to take stock of the tragic happenings and to call in the army, which was standing by, until the entire murky affair was over and the Congress-led mobs had done their duty by the dead leader and secured their future with the new party leadership.

Or so they thought. Harsh Mander, a former bureaucrat, who resigned in disgust from the Indian Administrative Service (IAS) after observing the dismal failure of his colleagues in the western state of Gujarat to do their duty by the Constitution and rule of law by colluding with a fanatical chief minister in facilitating the massacre of hundreds of Muslim men, women and children in cold blood in 2002, accuses the entire ruling establishment in Delhi of inaction or worse during the Sikh killings in November 1984. 'As Delhi burnt, Home Minister PV Narasimha Rao, Delhi Lt-Governor M.M.K. Wali and the entire battery of magistrates and police officers refused to take the help of the army to quell the riots,' he noted in a rather poignant article in *Hindustan Times*, New Delhi, on 26 November 2004.

Patwant Singh, a prolific writer on human rights issues and Sikhism, referred to the Sikh pogrom in Delhi and its handling by the Union government in an article in the *Times of India*, New Delhi, dated 15 October 2000 in these words: 'The pendulum of public opinion often swings erratically. So it is not surprising that Narasimha Rao is mostly seen as the man who helped liberalize the Indian economy. Not many recall his many acts of moral coarseness. One of these involved the loss of thousands of human lives in Delhi, which he could have helped save as India's home minister in 1984. But he allowed them to perish by doing nothing...The army was not called until the night of 3 November. Had it been given charge of Delhi on the first day, 3,000 Sikhs would not have died, nor their homes, shops, factories, trucks and places of worship destroyed under the indulgent eye of the administration'.

In an affidavit submitted to the Supreme Court of India, senior advocate H.S. Phoolka, who has been fighting for justice to the victims and retribution to the offenders for over two decades, states:

> Out of the total killing of 2,733 Sikhs (official figures) during the first three days of November 1984, about half of them took place on 1st November itself. The police at all levels, i.e., right from the commissioner of police to an ordinary constable, were only busy demobilizing the Sikhs. The first priority of the police officers seemed to be to disarm the Sikhs. There were innumerable instances when the police officers ordered their men to divest the Sikhs of their traditional kirpans and licensed arms. At several places, the police even arrested such Sikhs, who tried to defend themselves and their families and booked them in criminal cases. The police records show that most of the arrests made by the police on 1.11.1984 were of Sikhs. There were also instances when the police went out of their way to break up

peace committees set up in some localities. The object of the police was clearly to remove all the hurdles from the marauding mobs. The few places where the Sikhs or the peace committees refused to disperse, they succeeded in driving away the rioters and protecting their localities. This underlines the fact that the police had been as much a threat to the Sikhs as the rioters themselves....The first significant attack on a Sikh in the wake of Mrs Gandhi's assassination was on none other than the first citizen of India, President Zail Singh. It happened around 5 pm on October 31 at AIIMS, when Zail Singh's convoy arrived there from the airport. A mob not only raised slogans against Sikhs, but also stoned the President's convoy in the presence of the police deployed at AIIMS...The police's willful (sic) failure to take action on a matter as serious as that seems to have been part of a premeditated plan to give two distinct signals. One, no Sikhs to be spared, no matter how highly placed. Two, no action will be taken on any of those who attack Sikhs to avenge Mrs. Gandhi's murder.

Phoolka then goes on to cite specific instances of active collusion by the police in helping the culprits to more efficiently carry out their nefarious designs. Such horrendous scenes of sectarian violence had not been witnessed in the national capital of the world's largest democracy since the days of partition in 1947. However, there was one vital difference; while the 1947 riots were between Muslims on one side and Hindus and Sikhs on the other in which both sides were equally involved, in 1984, it was a one-sided affair, Hindu mobs going from house to house and systematically slaying Sikhs in an unbelievably cruel and barbaric manner.

*

Mercifully, a few voices of sanity did make themselves heard even during those dark days. A citizens' commission under the chairmanship of Justice Sekhri, a former chief justice of India, was the first to put together a credible, authentic and detailed account of the scale of killings, rapes, plunder and arson that had seized the city of Delhi during those horrible days following Mrs Gandhi's murder. It also brought to light the full extent of negligence, indifference, inefficiency and collusion that the police and general administration displayed in dealing with the carnage. Many other civil society groups too would later strive to uphold the spirit of democracy and rule of law by raising their voice against the blatant failure of an oppressive and arrogant state apparatus to protect the life, honour and property of a section of Indian citizens. The response of the state to the widespread outcry and outrage among the Sikhs and many sections of enlightened citizens against the massacres was on expected lines. It appointed a commission of inquiry under Justice Rangnath Mishra of the Supreme Court of India. After a prolonged exercise, where the victims and their advocates were hard put to adequately plead their cases before the commission, due to unusually stringent and intricate procedural requirements, the commission submitted a rather insipid report, which left both the victims and their lawyers far from satisfied. Justice Mishra, however, went on to become the chief justice of India and to occupy the posts of chairman of the country's national human rights commission, Governor of a state and a Congress member of the Rajya Sabha in quick succession. More such commissions would be appointed from time to time, especially on the eve of a national or state election, with various terms of reference and an eye on Sikh votes.

The last such body was the Justice Nanavati

Commission, appointed by the NDA government of Atal Bihari Vajpayee in 1999. It took the commission five years to submit a wishy-washy report, without clearly indicting any of the senior Congress leaders who had been held guilty by a number of inquiry committees earlier of the worst anti-Sikh carnage in the history of independent India. Successive Union governments, whether of the Congress party or the BJP-led NDA, were even more unmindful of their moral and legal responsibility to right a two-decades-old wrong committed by prominent political leaders in a manner that left little doubt that the highest political and bureaucratic authorities were themselves deeply involved in the matter. Arun Nehru, then minister for internal security, was reported to have said, 'Let Delhi burn for three days'. Nor did the conduct of other top leaders, during and after the killings, lead one to believe that they wished the killer gangs to be reined in. For, after all, they were only ensuring that the whole Sikh community suffer due retribution for the assassination of a prime minister at the hands of two of its members. Nanavati only found the then Delhi Lt-Governor and the police commissioner clearly guilty, forgetting that Delhi is under the full control of the Union home ministry and the then home minister and the prime minister failed to call in the army for all of three days.

No police force would stand by or do the disappearing act in situations of the kind that prevailed in Delhi during those horrible three days, unless the ruling establishment wanted it to do so. In the meanwhile, Sikh children, who had been mute and terrified witnesses to the brutal killings of their fathers and brothers, the molestation of their mothers and sisters and the plunder and destruction of their homes, have grown up into angry and bitter young men. The widows of the 1984 massacres, waiting patiently for over two decades for justice, are growing more bitter and despondent by the day, while the perpetrators of the butchery roam free, some of them even occupying ministerial office. Evidently, the wounds of 1984 will not heal as long as stern action is not taken against those guilty of the carnage, and the event will continue to fan resentment and despair.

Several officers were indicted later by inquiry committees. One of them, the Kusum Mittal panel, blamed five deputy commissioners (all IPS officers), four assistant commissioners, 22 station house officers and several subordinate officials. No action was taken against any; most of them, in fact, continued to receive promotions when due. Another committee comprising of a former high court judge Justice J.D. Jain, and D.K. Aggarwal, a former director-general of UP police, found as many as 292 police officers guilty of faulty investigations and tampering with records. Still another committee, the Rosha-Potti committee, was appointed soon after to go through the entire futile exercise once more.

Apart from whatever information was coming through the Punjab CID to me as the director general of Punjab police, I had to personally call up the Delhi police control room a few times to verify reports received from contacts and friends in Delhi. It was clear that the state had completely withdrawn its protection to the Sikh citizens of India's national capital, a blot the Delhi police will never be able to live down. While Sikh policemen were asked to cool their heels in the police lines, Sikh officers, even those belonging to the IPS, were not sent out into the field. It is standard practice for post-independence Indian governments to seek to inundate critical issues of civilized governance and democratic policing in a spate of inquiry commissions and committees without doing anything worthwhile to check the steep decline in administrative values and norms. Many a moribund FIR would subsequently be sought to be resurrected in Delhi under judicial direction, but without addressing the core issues of police and administrative connivance in the massacres. All political parties in office behave in the same manner when it comes to enforcing the rule of law, the latest such instance being the state-sponsored orgy of killing, rape, loot and arson in Gujarat, directed against the minority Muslim citizens. Police action against the rioters was, tardy, listless, half-hearted and evasive; few, if any, inquiries were pursued with vigour and competence, though there was no dearth of pious proclamations and cosmetic exercises in response to an outcry from many a civil society group.

As the Sikh community in Delhi and in Punjab grew more disillusioned and restive with the ruling establishment and its policy of masterly inaction against the killer gangs and their leaders and a studied apathy towards the victims, the Indian state and the Sikh people now seemed to be virtually at loggerheads. With the Sikh political leadership either in prison or in hiding due to the rising tide of militancy, the new crop of militant groups, assured now of implicit support of an outraged community and safe houses and plentiful supply of sophisticated weaponry by a neighbouring country, would soon acquire almost complete sway in large parts of Punjab. It would continue to grow at a rapid pace to become, after 1986, virtually invincible, and slowly envelop almost the entire Punjab and parts of Haryana, Rajasthan and UP, striking at will also in the national capital and many far off places.

However, let us revert for a moment to the horrific pogroms of Sikhs in November 1984 in many cities and towns, in railway trains and on roads spread across the country, but especially in the north and the west. In Jabalpur, a Sikh inspector general of police was shifted out apparently because he would not allow the mobs a free hand in the orgy of killings of innocent Sikhs, to be replaced by a more pliable officer. Carefully crafted but groundless rumours were disseminated in Delhi and other places that trainloads of dead bodies of Hindus were coming from the Punjab, that the water supply system in Delhi had been poisoned by the Sikhs and that large bands of armed Sikhs had attacked Hindu colonies. Reports were also rife that Sikhs given shelter by their Hindu friends had turned against their protectors and killed them in cold blood. It hardly needs a great deal of brainpower to guess who could have been interested in spreading such dangerous canards and why, despite the fact that there was not a single case of Hindu-Sikh clash in Punjab during those fateful days.

A rather sick joke doing the rounds of posh Delhi colonies went something like this: 'What is a *seekh kabab*? Answer, a burnt Sikh.' Sadly, the incidence of such light-hearted shots at demonization of the persecuted community was not confined to the adults alone. Many school kids too were part of such discourse. After a few weeks, when a shocked and bewildered citizenry realized the sheer enormity of the horrors perpetrated on a small but proud minority by marauding mobs enjoying the tacit support and approval of the ruling establishment and the coercive instruments of state controlled by it, several individuals and groups felt deeply disturbed at the tragic episodes. Many among them would come out openly in condemnation of the massacres and engage whole-heartedly in rehabilitation of the victims. Two of the more sensitive and perceptive of them, Uma Chakravarti and Nandita Haksar (one a teacher of history and the other a law student, later to rise to the top of her profession), spent years laboriously documenting the entire horrific course of events, through interviews with many of the survivors of the carnage, widows and orphaned children of the slain Sikhs. Their encounters with the traumatized survivors would change for ever the way they looked at the crucial issues of majorities and minorities in a plural society and impel them to make its study a life-long mission.

Their extended labours would, in due course, fructify in the production of a most touching account of the gruesome happenings in the form of a book *The Delhi Riots: Three days in the Life of a Nation*, published by Lancer International, New Delhi, in 1987. It would be best to describe the making of the book in their own words. 'As we went about helping in the relief effort, in whatever way we could, our awareness of the horror of the three days as an event in the life of the nation began to grow. Throughout the period we were becoming conscious of the fact that we were witnessing the unleashing of new political and social forces, which were bound to have far-reaching consequences for our country. It did not take us long to realize that what we were witnessing was the *birth of a new minority*; history was being made in our presence in a way in which we did not want it to be shaping or had ever conceived was possible', (italics added), they feelingly stated.

The shocking events of 1984 were unique in many other ways too. It was the first time that many middle class families came face to face with mob frenzy and organized violence, a traumatic experience that would soon get etched deeply in the collective consciousness of an entire people, especially when justice and adequate relief were denied to the victims by an indifferent and collusive state. The victims of the carnage found it impossible to come to terms with the suddenness and ferocity of the killing spree by people who had until the other day been close friends and neighbours. Past perceptions of serious outbreaks of communal violence, such as those in 1947, made the current bout even more perplexing. Many of the older victims of the 1984 riots, with vivid memories of the 1947 bloodbath, found it incredible that while most of them had been able to escape from Pakistan without losing a dear one, the Delhi mobsters attacked them in their own homes and kill every single Sikh they could lay their hands on. To quote the authors again, 'The impact of the November riots on many Sikhs has been such that not only is 1947 a reference point, a kind of backdrop to the events of 1984 and to their understanding of it, but through the events of '84, their understanding of the past itself has changed. Thus the perceptions in 1947 about what led to the partition have now been altered by what one of our interviewers described as a "more mature understanding" of what happened then, but also by what he witnessed and experienced in 1984. The past is thus being recast in the minds of many of our interviewees.'

From a conscious recasting of the past to relating the current carnage with similar episodes in Sikh history, such as the *ghallugharas* or great massacres, is but one short step. Together with Operation Blue Star, the 1984 killings contributed in a major way to the reassertion and sharpening of separate identities and agendas between the Hindus and Sikhs. The widening schism between these two communities, which still had much in common in social and familial terms, that took a serious turn for the worse in the wake of the events in Punjab in early 1980s, had now clearly reached a final point of rupture. In consequence, they would henceforth look at every major event in the country, starting with Blue Star itself, in a sharply dissimilar manner. Thus, while the Sikhs began to perceive themselves in terms of a 'marked' minority, not unlike what the Muslims had been feeling all along, the Hindus appeared to view the whole chain of events from Blue Star onwards as marking the final assertion of their rightful position as the dominant majority with an unquestioned right to primacy in the scheme of things.

The Sikhs also developed a more supportive perception of the problems faced by Muslims and other minorities in a country fast turning into a Hindu state, though not in formal terms. However, the transformation was apparent enough for all practical purposes and as frequently dictated by electoral compulsions. Like many other minority segments in the country, the Sikhs too started suffering from an acute sense of insecurity, a painful experience for a proud people for long conferred the status of a martial community, now dismissed as but a minuscule 2 per cent of the population.

Abraham Lincoln once famously endorsed the likely response of a minority people in such a situation. 'If by the mere force of numbers', he asserted, 'the majority should deprive a minority of any clearly-written constitutional right, it might, in a moral point of view, justify revolution—certainly would, if such a right were a vital one'. Having suffered two lethal and most humiliating blows to their sense of individuality and self-image, one after the other, at the hands of the Indian army during Blue Star and by Hindu mobs led by ruling party leaders in November 1984, the Sikhs felt deeply mortified and could not but look back into the past to construct a response in keeping with their historical experience to defend themselves against what they perceived as an oppressive and unjust state.

Surprisingly enough, Dr P.C. Alexander, then the principal secretary to the PM, devotes just about a page to the horrific events of November 1984 as against some 90 pages to describe how unreliable and deceitful the Akali leaders were, whether in the matter of launching their *morchas* or repeatedly backtracking on implicit agreements during negotiations. He astutely glosses over the role played by the media in inflaming passions among the Hindus against the Sikhs by repeatedly showing Indira Gandhi's dead body and tell-tale slogans raised by the mobs being telecast over national television. Nor does he make any mention of the support and direction extended to the murderous mobs by senior Congress leaders of Delhi, who incited the killer gangs to kill, plunder and molest Sikh populations in many Delhi resettlement colonies, most of whom had, in fact, been long time Congress supporters.

Eminent lawyer P.N. Lekhi, who defended one of Mrs Gandhi's killers Satwant Singh in the murder trial, would later question the need and aptness for making a special mention in the FIR that the killers were Sikhs. A watchful and tactful administration would surely have avoided that kind of description.

*

Dipanker Gupta, a close observer of the Punjab scene, was to note later: 'If there was any pride (*izzat*) left among the Sikhs after the massacre of their numbers in the Operation Blue Star, even that was being forced out into the streets. First, the Sikh library and museum in the Golden Temple complex was set on fire a full two days after Blue Star was officially concluded. Then again instead of allowing the SGPC to rebuild the Akal Takht and the bullet-marked sanctum sanctorum and recover its shame, the government handed over the task to an interloper from a renegade Sikh sect, the Buddha Dal, which further aroused the ire and resentment of the Sikh masses. This was followed by the arrest and torture of hundreds of Sikhs, reminiscent of the Naxalbari operation a decade ago. The crucial difference with the anti-Naxalite operation is that in this case it is enough to be a Sikh to be worthy of suspicion. Other identities do not matter. The country's military and paramilitary forces have come down heavily on the restless Sikh youth, both in the countryside and in the urban areas. The youth who were already frustrated with the tapering off of the green revolution were immediately incensed...All this makes a very volatile and inflammable situation.'[6]

Ironically, Indira Gandhi's politically naïve son and heir would be dexterously manipulated by the party veterans to exploit her slaying by Sikh security guards and the bogey of Sikh separatism as an effective electoral device to win a record three-fourths majority in the elections held within a month of the tragic episodes of November 1984. The Congress party, cleverly projecting itself as the only bulwark against the country's imminent break-up, and powerful enough to defeat the secessionist designs of misguided Sikh youth, in league with a hostile neighbour, and the devious and wily Akali leaders, was assured of overwhelming electoral support by the majority Hindus, with the RSS cadres too canvassing for the Congress rather than their own political outfit, the BJP.

The failure of the Rajiv-Longowal accord of July 1985 would turn out to be another important contributory factor in the process of intensification of militant sentiment in the community, manifesting itself in a marked extension of support to the militant groups. We will deal with the many ramifications of these disturbing events in the next chapter.

7

A Phony Accord

The intangible but strong bonds of trust and affinity that must exist between the state and sections of its people in as diverse a country as India, were now plainly in shreds so far as the tiny Sikh community was concerned. In this deeply disquieting scenario, the only state organs that still continued to function were the police and central security forces. Not unexpectedly, these forces would now occupy centrestage and set out to cope with the situation on their own, employing whatever strategies they were capable of, in an environment of complete collapse of the prescribed modes of judicial, magisterial or political accountability, built into the Indian law-enforcement system over a century-and-a-half. This would lead to a virtual police raj in the state, with the security forces pursuing their counter-terrorist operations in a most brutal and outrageous manner, especially in the post-1986 phase, when the sheer scale of militant activity acquired near-invincible proportions.

Although Indian police is not averse to resorting to unlawful practices on their own when faced with grave law and order situations, the tacit support of the authorities makes such practices more widespread. In post-1986 Punjab, the grave and routine infringement of legal provisions and rules of propriety by the police apparently enjoyed the full sanction of the highest political executive. The implied remit for the police seemed to be to eradicate the scourge of terrorism—within the law if possible, outside it if necessary. It needs no great perspicacity to infer that given the kind of climate then prevailing in the state, most counter-terrorism strategies adopted by an unaccountable police would conform to the second part of the above injunction. Inherent flaws in substantive law dating back to the mid-nineteenth century made it inevitable.

Meanwhile in Delhi, the supreme seat of national power, a young prime minister, flush with a record electoral victory in the parliamentary elections of December 1984 and surrounded by a bunch of friends from the world of computers and management jargon, had succeeded his mother as the prime minister at a rather young age, without adequate experience either in administration or politics, to govern a vast land and a disorderly and fragmented polity in deep crisis. In the peculiar version of parliamentary democracy practised in India, party leaders are normally chosen by consensus, not through a transparent election process. Rajiv Gandhi was appointed prime minister by a beleaguered President Zail Singh, then the target of attack for being a Sikh, even before a rump in the Congress parliamentary party elected him as the leader. This precipitate action was allegedly meant to pre-empt an ambitious senior leader from staking a claim. The name of Pranab Mukherjee, long-time Indira loyalist, was floated by the media as a possible claimant. The new government under Rajiv, somewhat flippantly labelled as a *baba log* government, nevertheless, started off well by introducing many radical changes in different spheres of governance, with the new prime minister exhibiting an uncommon fervour to infuse a brand new culture of innovation and modernism in administration, not only in the area of economic reforms but also in evolving an imaginative approach to the management of minority discontent in the north-east and the Punjab.

Passionate about his self-professed mission to radically reshape the style and manner of governance in the country, a youthful if impetuous Rajiv Gandhi went about his business with singular determination to clean up the Augean stables of a decrepit, effete and corruption-ridden administration that he inherited. It is a different matter that the systems and institutions of governance, rendered dysfunctional and capricious since long, would prove too much for him and his young colleagues and it was not long before he too would be sucked into the mire of sleaze and venality, though most allegations against him would remain unproved. Two of his closest colleagues in the ministry, Arun Singh and Arun Nehru, were to leave him midway in rather unsavoury circumstances, the latter would, in fact, desert his one-time friend and mentor and join an opposition party. Surrounded as they are by armies of sycophants and hangers-on, even the most conscientious and straightforward of Indian prime ministers, especially if they belong to the Gandhi-Nehru dynasty, tend to become arrogant and dictatorial in their functional styles in a short time, though Rajiv proved somewhat more resilient in this matter.

It was during this early phase of Rajiv Gandhi's prime ministership that the government of India started looking at an alternative approach to the concerns and grievances agitating many minority segments of India's hugely diverse population and setting off a variety of extremist movements in several parts of the country, but mainly in the north-east and north-west. In the first few months of his rule, he showed exceptional qualities of ingenuity and boldness in breaking with the past to pursue a policy of peace through negotiations and by signing what could be called, in the corporate culture, MoUs or memoranda of understanding with local leaders. This was the genesis of the Assam Accord, the Rajiv-Longowal Accord in the Punjab and another with the Bodos of Assam, but that was signed by the Union home secretary. The Indian people, for long fed on a diet of trite homilies by stuffy politicians, were greatly excited over the initiatives taken by the new prime minister to bring peace to the troubled regions, generating a heady sense of optimism all around, both among the masses and the intelligentsia.

Unfortunately, however, the optimism proved to be short-lived as the so-called accords came unstuck one after the other as they were found to be flawed in several respects. In the event, the much-vaunted policy of peaceful resolution of conflicts between an all-powerful Indian state and its myriad minority peoples received a serious setback. As the efficacy and the appeal of different accords in ending insurgencies and extremist violence in the disturbed areas faded and a sense of disillusionment set in among the affected peoples, the Indian state once again reverted to the earlier regime of suppressive policies to contain minority dissent, discontent and restiveness, while the challenges posed by various movements that they spawned were met with overwhelming, if brutal illegitimate and inapt, force. As British statesman William Pitt noted in a different age and context, 'Where laws end, tyranny begins'.

With the situation in the Punjab worsening rapidly, the Indian establishment was hard put to evolve a suitable and effective response. All that the wise men in Delhi could think of was to change Governors and police chiefs from time to time and enact a battery of repressive laws, which would, however, largely prove ineffective in containing the rising tide of militant violence. On the other hand, all such draconian laws would provide a handy instrument to the police for the harassment and torment of scores of innocent citizens during a period of heightened militancy in the post-1986 phase.

*

The worst and the most frequently misused of such laws was the infamous Terrorist and Disruptive Activities (Prevention) Act (TADA), passed by Parliament on 20 May 1985. This was an omnibus provision, which greatly broadened the definition of criminality to include a whole range of actions such as preaching or proclaiming secession, questioning national sovereignty over any part of the country, the recitation or dissemination of speeches, ballads, songs or other material whether by word, print, cassette or otherwise, calculated to cause terror, pain, disaffection, communal disharmony and the like; or to do anything that might cause death or injury or damage to property or disrupt any essential supplies or services. TADA was applicable also to Indian citizens living or traveling abroad and to persons aboard ships or aircraft registered in India, wherever they might be. The penalties for an offence under the Act included death, even for those found guilty of advocating, inciting, advising, abetting or in any way facilitating or predicting the commission of any offence, defined as such in the Act. The Act empowered the police to enter any place whatsoever suspected to be in use for terrorist or disruptive activity, as defined in the Act, for the purpose of search and seizure; internment, control and regulation of movement and conduct of persons in any area; interception or scrutiny of mail or telecommunication; prevention of impersonation and forfeiture of equipment or property etc. The rule-making powers under the Act were vested in the executive, without any worthwhile judicial oversight.

The trial of offences under the Act was to be conducted *in camera* and in absentia in courts specially designated for the purpose by the Union government and normally convened in a protected place. Further, the names and addresses of witnesses were to be withheld from public knowledge. There were some other extraordinary provisions too, like long periods of police remand and relaxation in the time limit for submission of challans or final reports. In short, the new law evoked bitter memories of the Rowlatt Act passed by the British Indian government many years before independence, to contain the widespread national upsurge in the wake of the II Lahore conspiracy case, involving the legendary revolutionary Bhagat Singh. As noted by a perceptive analyst, 'The cumulative impact of this Act together with the provisions of the disturbed areas and anti-terrorist legislation adopted earlier in the Punjab is that any person can be lawfully sentenced to death after proceedings held *in camera* in his absence, in a special court, on the basis of testimony of unnamed persons, for having predicted that an offence calculated to cause communal disharmony is to be committed!'[1] However, despite such stringent laws and brutal suppression, the administration was unable to make a noticeable dent in the ongoing dance of death and destruction in the state.

According to one estimate, out of the over 13,000 TADA cases registered in the state, the conviction rate was less than 0.5 per cent, mostly under minor offences. The way in which TADA and other stringent special legislation for tackling terrorism was implemented on the ground showed the utter inadequacy of the Indian criminal justice system to utilize them to the maximum extent to achieve the desired ends, although the police would frequently misuse the special powers conferred on them under Acts such as TADA to hold the accused persons in long periods of custody for interrogation—sometimes also for extortions. The clause making confessions before senior police officers admissible in evidence was never fully utilized, presumably the officers so empowered were disinclined to appear in court, apprehending embarrassing cross-examination. The conviction rate under TADA was actually even less than 0.5 per cent and most convictions were obtained in Arms Act and Excise Act cases and not for serious IPC offences. Over two-thirds of all TADA cases, or 88 per cent, ended in discharge, i.e., there was not enough evidence even to frame charges. A report in the *Hindustan Times* of 9 December 2001 revealed that out of 17,890 offences registered in Punjab until then only 10,562 were charge-sheeted. By the end of that year, merely 190 were convicted and the rest acquitted; the rate of conviction being as low as 0.2 per cent.

TADA was finally allowed to lapse in 1995 due to stiff opposition to its extension from sections of the intelligentsia and civil liberties groups as well as the National Human Rights Commission. Provisions similar to that in TADA were sought to be incorporated in another law in 2001 called Prevention of Terrorism Act (POTA). However, it could be passed only after the ruling coalition took it to a joint session of parliament, in itself a very rare occurrence. Later, this new anti-terrorist Act would more often be used against difficult political opponents in states like UP and Tamil Nadu rather than against terrorists, obliging the Union government to considerably strengthen the review mechanism. POTA too was allowed to lapse a few years later.

*

In order to initiate the so-called peace process in the Punjab, it was necessary to place a highly astute political operator to head the state administration. The state had been under central rule since 1983, which meant that there was no elected government and no chief minister. So, the then Governor, the suave and upright K.T. Satarawala, formerly of the IAS, was asked to pack up in a hurry to be replaced by Arjun Singh, who had only recently taken over as the chief minister of Madhya Pradesh. True to tradition, Satarawala was not even informed of the impending change, much less being extended the courtesy of being consulted about it. He had to wait in Delhi for months before securing his next assignment as Indian ambassador to Mexico. The selection of Arjun Singh as the new Governor of Punjab was obviously the result of a well-orchestrated strategy, although his abrupt removal from Madhya Pradesh set off plenty of rumours.

Arjun Singh had inherited a small estate in the erstwhile princely state of Rewa in central India from his father Vijay Bahadur Singh, minister of industries in the small part C state of Vindhya Pradesh in the early years after independence. Rumours, never substantiated, had it that the minister had somehow got entangled in a trap laid by the special police establishment in Delhi, on a complaint from a Bombay industrialist close to Sardar Patel, free India's first home minister. As bazaar gossip would have us believe, an impressionable Arjun could never forget the indignity to which his father was subjected during the Congress regime presided over by the charismatic Jawaharlal Nehru. Apparently, as the son of a man whose political career had been all but destroyed by a shady operation, Arjun Singh had to carry the cross all his life, and despite his oft-professed fealty to the Nehru-Gandhi dynasty, was always hostage to a degree of suspicion on this count. The story, probably apocryphal, would refuse to fade away with the passage of time. It would, in fact, gather more currency whenever Singh was seen to be gaining political importance.

Be that as it may, Arjun Singh was among the smartest of political operators that Indira Gandhi and Rajiv would frequently fall back upon to handle many tricky situations. He was initiated in the craft of politics by D.P. Mishra, a contemporary of Jawaharlal Nehru since before independence, but hardly a favourite with the latter. Mishra, also known as the modern-day Chanakya of Indian politics, took good care of the young Arjun for reasons of his own and groomed him good and proper to emerge as a powerful rival to the new generation of political heavyweights from the various regions of the new state of MP. The disciple exhibited an uncanny talent to readily absorb the sundry nuances and shades of the art of political manoeuvring and manipulation, for which his mentor was universally known—and feared. He was elected as the chief minister of MP in 1980, allegedly after Prime Minister Indira Gandhi's wayward son, Sanjay, overruled the legislature party's majority verdict in favour of a long-time tribal legislator and rival candidate, Shiv Bhanu Singh Solanki, the sort of underhand dealings only too common in an intrigue-ridden Indian polity. Arjun Singh was re-elected as CM in December 1984. However, before he could fully settle down in the CM's chair, he was moved to the government house in Chandigarh as the Punjab Governor in March 1985. Apart from his acclaimed talent for political management and administrative acumen, Arjun Singh was also known to have developed fairly good relations with the top Akali leaders, who had spent a few years in detention, during the Emergency years, in Pachmarhi, a salubrious hill station in Madhya Pradesh. This was expected to prove immensely helpful in opening a valuable new channel of interaction with the Akali leadership.

Master tactician that he was, Arjun Singh promptly set about exploring the various aspects of the situation, with a view to examining possible policy options for unraveling the tangled mess that he confronted in the state. His profound insight into Indian historical processes led him to make use of a significant episode in the Indian freedom struggle, which also carried a deep emotional appeal for the Punjabi people. For it was in the month of March 1930 that the then British Indian government had surreptitiously transported the dead bodies of the legendary Sikh revolutionary, Bhagat Singh, and his two associates, earlier hanged in the central jail Lahore, to Hussainiwala in district Ferozepur for a hush-hush cremation, in order to avert a possible outbreak of violence in an emotionally-charged Punjab capital. So the anniversary of the cremation of the three valiant freedom fighters was proposed to be observed that year by holding a huge public rally at the hallowed spot, with a view to reminding the Sikh youth of the great sacrifices made by their people in India's freedom movement, hoping thereby to wean them away from the course of extremism and militancy.

Collecting massive crowds for public meetings in India poses no great problem, especially when the state itself is the sponsor and a VVIP presence is assured. Even the prospect of a helicopter sighting would attract multitudes of curious spectators. District officers, tahsildars and police station officers are directed to ensure maximum attendance from their jurisdictions, while truck and bus owners are asked to ferry the maximum number of free travelers to the meeting place. In return, they are allowed to flout many legal and procedural constraints to make up the losses they may have suffered in the process.

With the young and handsome PM likely to attend, the Hussainiwala rally attracted a mammoth gathering of rural Sikhs to hear the many VVIPs make long and impassioned speeches in praise of Bhagat Singh and the Congress triumvirate of Jawaharlal Nehru, Indira Gandhi and Rajiv Gandhi. A somewhat bizarre incident may be narrated here, if only to provide comic relief. The strong draft of air produced by the PM's chopper, while landing at a newly-built helipad, blew away the turban of Buta Singh, a senior cabinet colleague of the PM. This led to a great deal of mirth among the small crowd waiting for the PM, obviously at Buta's expense, who was wearing a Rajasthani, not a Sikh-style turban on account of being an MP from Rajasthan. The irony of the situation was not lost on the young PM, as, unlike the Rajasthani headgear, Sikh turbans are tied much more securely. On sighting his senior colleague chasing his turban in the sprawling wheat fields, a visibly amused PM could not help having a dig at an embarrassed Buta Singh. 'Buta Singh*ji, apni pagri sambhaliay, kahin udh na jaey.* (Mr Buta Singh, take care of your turban lest it flies away). No doubt a light-hearted remark, it could not but ruin the rest of the day for Buta Singh. The rally went on until late evening, ending only after every VIP worth his salt had had his say. The audience listened to the speeches and sermons somewhat grimly, waiting for the event to conclude so that they could trudge back to their villages and resume their humdrum lives. The rally apparently made no difference to the ongoing alienation of the Sikhs from the Indian state, though it did provide a unique platform to the new Governor to showcase his political dexterity to the powers that be in Delhi. It is another matter that preparations for the gathering and the construction of the helipad and the many roads and tracks leading to the site required that acres of wheat crop, ready to be harvested, be destroyed to clear the ground. Months after the experiment for bringing the Sikh youth into the so-called mainstream of national life by invoking historical legacies was over, the promised compensation for the losses suffered by poor farmers remained a distant dream.

As expected, the Hussainiwala rally did not materially alter the overall situation in Punjab, nor did it lessen the enormity of the collective hurt caused to the Sikh people by the army action in Amritsar and the Sikh killings in Delhi. The peace process was sought to be stepped up by an announcement by the Governor on 28 June 1985 that all those held in custody against whom no specific charges of sedition, murder, dacoity and arson had been framed, would be released, compensation would be paid for all those killed in the Punjab since 1 August, 1982, and a special committee constituted to review the progress of relief and rehabilitation of the victims of the Delhi Sikh killings of November 1984. This was followed by the release of most of the Akali leaders and other detainees not involved in heinous offences but interned since

Operation Blue Star, and the lifting of the ban on the All India Sikh Students Federation (AISSF). The Governor added for good measure that all these initiatives signified 'an act of grace' and 'a gesture of magnanimity' on the part of the prime minister (the *Tribune*, Chandigarh, 29 June 1985). The process entailed lot of hard work for the police, as they were required to compile lists of internees from time to time, whose release would not lead to an upsurge in violence. The number of persons to be released every now and then was arrived at arbitrarily by the Governor in consultation with his advisers in Delhi, without taking the local administration into confidence. This exercise, i.e., the periodical release from custody of a given number of persons, was meant to create a conducive climate for reviving the apparent peace process in Punjab.

However, the rhetorical claims made by the Governor about the favourable environment resulting from these policy initiatives were not borne out by ground realities, because of the huge gap between the announcements and their implementation. According to media reports and statements issued by Akali leaders, a large number of persons claimed to have been released were not in custody at all but on bail. A report in the *Tribune*, Chandigarh, clarified the position without the spin the Governor wanted to put on the exercise. It stated, 'The Punjab government today (17 July 1985) conceded yet another Akali demand by making public the names of 1,371 persons whose release has been ordered under the partial amnesty announced by the Governor, Arjun Singh, at Amritsar last month. Referring to the criticism that the actual number of persons released was much less than that claimed by government, an official spokesman explained that while the release of 1,371 persons arrested during or after Operation Blue Star had been ordered, courts had to date

allowed the withdrawal of charges against 816 persons.
The spokesman admitted that only 205 persons had so far
been actually released from various jails. The remaining
611 against whom cases had been withdrawn were already
on bail. Officials did not rule out the possibility that
certain persons involved in violence during recent weeks
have been arrested. In certain cases, persons wanted in
crimes committed several months earlier were arrested.

In other words, the number of those being released
was sought to be made up with fresh arrests. On the flip
side, however, the army and the central security forces,
with or without the active cooperation of the Punjab
police, would see to it that the earlier suppressive policies
remained unchecked. Lt-General J.S. Aurora observed in
an article titled 'Rajiv Gandhi Has to Undo the Damage'
in *Probe India* of Allahabad in May 1985, 'The Indian
army, which rolled in the rural areas of the Punjab to
ferret out extremists, created mistrust in the local
population because it detained and questioned a lot of
youths. Having fought the 1965 and the 1971 wars, I
know how essential it is for the army and civilians to walk
shoulder to shoulder. In Punjab, young men were arrested,
a few were killed in encounters, of which some were fake.'

*

The release of Akali leaders did not materially improve
the prospects of peace in the state for the simple reason
that the moderate sections within the party were fast
losing ground to the extremist elements. Barring Longowal,
no Akali leader of note was prepared to join issue with
the advocates of a militant approach. While Tohra and
Talwandi were openly critical of the Longowal approach,
Badal's position was fickle and wavering as usual in trying

to guard all his flanks in the true style of a power-hungry politician, seeking to keep all possible avenues to political office open. Differences between Longowal and the others mainly revolved around resuming a dialogue with the government after the latter accepted the basic demands of the party, voiced since long. Whereas Longowal maintained that the Akali movements and demands should be pursued strictly within the constraints imposed by India's constitutional framework, Tohra asserted that no solution of the Sikh grievances was possible within the Constitution. Badal was ambivalent. As for the ruling Congress party, it had its own cynical designs to seek to demolish the Akali party as a long time political voice of the Sikh people.

In the event, it once again chose to tread the old familiar path it had opted for earlier when Sant Bhindranwale was projected as a counterfoil to the Akali leadership, with disastrous results, as we have seen already. It now zeroed in on the late Sant's father, Baba Joginder Singh, to serve the same purpose. The latter was persuaded by a couple of emissaries, known to be close to Zail Singh and other Congress leaders, to float another Akali Dal, to be called Akali Dal (United), and become its president and then dissolve all the existing factions, including the one headed by Longowal, with which the government of India had been in dialogue for many years. Such a process of periodical fragmentation and reunification of the Akali movement was to repeat itself many times over in subsequent years, severely undermining the reputation and credibility of the premier channel of Sikh political assertion. All such endeavours, it need hardly be added, owed their inspiration and success to the manipulative genius of some top Congress leaders. It would be interesting to recapitulate what long-time Punjab watcher Kuldip

Nayar had to say on Joginder Singh's rapid ascent to power in Sikh politics:

> Three other Sikh leaders met Joginder Singh. They are not Akalis. They have been Giani Zail Singh's men or Mr Darbara Singh's supporters (now, perhaps, they are in the Darbara Singh camp). And then suddenly Sant Jarnail Singh's brother was released on bail. The government had reportedly opposed the move for 10 months! Who pulled the strings and for what purpose? This is anybody's guess. It is openly said that the release was ordered at the instance of Buta Singh who is close to Mr Jagdev Singh. Then two persons persuaded Mr Joginder Singh to jump into the fray. They are Mr Trilochan Singh Riyasti, a Congress (I) leader and Mr Inderjit Singh Sekhon, a lawyer from Faridkot, who till recently was a Congress (I) leader...After Mr Jagjit Singh's release, Mr Joginder Singh announced the names of the committee members, giving an overwhelming majority to the extremists. Mr Joginder Singh made the announcement of the committee, when Sant Harchand Singh returned to Punjab after his successful visit to Delhi. This appears to be more than a mere coincidence. The Sant seemed to have regained some of his old poise and it appeared that he might be able to win back his credibility with the Sikhs and Hindus both. That apparently did not suit the extremists.[2]

And their supporters elsewhere, he might have added.

For the record, Jagjit Singh was the real brother of Bhindranwale, who had exhibited no political ambitions until then—nor had Baba Joginder Singh, for that matter. What kind of goals inspired the central leadership to have suddenly developed a fondness for late Bhindranwale's family could hardly be rated as the best kept secret of the times. Almost every male member of his family was deftly wooed and sought to be inducted into Sikh religio-political institutions. This included his father Joginder Singh, brother Jagjit Singh, nephews Gurjit Singh and Jasbir Singh and uncle Harcharan Singh, a former junior commissioned officer in the Indian army. It was all so patently Machiavellian in conception and design. Gurjit would later play a leading role in one of the more prominent militant groups, while Jasbir Singh will figure in this narrative in a major way a little later.

Kuldip Nayar pointedly describes how earnest Sant Longowal was in pursuing a conciliatory approach towards New Delhi and how he deferred his morchas again and again so as not to close the peace options with the government. He was also constantly on the move in Punjab to reach out to the Hindu population, many of whom had been planning to migrate out of the state. Since most other Akali leaders, including his principal associates Tohra and Badal preferred to sit on the fence at this most critical stage in the state's history, the full responsibility for normalization of the situation had devolved on Longowal, of which he was only too well aware. Apart from frequent insinuations against top Congress leaders in respect of their close but covert relations with Sikh militants, media reports also spoke of overt links that some Congress leaders allegedly maintained with the former. In one case, a hardcore militant Gurinder Singh, shot dead in an encounter in Chandigarh on 13 May 1985, was found to have been a protégé of Santokh Singh Randhawa, then Punjab Congress president. Randhawa had to quit office soon thereafter in a damage control exercise. Obviously, a battle of sorts was raging between the Congress and Sant Longowal, now progressively emerging as the only Sikh leader genuinely interested in promoting a durable process of peace and gaining increasing credibility among both Hindus and Sikhs, to appropriate maximum political space in the Punjab.

Unfortunately, the Delhi establishment had once again chosen to disregard overall national interests by adopting shady and manipulative measures, freely using intelligence and other state institutions under their control in Delhi and Chandigarh, to worst a political adversary, who should, in fact, have been recognized as the best bet for ushering in an era of peace and communal harmony in the region and supported in his endeavours. Instead, the establishment would do all it could to weaken his hold on the Akali Dal and lessen his growing influence in Sikh politics by trying to personally discredit him. Realizing that Sant Bhindranwale had earned a hallowed status in the collective Sikh consciousness by virtue of his demise in Operation Blue Star as against the Akali leaders who had meekly surrendered before the invading army, the ruling establishment proceeded to co-opt almost every male member of Bhindranwale's family for the purpose. Such a no-holds-barred battle for the acquisition of maximum political space in the strategic border state would one day devour Sant Longowal himself as the only Sikh leader capable of stemming the rising tide of Punjab militancy. Was the Indian state banking upon the growth of terrorism as an essential component of its agenda of finding the ultimate solution to the nationality question of India? In the confusion and disarray that typified the decision-making processes in the state administration during that critical phase in its history, nothing could be ruled out. We will deal with some of the more baffling aspects of the assassination of Longowal a little later.

*

In a bold move to create a more propitious political climate, the top Akali and Shiromani Gurudwara Prabandhak Committee (SGPC) leaders held their first formal meeting after Blue Star on 30 April 1985 at Anandpur (a hallowed site in Sikh history because it was there that Guru Gobind Singh created the Khalsa in 1699) to discuss what Badal called the past, present and future course of events in Punjab. The general mood in the conclave was described by the media as positive, with leaders strongly favouring a pragmatic approach in pursuit of a lasting solution to the lingering Punjab problem and hoping that the government too would be more cooperative so as to restore the dignity, honour and confidence of the Sikhs. However, with the obvious official backing enjoyed by Baba Joginder Singh and his newly floated Akali Dal (United), and the dissolution of all other Akali Dals under his diktat, including Longowal's, it became difficult for the mainstream Akali leadership to strongly pursue their political agenda. It must be said to his credit, however, that Longowal did not renounce his mission even under intense multiple pressures, to soon emerge as probably the most influential of contemporary Sikh leaders, despite formally resigning from all party positions on 11 May. According to the Sant, 'Certain selfish powers are conspiring to spoil the cordial relations between the two communities and blaming the Sikh community for the situation'.[3]

On 22 May, a largely-attended meeting of district presidents and state leaders of the party pressed both Longowal and Badal to withdraw their resignations, which they did a couple of days later. Nevertheless, all these unseemly developments and the formidable challenge posed by the Joginder Singh phenomenon could not but critically corrode the authority and influence of these long-time

Akali leaders. Joginder Singh's Akali Dal organized a *panthic* convention in the Golden Temple complex to observe the first anniversary of Operation Blue Star, which was 'dominated by the spirit of Sant Jarnail Singh Bhindranwale,' as described by the *Tribune* of 7 June 1985. The report went on to state further:

> The tone and tenor of the speeches made and the resolutions passed at the convention left no one in any doubt that the organization's aim was to promote the Bhindranwale cult...The convention through a resolution eulogized the killers of Indira Gandhi. It gave a call to the Sikhs to get baptized and arm themselves to defend their religion, honour and dignity. The speakers refused to believe that Sant Jarnail Singh was dead and maintained that he would reappear. Every time his name was mentioned, the audience became hysterical and raised full-throated slogans... A handful of youth seated in the galleries repeatedly disturbed the proceedings by chanting pro-Khalistan slogans. They also raised (other) slogans like Sikh *quom de tin ghadar* (the three traitors of the Sikhs), Badal, Tohra, Longowal...The Akali leaders were blamed for surrendering to the armed forces during Operation Blue Star in violation of the pledge taken by them before Akal Takht....In a fiery speech, the All India Sikh Students Federation ad hoc convener, Mr Harinder Singh Kahlon said...We shall not forewarn the enemy before we strike and asked the youth to mobilize Sikhs under the leadership of Mr Joginder Singh. He (also) gave a call to the minorities, especially the Muslims, to lend support to the Sikhs to fight against injustice if they wanted to protect the honour of their own community. Mrs Surjit Kaur, a leader of the Istri (women) Akali Dal, talked of Mrs Gandhi's assassination as a revenge for

> the desecration of Akal Takht and said that Mr Rajiv
> Gandhi would meet the same fate for his role in the
> anti-Sikh riots...By another resolution, the
> convention...deplored the injustices perpetrated by
> the government on Muslims, backward classes and
> other minorities.

Neither Joginder Singh, nor the other leaders present at
the venue prevented the speakers from making such
outrageous remarks. One can be sure that every word of
what was said in these speeches and the general ambience
of the proceedings must have been reported faithfully by
intelligence agencies to bosses in Delhi and Chandigarh.
The attendance at the convention was estimated to be
around 15,000.

Three days later, the Longowal Akali Dal too held a
convention in the Golden Temple complex, which
reportedly attracted a much larger attendance than the
one organized by Joginder Singh. This convention, while
supporting the revival of Akali-Centre talks to resolve the
Punjab crisis, demanded the unconditional release of all
detained Sikhs, revocation of all black laws, closure of the
special courts and withdrawal of the army. Some young
men tried to disturb the proceedings by shouting pro-
Bhindranwale and pro-Khalistan slogans and distributing
leaflets, accusing the Akali leaders of betraying the *panth*
and being in league with the establishment. The commotion
lasted some 20 minutes, after which the miscreants were
chased out of the premises by Longowal supporters. The
Akali leaders met again at Anandpur on 8 July to draw up
their future plan of action. They once again reiterated
their earlier demands and wanted an assurance from the
authorities regarding their fulfillment before agreeing to
any further talks with the latter. By this time, however,
the Akali Dal (Longowal) was hardly a cohesive party and

relations between Longowal on the one hand and Tohra and Badal on the other were getting increasingly strained, Tohra because of his suspected militant leanings and as for Badal, he liked to keep his options open as he was forever on the lookout for opportunities to manoeuvre his way to power. Longowal now proposed to devote most of his time to touring the state to re-establish contact with the Hindu community and assuring them that the Sikhs were never interested in anything but peace and harmony in the country. Rajiv Gandhi too was reported to be appreciative of the changed attitude of the Sikh leadership as voiced by Longowal. For a brief interval, a ray of hope lighted up the mood in the entire region and it appeared that some kind of a *modus vivendi* had been worked out between the government and the Akali leadership and it was only a matter of time before peace would return to the beleaguered state.

However, subsequent events would not only dispel any nascent prospect of peace and security, they would also contribute in a major way to the intensification of militant sentiment in the Sikh community as a whole and the growth of militancy and terrorism at a scale never experienced earlier. We will deal with that phase a little later.

In the meanwhile, a series of bomb blasts in Delhi and a few other towns in the region in early May caused the death of some 80 persons. Thanks to an unrelenting campaign of slander and calumny against the whole Sikh community since the early 1980s, the media and the bulk of national leadership lost no time in holding the Sikhs responsible for the dastardly crimes, overlooking the possibility that it could as well be an act of an agent provocateur. Another major terrorist act was the bombing of Air India flight 182 on 23 June off the Irish coast in which 239 persons perished. The crime was traced to a powerful Babbar Khalsa International cell in Winnipeg and Vancouver in Canada, set up by some Canadian Sikhs of Indian and Malaysian origin. Four persons were prosecuted for the offence and tried in a Canadian court. After a protracted trial lasting almost two decades, two of them, Ripudaman Singh Malik and Ajaib Singh Bagri were acquitted by the court in March 2005 for lack of conclusive evidence. Of the other two accused, Talvinder Singh had been killed in an encounter in the Punjab in 1992, while Inderjit Singh Reyat had already been sentenced in 2003 to five years imprisonment in another case.

Predictably, the acquittal set off a deep sense of disappointment and outrage in India, especially among the families of the victims. The Indian government too took up the matter with the Canadian authorities. The Canadian parliament recommended to the government that an inquiry be conducted to find out the causes of the failure of the case in the court. In Punjab too, militants were becoming bolder and more organized in their operations, despite continuing accretion to the operational capacity and strength of central security forces on deputation to the state, as well as strengthening of the arsenal of repressive laws in the hands of the executive.

*

It was against this backdrop that Sant Longowal finally accepted an invitation from the prime minister, conveyed through the state Governor, to visit Delhi to enter into an agreement with the Indian government, as the president of his party, aimed at the resolution of all the problems afflicting the region for long. Evidently, it was not easy for the Sant to take such a crucial decision all by himself as none of the senior party leaders was prepared to back him in case the gamble misfired. The one and only Akali leader of any standing who offered his counsel to the Sant at the time and who would, in due course, accompany him to Delhi, was Balwant Singh, a Kamboj Sikh and thus not very popular with the Jutt Sikh rank and file of the Akali Dal. Nor was he known for political morality. Arjun Singh had deftly used Balwant's good offices to create a personal equation with Longowal and persuade him to visit Delhi for a meeting with the PM. As noted by Shubhabrata Bhattacharya, editor of the Calcutta weekly *Sunday*, 'Five days before the Punjab accord was signed, the Akali Dal chief, Sant Harchand Singh Longowal, faced with stiff opposition from his colleagues, Parkash Singh Badal and Gurcharan Singh Tohra, decided to seek God's verdict on his peace move. As per Sikh custom, after offering *ardas*, he at random opened the *Guru Granth Sahib*. The first stanza of the holy book, which attracted his attention said, 'If invitation has come, then go ahead.' When Sant Longowal left the Chandigarh residence of Akali leader Balwant Singh after this *ardas*, he had made up his mind: he was going to New Delhi to negotiate peace with the Union government'.[4]

Another version is offered by D.R. Ahuja of the *Tribune* in his report published on 26 July, according to which it was suggested to Sant Longowal that he take a *vak* or guidance from *Guru Granth Sahib* to surmount his sense of unease and irresolution. 'The Sant went to the adjoining room where the holy book was kept. Before opening the book, the Akali Dal chief offered *ardas* seeking the blessings and guidance of the Gurus, saying that the Sikh community was at a critical juncture and prayed to Waheguru to show him light. Then he took the *vak* from *Guru Granth Sahib*. It read: *Duvidha chhad, Guru tere ang-sang* (Abandon indecision, the Guru is with you). The Sant immediately made up his mind to accept Mr Gandhi's invitation'.

The Sant left for Delhi along with Barnala and Balwant Singh, where they were lodged in a wing of the stately Kapurthala House, a Punjab government guest house in Delhi. Arjun Singh made himself at home in another part of the mansion. Basically a man of religion, the art of political bargaining and equivocation did not come naturally to Sant Longowal and, in any case, he could never match the penetrative and manipulative skills of Arjun Singh, now intent upon creating history by bringing about an improbable agreement between the Akali Dal president and the Indian prime minister. Isolated completely from his senior colleagues and their counsel, with only the shifty Balwant as his adviser, Longowal must have felt trapped in a most awkward situation. Having come all the way from Chandigarh in search of a final solution to the Punjab tangle, armed with what he naively believed to be divine intervention, he would surely have felt deeply and emotionally committed to reach a settlement. Even then, he would have very much preferred to consult party colleagues, rather than rely solely on Balwant Singh, who was commonly believed to be more loyal to Arjun Singh than the Sant. The latter was understandably fidgety and unsure of himself during the talks and wanted to go back to Punjab to consult the party. This was subtly ruled out as it would have meant the virtual failure of the entire exercise, so adroitly worked out by Arjun Singh and his close advisers. The upshot was that Longowal was more or less conned into signing what was called the Rajiv-Longowal accord on 24 July 1985.

The accord, which purported to 'bring to an end a

period of confrontation and usher in an era of amity, goodwill and co-operation, which will promote and strengthen the unity and integrity of India' was widely applauded as a most welcome initiative by a young prime minister to reach out to the agitated Sikh community. Even the Pakistani media acclaimed it as a significant development. In an editorial comment 'Defusing the Sikh Crisis' on 26 July 1985, *The Muslim*, Islamabad, called it 'a personal triumph for Rajiv Gandhi' for which he should be 'complimented'. The Indian media too was upbeat about the prospects of peace and order returning to the region as a result of the accord. This was strange because barring Longowal, Barnala and Balwant Singh, nearly the entire Sikh religio-political establishment, ranging from Joginder Singh's Akali Dal to minor Akali leaders like Talwandi and Cheema, was openly critical of the Sant for signing a dubious accord, and that too without the government accepting any of the conditions set out by the Akalis. Not even Badal and Tohra, the two key associates of Longowal, were prepared to support it, claiming that they were not even aware of the secret negotiations between Longowal and the government of India and were thus not a party to it. Not endorsed by a vast majority of the Sikh leadership and condemned in no uncertain terms by the swelling ranks of militant groups, the accord soon lost its shine as far as the Sikhs were concerned.

To make matters worse, the document itself turned out to be seriously flawed in many respects. Its major clauses, especially those relating to territorial claims and sharing of river waters were virtually unimplementable due mainly to its vague phraseology hedged in with built-in contradictions, the result either of poor draftsmanship or intended obfuscation. Who actually prepared the draft and who vetted it at various stages remained unclear for long, though several conjectures were doing the rounds at the time. Among those mentioned as its authors were a reputed teacher of Punjab university and a couple of young Congressmen often seen with the governor. One can be sure, though, that the final product must have received the most careful attention of Arjun Singh and if the failure of the accord were to be attributed to its interpretative ambiguity, it must have been drawn up with that purpose in view. For, it is inconceivable that a meticulous draftsman like him, in more senses than one, would let a poorly drafted document pass out of his hands, unless he meant it to be so— which, in this case, appeared to be a distinct possibility.

To add to the confusion, the neighbouring states of Haryana and Rajasthan, both ruled by Rajiv Gandhi loyalists, and affected by the terms of the accord in many significant aspects, were not made parties to it. As if on cue, Haryana soon refused to cooperate and the much-acclaimed peace process came unstuck. It soon became clear that the accord could not pass muster even as a genuine effort to address Sikh grievances voiced over the years and to heal the traumatic hurt caused by operations Blue Star and Wood Rose and the Sikh killings of November 1984. In consequence, the accord miserably failed to bring peace to the region, partly because of the way it was framed but largely because of the forces working against it. The inability or indisposition of the central government to implement the accord was perceived by the Sikh community as a calculated attempt to hoodwink them. However, it was the sundry militant groups, gradually re-establishing their supremacy in *panthic* affairs with the active connivance of radical elements in Joginder Singh's United Akali Dal, who would feel most incensed at the developments and let loose a wave of terrorist attacks to soon transform the region into a veritable battlefield against the state.

As commission after commission failed to arrive at any workable proposal for the implementation of various provisions of the accord acceptable to all parties, the whole charade became too bizarre to carry credibility with most civil society groups in the country. For the time being, though, both the accord as also its principal architect Arjun Singh received copious accolades from all sections of the media, not only across India but also internationally. The former was, of course, too shrewd an operator to let grass grow under his feet. He knew very well that the Punjab Raj Bhawan was a virtual graveyard of gubernatorial ambitions, and was only too eager to leave the state as soon as possible, while the going was good.

*

It did not take long for Sant Longowal to realize that he had been virtually tricked into signing a document that had no takers among his colleagues in the Akali party nor inspired enthusiasm in the community as a whole. Moreover, the militants had found in the accord and its imminent failure a powerful impetus to revive their activities with greater force and to seek more assured support in the countryside. With almost every Akali leader of any consequence, except Balwant Singh and Barnala, intent on distancing himself from the accord, the foremost responsibility to push it among the Sikh masses fell exclusively upon Longowal. He, therefore, took it upon himself to promote the accord as a peaceful alternative to the violence and terrorism rampant in the area for some time, by embarking on extensive mass contact visits throughout the length and breadth of the state. An extremely devout Sikh, he also intuitively turned to scriptural sources for solace and inspiration, frequently visiting gurudwaras and other holy places, prominent among them his own *dera* or religious centre at Longowal village in Punjab's Sangrur district. In an effort to establish a modicum of rapport with the militants, he also started attending the *bhog* ceremonies (last rites) of militants slain in police encounters. However, despite the outward calm and poise, the Sant was clearly a sad and troubled man, shunned by his colleagues and berated by militant sections for having entered into a phony accord with a repressive regime in Delhi.

As it happened, within a month after he put his signatures to the accord document, he was mysteriously assassinated while attending a religious function in the Longowal village gurudwara. Who actually killed him and for what reason was never conclusively established. An inquiry was conducted by Lt-General Gowri Shankar, security adviser to the state government and the corps commander at Jalandhar within days of the murder but his report was never made public, although a few Punjab Armed Police (PAP) officials were suspended or dismissed in the process. Another inquiry was conducted later under orders of the Akali government that came to power after the legislative elections in August 1985, this time by a high court judge. The findings of this inquiry too remained buried in the cavernous godowns of the Punjab government secretariat in Chandigarh, along with several other murky secrets of those dark days.

The prolonged labours of state and central investigation agencies too failed to clear the air and dispel the many doubts and suspicions in the public mind regarding Sant Longowal's assassination at such a crucial juncture. The official version that the crime was the handiwork of

militants, as the late Sant was deemed to have betrayed
the community by signing the accord, perceived by them
as a sell-out, had few takers in the Punjab. Even after the
CBI charge-sheeted some Sikh militants, a number of
significant questions, raised in the inquiry and otherwise,
continued to baffle close observers of the scene for a long
time until the event, crucial though it was for the future
of peace and order in large parts of the country, itself
slipped from public memory. We will revert to the subject
presently, but first let us take a look at the various
provisions of the accord and how far did they address the
Sikh grievances and demands.

*

We may recall that the Akali Dal had always insisted on
the acceptance of certain preconditions before resuming
talks with the Centre. While signing the accord, the Sant
apparently missed out on the preconditions as the document
was either silent about them or addressed them only
partially. Nor were any of the major demands of the Sikhs
adequately dealt with. The preconditions were: the release
of all innocent Sikhs, abolition of special courts and
scrapping of the black laws. The accord promised to
withdraw notifications applying the armed forces special
powers Act to Punjab at a future unspecified date. They
were, in fact, not withdrawn for the next decade and a
half. It said that the existing special courts will try only
offences relating to waging war and hijacking, but almost
all Sikh activists were charged with precisely those classes
of offences. About withdrawal of cases against army
deserters, the accord merely promised to make efforts to
find alternative employment for all those discharged from
the army. About acceptance of the Anandpur Sahib

resolution: it stood referred to the Sarkaria commission in so far as it relates to Centre-state relations, *on being assured by Sant Longowal that it was not meant to be secessionist in nature.* Regarding action against those responsible for Sikh killings in Delhi and elsewhere, the accord merely promised to extend the terms of the ineffectual Ranganath Mishra commission to two more towns of Bokaro and Kanpur. The last precondition asked for a judicial inquiry into violence against Sikhs, the accord made no mention of it.

More or less the same vague approach is noticeable with regard to the specific demands put up by the Akali Dal from time to time. About recruitment of Sikhs to the armed forces, the accord states, 'All citizens of the country have the right to enroll in the army and merit will remain the criterion for selection.' There is no mention of enhanced recruitment quota for the Sikhs in keeping with their traditional prominence in the Indian army. On Punjabi, the accord said, 'The central government may take some steps for the promotion of the Punjabi language.' About representation of minorities, it promised that 'Existing instructions regarding protection of interests of minorities will be recirculated to the state chief ministers.' On an All India Gurudwara Act, the accord stated blandly, 'The government of India agrees to consider the formulation of an All India Gurudwara Bill.' While the minor issues were couched in plain and easy vocabulary, the more critical issues of territorial adjustments, sharing of river waters and the status of Chandigarh were sought to be buried in terminological and interpretative ambiguities, which would make their implementation a virtual impossibility.

On the question of transfer of Chandigarh to Punjab, for example, the accord stated: 'The capital project area of Chandigarh will go to Punjab...It has always been maintained by Smt. Indira Gandhi that when Chandigarh is to go to Punjab, some Hindi-speaking territories in Punjab will go to Haryana. A commission will be constituted to determine the specific Hindi-speaking areas of Punjab, which should go to Haryana in lieu of Chandigarh...The actual transfer of Chandigarh to Punjab and areas in lieu thereof to Haryana will take place simultaneously on 26 January 1986.' The reference to some Hindi-speaking territories in Punjab to be transferred to Haryana in this clause clearly pointed to Abohar and Fazilka areas, a rich cotton-growing tract, and not to territorial claims and adjustments, based on linguistic factors, because another clause dealt specifically with that problem. The Akalis had, however, always been opposed to the issue of Chandigarh being linked to Abohar-Fazilka, a stand endorsed even by the Punjab Congress party.

Similar ambiguities and fudging marked the clauses relating to river waters and territorial claims, making their implementation virtually impossible. No wonder a majority of political analysts soon came to realize that the much-applauded accord was a seriously-flawed document, deceptive in design and incapable of being fully implemented, an exercise intended primarily to entice an upright man of God into signing away his party's long-time stance, rather than to find a lasting solution to the festering sore of the Punjab tangle. If, in the process, the already fragile unity in the Sikh religio-political establishment gets further dented, it will be an additional bonus for the Indian state; it will make it easier for the latter to deal with the uppity Sikh community from a position of strength.

To ascribe all such linguistic flaws and incongruities to poor draftsmanship would be the height of naiveté and a willing suspension of disbelief as to the manipulative genius of the principal architect of the so-called accord. For, no document as vital to the peace and tranquility of an entire region as the Rajiv-Longowal accord could afford to be the product of slipshod drafting, unless meant to be so. In consequence, commission after commission would go into the many sticky issues to unscramble the maze, probably purposely crafted by the authors of the memorandum of (un)settlement, and to pressurize a simple man of religion to put his signature on it in all good faith and, as an upshot, lose his life. It is another matter that the subsequent collapse of the accord, whether intended or otherwise, would also plunge the entire north-western India into one of history's worst phases of terrorist and militant violence, heaping indescribable suffering on the populace for several years to come. But maybe that too was part of a diabolical and well-orchestrated design to solve the intractable nationality question of India. What was quite obvious, however, was that the Indian establishment had succeeded in consolidating the radical elements in the Sikh leadership, while considerably weakening the moderates. This end was achieved by extending tacit and not so tacit support to the hardliner sections within the community, even patronizing some of the emerging militant groups and *panthic* committees.

We will go into these particulars later. For the present, let us turn to some extraordinary circumstances attending upon the assassination of Sant Longowal.

*

Sant Longowal returned to Chandigarh after signing the accord on 24 July 1985, somewhat sad and dispirited at the turn of events, as reported by media persons, who tried to draw him out on the deeper implications of the document he had signed in Delhi. He did not stay long in the state capital, nor did he call a meeting of the party working committee. Instead, he left the very next morning for his village, where he would engross himself in prayers in the gurudwara. I gathered from reliable sources that legislative elections were proposed to be held in Punjab soon after the accord was formally ratified by the Akali Dal. Badal told me after the assassination that the Sant had wanted him to take over as chief minister after the elections but he sounded visibly unhappy because now that the Sant was no more, his promise meant nothing. This was somewhat strange because how could the late Sant presage an Akali victory in the elections still to be held unless there was a tacit understanding between the Sant and the Centre that the elections to the Punjab legislature would be 'managed' in such a manner that an Akali government would assume office in the state. Later events would seem to indicate that there was, indeed, such an arrangement. For the present, however, Sant Longowal, as the co-signatory of the Punjab accord, which was more or less disowned by almost the entire Akali leadership, including its various factions, was under increasing threat from the many militant groups, who were steadily gaining support within the Sikh community and taking to militancy and extremist violence in a major way, especially in the border areas. These groups clearly blamed the Sant for having signed away the vital interests of the community by entering into an inequitable agreement with a tyrannical Delhi durbar (remember the collective historical perception of the community).

In view of the enormity of the threat perception to Longowal's life, the Punjab government, in consultation with the Union home ministry decided to provide him with a high level of personal security, although he continued to adamantly refuse to accept any kind of visible security cover from the state, for obvious reasons. Obviously, the matter had to be handled very tactfully in view of the extremely sensitive nature of the task and the kind of situation then developing in the state. It also required considerable persuasion to convince the Sant about the urgent need and imperatives of personal security. I asked the inspector general intelligence to visit Longowal village and draw up a comprehensive security plan for the Sant. Accordingly, a high-level meeting was held at the district headquarters to which Sant Longowal belonged. This meeting was attended by the inspector generals of intelligence and Punjab armed police (PAP), deputy inspector general (security), Sangrur's superintendent of police and other concerned officers. The Sant was also informally consulted about the plan, to which he reluctantly assented. An officer of the rank of a police superintendent, who enjoyed the Sant's confidence, was placed in overall charge of the security arrangements. A small but reliable group of officials in plain clothes was placed at his disposal for ensuring the Sant's proximate security. In addition, a uniformed detachment was stationed nearby to supplement plainclothes personnel in case of need. Both these security details were provided with high-level communication equipment so that they remained in constant touch with each other as well as with the state intelligence headquarters.

In conformity with the time-tested procedures laid down for such highly sensitive duties, the entire security unit detailed for the Sant was placed under the operational and supervisory charge of IG intelligence and DIG security. These two officers were also responsible for their postings, transfers, replacements, training schedules, briefings and, of course, necessary security clearance. Thus, the entire package of functions impinging on the Sant's security was to be closely monitored by them, though they were also required to keep the director general of police informed of any important developments, if and when they thought it necessary. For logistical and other reasons, however, the bulk of the security detail was borne on the strength of the PAP headquarters at Jalandhar.

Along with Arjun Singh came several officers from his home state of Madhya Pradesh, known to be personally loyal to him, including both his special assistants, his personal security officer and other staff, apart from almost a battalion strength of the MP special armed force for personal security. A close relative then serving in a top post in the CRPF was frequently seen visiting Raj Bhawan and undertaking extensive tours of the state, as was another IPS officer from MP, reputed to be an exceptionally smooth operator and *fixer*, with long experience in the intelligence field. A former director general of a central paramilitary force, who had earlier served as an inspector general with the CRPF at Amritsar during operations Blue Star and Wood Rose, was brought as an adviser to the Governor, presumably on the recommendation of a close relative, then serving in the same force. Even the inspector general, intelligence, Punjab, was a trusted loyalist, who had worked as joint director of the state intelligence bureau at Bhopal, when Arjun Singh was MP chief minister. It is not unusual for Indian politicians to surround themselves with familiar and loyal officials, for obvious reasons. However, when such practices lead to the undermining of established norms and proprieties of administrative culture and tradition, they end up destroying the unity and effectiveness of the local system of command and control. Such a style of governance, then obtaining in

Punjab, needs to be taken note of, because the institutional damage resulting from such a personalized and devious system of decision-making was seriously responsible for the emasculation of the Punjab administration in coping with the critical situation following Sant Longowal's assassination and the failure of the accord he had signed less than a month earlier.

To come back to the assassination, the most serious of many lapses that most likely led to the catastrophe was the substitution of the officer in overall charge of the security detachment, posted by the intelligence headquarters after a careful vetting from the security angle, with another officer by the PAP top brass, within days of the security scheme being approved by the government. Strangely, the officer selected as replacement had only recently faced a departmental inquiry for having links with militants, for which his dismissal from service had been recommended by the police and home departments. The case was pending with the state Governor for final orders. What is more, no prior clearance for the crucial replacement was obtained from the state intelligence branch, as required under the standing orders and the circumstances of the case. To assign such a sensitive and crucial responsibility to an officer whose very credibility was in serious doubt and that too without conducting a proper security check was a highly irresponsible act, if not outright culpable. Sadly for the late Sant and prospects of peace in Punjab, such a serious lapse did not come to notice until after the foul deed had been done. It was only then that the Governor called for the case file and ordered the dismissal of the concerned officer. On the face of it, it does seem strange that so many worthies, from the Governor downwards, would sit on such a volatile case for months—whatever the usual bureaucratic reasons behind it. The dismissed officer would later join the radical Sikh leader, Simranjit Singh Mann, as his secretary.

A few among the shocked members of the congregation at the Sherpur gurudwara, eyewitnesses to the assassination, gave some startling details of the actual sequence of events, when questioned right after the incident. According to these accounts, two young men sitting behind the Sant whipped out their revolvers and shot at the Sant as he bowed in prayer after the *ardas*. The Sant fell down but was unhurt. Predictably, the firing led to much confusion among the worshippers, though many of them had the presence of mind to lie on top of the Sant, thus shielding his body from further attack. A senior police officer reportedly came on the scene at this point and asked the persons covering the Sant's body to let him get up as the alleged killers had already been taken into custody. It was then that the Sant was fatally shot at again. Expectedly, none of these disclosures would have formed part of the recorded evidence, as neither the police nor the witnesses would be too keen to place themselves in a situation, pregnant with embarrassing and hazardous possibilities. Understandably, all such baffling goings-on of that dark period were sought to be glossed over by the authorities, though some of them did probably catch the eye of the judicial commission, appointed by the successor Akali government. Not unexpectedly and true to the hallowed traditions of an unaccountable and authoritative colonialist administration, all adverse inferences were firmly suppressed.

Who was really behind the crucial replacement in the proximate security set-up of Sant Longowal, which presumably facilitated the foul deed and what could have been the motive for elimination of the Sant, who was poised to play a historic role at that critical stage in the history of the Punjab? Was it a plain and simple act of negligence or was there something more to it than the versions put out by the establishment? It is not as if the PAP top brass was unaware of the antecedents of the officer they posted to guard the Sant against militant attacks. The inquiry culminating in his dismissal from service was conducted by the same DIG and the same IG, who had now made the controversial replacement. These and many other questions posed by political analysts from time to time in an effort to comprehend the logic and raison d'être of a militant movement, alien to Sant Longowal's scheme of things, that followed his slaying, are not merely rhetorical, they seek to ascertain the true ancestry of many catastrophic events that marked the course of events in the region after his assassination.

*

An analysis of political developments as attempted above would show that apart from the army operations of June 1984 and the Sikh killings later that year, two events that would prove to be of critical significance in the intensification of Sikh militancy in its post-1986 phase, were the assassination of Longowal and the fading prospects of implementation of the accord, he had signed with Rajiv Gandhi. The first of these events would lead to an obvious wilting of the political leadership of the community and making them overly defensive and fearful of losing their lives if they opposed the militant gangs, while the second would effectively silence the moderate elements within the Sikh community, who now had no answer to the line of reasoning put forward by the radicals regarding the basic insincerity of the Congress party and its government. In other words, the elimination of Longowal and the sidelining of the moderate Akali leadership left the field wide open for the militant groups to take centrestage in asserting the demands and grievances of the community. In the process, an essentially political struggle of the early 1980s had assumed the character of a militant movement of the classical type, ostensibly motivated by ideological goals. Under the circumstances, the militant groups, now operating under what were called *panthic* committees and assured of ample support from the community, emerged as the sole advocates of the so-called Sikh demands and complaints for the next few years. Since all the principal Sikh grievances, i.e., allocation of waters from Punjab rivers to non-riparian states of Haryana and Rajasthan (thus depriving the Sikh farmers of adequate water from Punjab's rivers for irrigation purposes), exclusion of some Punjabi-speaking areas and the city of Chandigarh from the new state, and the failure of the government to bring to book guilty persons involved in the 1984 anti-Sikh riots had remained unaddressed, militant groups found no great difficulty in using the existing discontent of the Sikhs to arouse strong passions in the community against the state. Soon, however, militancy and terrorism would assume a self-sustaining character, pushing into the background all other factors that may have triggered the movement in the first instance.

We will conclude this chapter with a quotation, with which most of us are familiar, but in which few ever discovered an argument in favour of militancy and extremism.

> To be or not to be—that is the question,
> Whether it is nobler in the mind to suffer
> The slings and arrows of outrageous fortune
> Or to take arms against a sea of troubles
> And by opposing end them...
>
> —Shakespeare in *Hamlet*

8

Intensification of Militancy

The assassination of Sant Longowal in some highly mysterious circumstances was to prove calamitous in several ways that will find mention in the following paragraphs. It was also to crucially impinge on me and my career. I was on tour to Delhi at the time for a meeting with the Union home secretary to work out the logistics of the projected elections to the Punjab legislative assembly. On learning of the tragic event, I rushed back to Chandigarh and found that the Governor had already left for the scene of the crime. When I got in touch with him on telephone, he asked me to stay on at the headquarters and monitor the progress of the investigation and feed the necessary details to Delhi. N.N. Vohra, the state principal secretary, home, and I stayed on in my office the whole night, dealing with a very critical situation indeed and answering endless queries from the PMO, home ministry, intelligence bureau and sundry other officials in Delhi, besides, of course, making transport and other arrangements for a horde of VIPs landing in Chandigarh in special planes to travel to Longowal village for the funeral of the slain Sant. I remained in constant contact with the Governor all through the time he was out of station, first in Longowal village until the funeral and then in Delhi, where he had flown after a short halt in Chandigarh, to brief the PM and his advisers with regard to the assassination. After a day or two, he refused to take my calls and I learnt from my friends in Delhi that a decision had been taken by the government to relieve me of my post and send me back to my home state of MP, as a damage control exercise.

It is not unusual for South Asian ruling establishments to find scapegoats for flawed policies and botched operations. It happened to several of my predecessors in Punjab as well as to a Governor in Tamilnadu and a Lieutenant-Governor in Delhi, besides many others. It seemed strange, though, that the DG be held responsible for a security lapse in a matter, which was being handled directly by the Governor with the help of his security adviser and the inspector general, intelligence. IPS officers of our generation were trained to obey orders and not to question the decisions taken by the establishment in their supreme wisdom. I handed over charge to the seniormost IG on 22 August 1985, and left the state, though not without an acute sense of disillusionment and plenty of cynicism.

With Sant Longowal no longer on the scene to exercise a moderating influence in Sikh politics, the Punjab situation would change radically. The views of the extremist sections would become central to the conduct of the struggle for justice and fair play. This would open the floodgates of violence, which would soon envelop the entire state. As the prospects of implementation of the Rajiv-Longowal accord faded, Sikh militancy acquired a fresh new impetus and intensity, marking the onset of its fourth and most deadly phase (1986-1992). In an obvious effort to consolidate the transient gains of the accord, the authorities decided to hold legislative elections in the state soon after. This was evidently a very hazardous proposition, given the highly volatile situation. Various militant groups, soon to be organized under some sort of unified command structure called the *panthic* committee, rejected the electoral option, unless the long-pending Sikh grievances were appropriately addressed and warned those who dared to contest of dire consequences.

However, the elections held in September 1985 under heavy security arrangements passed off peacefully, with the Akali Dal (Longowal) securing the highest number of seats ever in the Punjab assembly. An Akali ministry was installed in office by a beaming Arjun Singh on 29 September, with Surjit Singh Barnala as chief minister and Arjun's long-time friend Balwant Singh emerging as a power behind the throne as finance minister. Parkash Singh Badal and Gurcharan Singh Tohra were understandably not too happy with the outcome of the electoral exercise as they both felt short-changed, having been denied any share in the power structure that emerged from the elections. A recurring view being voiced in political and media circles was that the elevation of a mild and politically weak Barnala to the chief ministerial chair had been manoeuvred by the Congress party so that the state Governor continued to call the shots. This remarkable feat had been achieved simply by fielding weak Congress candidates against Barnala-backed Akali candidates and denying tickets to Akali contestants opposed to the Barnala-Balwant Singh faction. This election would, thus, go down in history as a unique event; a Congress Governor exercising the rare privilege of selecting the candidates of both the opposing parties, his own as well as the rival Akali Dal.

The rule of the unremarkable Barnala government did not last long, nor did it cover itself with glory during the period it lasted although—expectedly—the swearing in of an Akali government aroused high expectations in the Sikh masses, who hoped that the new government would, at least, curb the brutal behaviour of an unaccountable and oppressive state administration. However, leave aside the rectification of the principal grievances of the Sikh community, the new government soon proved to be too ineffectual even to provide relief to the masses from the atrocious conduct of the police and central security forces, hamstrung as it was by excessive subordination to the Congress government in Delhi through the state Governor.

Even the cardinal principle of democracy that when nothing else works, go to the people for guidance, failed to work in the Punjab of 1985. This exercise in democracy was sought to be utilized by the ruling party to entrust the reins of power to the Akali party under a hand-picked and pliable chief minister, who would for ever be looking to the state Governor for guidance and advice. This served two purposes: first, the central government would continue to call the shots and rule by proxy through the Governor, a shrewd politician and able administrator in his own right. And second, it would cozily shift the responsibility for implementing the accord on the Akalis themselves. If the accord failed, as was inevitable, the Akali government would be an obvious scapegoat. What is more, an Akali—not a Congress—government would now have to deal with Sikh militancy that would absolve the Centre of all blame for whatever may happen in the region. Or so they thought.

*

Many Akali leaders were able to see through the strategy, and started distancing themselves from the newly installed chief minister. Since the Akali leadership was neither able to provide quality governance to the oppressed citizenry nor prevail upon the Union government to address some of the long-standing demands of the community, the 1986 elections could achieve none of the goals of a democratic exercise. On the other hand, militant violence escalated exponentially, the Akali leaders themselves now became frequent targets of the gun, many of them losing their lives, including several ministers and high-ranking officers. Almost the entire leadership went into hiding. The weak-kneed Akali government did not last long and was dismissed as incompetent after a series of mass killings by the militants.

This marked the commencement of a long spell of central rule, facilitating extensive backseat driving by faceless bureaucrats in various Union ministries, at the cost of local initiative and autonomy. It also enabled intelligence agencies to launch undercover operations, supposedly in pursuit of establishing a bridgehead within the militant hierarchy and for other dubious ends. Central rule also opened innumerable doors of opportunity for the political classes to dispense favours to their supporters and flunkeys. While the gross mismanagement of the situation by the authorities would play a major part in fanning the flames of Sikh militancy, the growing interest exhibited by Pakistan in the fast-moving events across the border aggravated an already thorny problem. The convergence of the growth of Sikh separatism with the Indo-Pakistani hiatus had been fuelling suspicions and tensions on both sides of the border for some time. Now it became a more sustained and calculated process, with Pakistan actively assisting the militants in many ways, logistically and otherwise. Also, the large Sikh populations settled abroad were only too willing to provide to the community a transnational base, apart from Pakistan, to plan, conduct and sustain terrorist activities.

Many overseas Sikh organizations and prominent individuals were now lending active support to the propagation of militancy, both in financial and logistical terms, prominent among them being Ganga Singh Dhillon and Jagjit Singh Chauhan. The latter had set up a 'republic of Khalistan-in-exile' as early as 1971 and a 'national council of Khalistan' under his chairmanship shortly thereafter. The council continued to canvass support and collect funds from Germany, Canada, the United States and the UK, countries with sizeable expatriate Sikh populations. Chauhan would quietly resurface in the Punjab in late 2001, apparently under some tacit agreement with political authorities. After lying low for some time, he would resume political activity through a new outfit called the Khalsa Raj party.

*

The failure of the accord considerably reinforced radical perspectives in the Sikh religio-political arena. While each of these factors acting singly could probably not have led to the intensification, all of them acting together were sure to create conditions for the emergence of a conscious, common and shared objective and its pursuit by an increasing number of militant groups, now acting under the guidance of a *panthic* committee headed by Dr Sohan Singh, a former director of health services, Punjab. Dr Singh provided a much-needed ideological prop to the movement, and although it would soon go through a process of fragmentation and, at a later stage, that of lumpenisation, he would continue to be the most influential of militant ideologues, upholding the need for the adoption of a militant stance at that point of time in Sikh history. His *panthic* committee would, thus, retain its primacy in the militancy-driven Sikh movement for reassertion, even after several such committees had been formed. This is what led the prime Pakistani secret agency to zero in on him as its principal contact man in the Sikh militant movement.

The militants were now clearly seen by the community as being seriously engaged in seeking the redressal of Sikh grievances, in whatever manner possible. This is what earned them the necessary social recognition and support of the community, especially in the countryside, during the early phases of militancy, which was supplemented by the frequency of (fake) encounters and the failure of the courts to dispense speedy justice. Since all other organs of the state had become dysfunctional by this time, the police and central armed forces, as the only fully operational state agencies, unleashed a full-blown police raj, characterized by oppressive, callous and insensitive behaviour towards citizens. The people were in no position to complain as they were twice oppressed, at the hands of both the police and the militants. Towards the end of the 1980s, the militant movement would split into many factions, each apparently operating under a separate *panthic* committee, often engaging in internecine conflicts. While the scale of extremist violence would rapidly escalate, peaking around 1990, the movement itself was fast losing sight of its initial focus and unity of purpose, resulting in an extreme degree of fragmentation and inter-group rivalries, a situation tailor-made for the police to sow seeds of suspicion and mistrust between different groups, even to help set up new groups of fake militants to discredit the Sikh militants by engaging in blatant criminal activities.

This and some other developments would set the stage for a final showdown between the security agencies and the militants, most of whom had by now degenerated into pure and simple criminals. We will deal with that phase a little later in this study.

*

To revert to 1986, a Sarbat Khalsa convention was held at the Akal Takht on 26 January, India's republic day. The tradition of summoning Sarbat Khalsa congregations at critical junctures in Sikh history had originated shortly after the Guru period. Besides nominating a five-member *panthic* committee under Dr Sohan Singh to guide the militant struggle in the ensuing years, the convention adopted a bulky resolution, a *gurmata* in Sikh parlance. The preamble of the *gurmata* read: 'This function of today meant to evolve a consensus and delineate a strategy to tackle the problems confronting the whole Sikh world is an expression of real Sikh traditions'. The text dwelt at length on the problems facing the community and identified by name the enemies of the *panth*. It also expressly rejected the Rajiv-Longowal accord of 24 July 1985 as it did not measure up to the Sikh demands contained in the Anandpur Sahib resolution, and decided to demolish the Akal Takht, built by the renegade Nihang chief Santa Singh with government help. It would be reconstructed through voluntary labour or *kar sewa*, as ordained by Sikh tradition. Apparently, the *gurmata* sought to define in ideological terms the objectives of Sikh militancy, ironically on a day when the rest of the country was celebrating its nationhood.

Three months later on 29 April, the five-member *panthic* committee issued a document for the Declaration of Khalistan, claiming to 'fulfill the most cherished dream of the Sikhs'. This declaration was a sequel to a resolution passed at another Sarbat Khalsa, held at the Akal Takht a few days earlier on 13 April on the occasion of Baisakhi celebrations, in a way, signifying the fulfillment of Bhindranwale's prophecy that 'the foundation of Khalistan would be laid the day army enters Harmandir Sahib'. After elaborating the problems and issues that then faced the Sikhs, the document dealt with the working of Khalistan broadly under two heads—political recognition and social structure. It also affirmed, 'In this difficult situation, having made the declaration of Khalistan alone, we have observed reluctance in declaring total war against India in retaliation so that we may not be charged with impetuosity in the world court.' It was also announced that the Khalistan commando force (KCF) under 'general' Hari Singh would serve as the nucleus of the defence organization of Khalistan.[1]

The fact that more Sarbat Khalsa conventions were held during this period than ever before in Sikh history was a sure indication that Sikh society was passing through a turbulent phase and assailed by a severe crisis of confidence. Another lengthy *gurmata* was adopted at the Sarbat Khalsa held on 26 January 1987, confirming the decisions made at the earlier conventions, including the declaration of Khalistan and appointments of *jathedars* and head *granthis*. It held the 'Barnala-Balwant government responsible for atrocities on Sikhs, since it was playing into the hands of the communal government in Delhi.' The *gurmata* further affirmed that 'This convention refuses to recognize the Barnala-Balwant clique as a representative government to protect the interests of the people of the Punjab.'

A few months later, a world Sikh conference was convened on 4 August to take stock of the grave situation that then confronted the *panth*. In the following month, the *panthic* committee-appointed high priests too backed the Khalistan declaration. Evidently, neither the government nor the moderate Akalis possessed the capacity to check the fast deteriorating situation, with extremist elements having seized complete control of the Golden Temple complex. It was they who were now increasingly calling the shots. Whether such a contingency came about due to government incompetence or an ingeniously designed political strategy remains unclear, though the many strange developments in the ensuing period would tend to point to the latter possibility. In a couple of months, Arjun Singh would manage to join national politics, with the famed accord in shambles and the region in the grip of fast escalating militant violence. However, he would continue to carry the aura of being a friend of the Sikhs for quite some time and also retain his position as the principal adviser to the prime minister on Punjab affairs. Back in Delhi, he posted an impressive win in a parliamentary by-election in a Sikh-dominated constituency, apparently because of his assumed success in resolving the Punjab problem.

*

As if to mirror the developments in the Golden Temple, militant violence registered a huge upsurge, rising from 63 incidents in 1985 to 520 in 1986. Militant activity had also acquired a more organized and professional character, due mainly to the recognition accorded to KCF as the official militia of Khalistan. The KCF had now on its rolls about 400 well-armed militants, operating within a centralized, hierarchical and cohesive structure.[2] Big ticket robberies to raise huge sums of money for the procurement of weapons became common, the biggest of them being the one in Ludhiana in February 1987, involving a sum of nearly Rs 60 million. It was only after this robbery that Chinese-made AK-47 rifles made their presence felt. As militancy grew, militant groups multiplied and became bolder by the day. The KCF would, however, continue to occupy the central position in the movement right up to the liquidation of 'general' Labh Singh in July 1988, despite the fact that inter-group rivalry and fragmentation had already weakened the command structure. This and the fast-deteriorating situation within the Golden Temple complex would prompt the government to launch Operations Black Thunder to free the Temple from the control of extremists.

By the last quarter of the year 1988, the Babbar Khalsa International (Pakistan-based Sukhdev Singh Dassowal, Sukhdev Singh Sakhira and Talvinder Singh Parmar groups) had clearly emerged as the leading militant group, owing allegiance to the five-member *panthic* committee of Dr Sohan Singh.[3] Although, the origin of Sikh militancy in the 1980s is generally attributed to Sant Bhindranwale, its precise relationship with Jagjit Singh Chauhan's national council of Khalistan and other foreign Sikh entities remains unclear, except that there must have been substantial financial support from abroad. One of the more fanatical militant organizations, the Dal Khalsa, was formed by Jagjit Singh Chauhan in 1978, allegedly with the support of some senior Congress party politicians, who wished to cause a split in the Akali Dal and remove it from power in the Punjab (remember Zail Singh?) A prominent Dal Khalsa leader, Gurbachan Singh Manochahal, later to head one of the *panthic* committees, was for long one of the most wanted men in India. The outfit also claimed responsibility for the 1986 murder of General A.S. Vaidya, chief of army staff during Operation Blue Star.

Another group, the 'Dashmesh regiment', founded around 1982, was believed to be the brain-child of Bhindranwale's close associate Major General Shabeg Singh, a well-decorated Sikh general with wide experience of guerrilla warfare, later cashiered from the Indian army for professional misconduct. Its name derived from the tenth guru, Gobind Singh, who imparted the unique militaristic character to the Sikhs. The 'Dashmesh regiment' was responsible for a number of assassinations and cases of arson and bombings. Several other outfits would surface with the passage of time and due to police infiltration. Some more prominent groups were Khalistan liberation army, Jarnail Singh-Babla group, Mathura Singh group, Roshan Lal Bairagi group, Khalistan armed police (allegedly floated by the police), Khalistan liberation force, Bhindranwale tiger force of Khalistan, Mai Bhago regiment and Mata Sahib Kaur commando force—the last two being women's groups. As police pressure mounted and the ideological content of the movement dwindled, each of these groups would split into several factions. Even Buta Singh, then Union home minister and a major player in the Punjab imbroglio ever since Indira Gandhi's assassination, had an underground outfit of his own called 'Rangreta Dal', *rangreta* in Sikh folklore referring to the Mazhabi Sikhs, a Sikh scheduled caste to which Buta himself belonged. (See M.K. Dhar's recent book *Open Secrets*). One other group, the All India Sikh Students' Federation, which began as a youth wing of Akali Dal and was allegedly involved in many terrorist acts, appeared to have acted more importantly as a breeding ground for extremists than as a pure and simple militant outfit, although it always nursed fairly strong ambitions to finally become a powerful political force.

*

The dismissal of the Barnala government and the import of a police chief from distant Maharashtra in 1987 would seem to mark a clear watershed in the history of militancy in Punjab. The new Director General of Police, Julio F. Ribeiro, a former police commissioner of Mumbai, with a well-earned reputation for controlling the crime mafia in that metropolis, was the personal choice of the then Union minister of state for internal security, the portly Arun Nehru. Not realizing that Sikh militancy could not exactly be compared to Mumbai's mafia crime and that it enjoyed, at least until then, considerable community support and approval, the new DGP set about outlining his priorities through some controversial public statements, among them his infamous 'bullet for bullet' assertion that won him a lot of dubious publicity in the media. Whether such rash assessments also led to the triggering of a more destructive wave of terrorism after 1986 remains a matter of debate among political analysts. What is, however, clear is that the subsequent months did witness a phenomenal escalation in terrorist violence.

According to a news agency (UNI) report dated 1 January 1988, for instance, more than three persons, on an average, lost their lives daily in the year 1987, recording an unprecedented casualty figure of 1,216 during the year. Official data revealed that terrorists killed 822 civilians and 97 policemen, while 327 terrorists were killed by the security forces. As against this, 520 civilians, 42 policemen and 78 terrorists were killed in the previous year. The month of July 1987 experienced the height of terrorist violence when as many as 126 civilians were shot dead, including 42 bus passengers near Lalru, close to the state capital Chandigarh, on 6 July. The following day, 32 bus travelers were gunned down in neighbouring Haryana. In the stepped up anti-terrorist drive, while the security forces apprehended 3,687 terrorists and eliminated another 327, the police too lost 71 officials, including two IPS officers.

A report carried by the widely-circulated weekly *India Today* of 30 April 1988 by Inderjit Badhwar painted an alarming picture of the Punjab situation during the first year of central rule. 'Punjab continued to hold the nation's attention all of last fortnight in a vice-like group', the report ruefully stated. 'As President's rule in the strife-torn state tumbled into its eleventh month, and even as the killings multiplied relentlessly, the government seemed to be drawing up a new game plan. It announced the release of more militants from prison and asked security forces to play a low-key role for a while in the worst affected areas. Central ministers and home ministry officials rushed back and forth between Delhi and Chandigarh for urgent meetings. The questions being asked most often were: How serious is the government in implementing a workable policy in Punjab? What is the result of prolonged central rule in the state? Are the militants 'on the run' or have they regrouped with fearsome firepower? What is the role of jathedar (high priest) Jasbir Singh Rode?'

*

Jasbir Singh Rode, who liked to be known as Jasbir Singh Khalsa, was Bhindranwale's nephew and one of the many close relatives of the late Sant who suddenly surfaced in the Golden Temple soon after the Akalis came to power in Punjab and went on to occupy important positions in Sikh religio-political sphere as a corollary of an undercover operation undertaken by the intelligence bureau (IB). Jasbir had disappeared after Operation Blue Star and was brought back to the country by intelligence sleuths after an extended chase across several foreign lands. He was now suddenly released and anointed as the jathedar of Akal Takht, a position of immense prestige in the Sikh tradition. Obviously, the authorities hoped to use him as an intermediary to open a dialogue with the militants, a hope that was soon to turn into a nightmare for the security forces, when Rode started playing dubious games of his own. This clumsy attempt at manipulation of the Akal Takht and its jathedar for unspecified and dubious ends was one of the many moves that were made by a powerful and heterogeneous group in the Delhi establishment, backed by the abundant resources of the IB, either ignorant of or unconcerned about the history of the Sikhs and the character of the militant movement at that point of time. Little wonder that most such moves backfired.

The attempt to open a window to the movement through Rode was a continuation of the tactical line pursued by the Centre all along, intended obviously to keep the moderate Sikh leadership out of the reckoning in the political field. With a youthful and impetuous prime minister in Delhi still to fully grasp the political and administrative intricacies in ruling a vast heterogeneous country, his minions in Delhi and Chandigarh continued to stumble from one inept step to another amidst unending political and bureaucratic intrigues. As for Jasbir Singh Rode, he had obviously been in touch with Zail Singh, then the Union home minister, for several years. M.K.

Dhar, then a senior IB officer closely involved in its Punjab operations, recalls an instance of May 1981, when he was asked to contact a close relative of Bhnidranwale and bring him to Delhi to meet Zail Singh. 'I picked up young Jasbir Singh and a personal aide to Jarnail Singh (Bhindranwale) from Shardulgarh on the Haryana border and drove them straight to the official residence of the home minister. They were back with two fat shoulder bags. I was asked to drop them at Mansa near Bhatinda. I did my job with the characteristic silence of a deaf, dumb and blind intelligence officer'.[4] Dhar terms the authors of most such bizarre moves as 'the immature political kids and bandits in Delhi, who played with the Punjab fireballs during Indira Gandhi's second tenure, as well as Rajiv Gandhi and his corporate whiz kids.'

In his recent book *Operation Black Thunder*, Sarab Jit Singh, who had a ringside view of the events at that critical juncture as the deputy commissioner of Amritsar, vividly describes the shadowy goings-on in the Golden Temple at the time, including the appointment of Rode as Akal Takht Jathedar and the excessive trust reposed by the Centre in his ability to reach out to the militants to find a way out of the tangled web of Punjab militancy. Apparently, Sarab Jit Singh was ignorant of the long-time links between Rode and the then Union home minister.

*

Several other so-called peace moves were also in progress simultaneously. A Jain holy man Muni Sushil Kumar claimed to have met and negotiated with many extremist and militant leaders over the years, starting with Bhindranwale himself. He also maintained that his peace campaign enjoyed the full backing of prime minister Rajiv

Gandhi himself, no less. However, his moves too came a cropper. An embittered Muni later revealed: 'The reason nothing happened is because some people who will lose power and standing in Punjab just do not want solutions...The militants who were backing the violence are now opposed to it. So you have to ask who is now committing it' (in an interview published in *India Today* of 30 April 1988). He also made some other startling disclosures questioning the anti-militant policies and objectives of the Indian establishment.

However, a very different take on Sushil Muni is provided by M.K. Dhar, who claims to have been asked by Rajiv Gandhi to liaise with Sushil Muni in his peace mission:

> I met the Muni at his illegally constructed ashram on government land at Shankar Road. In cahoots with Buta Singh the Union home minister, the Muni had roped in Tarlochan Singh Riyasti, a veteran politician, for influencing a section of the terrorists. I gathered a clear perception that Sushil Muni was not loyal either to the PM or the HM [home minister]. He was loyal to himself and was angling for three steps towards nirvana: money, membership of the upper house of parliament and a Padma award...Riyasti gave me to understand that he was in touch with a young group of Khalistanis and they were ready to meet the PM. To my horror, I discovered that Riyasti had not even discussed the "operation" with the prime minister. In fact, he was not allowed by Buta Singh to meet Rajiv Gandhi and insisted that he should operate only through Sushil Muni...I was directed to bring the militant leaders to Delhi for a meeting with the PM...I reached Bhatinda at about 1 a.m. with two departmental officers and a

professional friend...My rendezvous with Riyasti was
fixed for 4.30 a.m. at a park frequented by morning
joggers.

To cut the story short, Dhar and Riyasti were able to meet
a group of hard core militants including Atinderpal Singh,
later to get elected to India's parliament, Gurjit Singh,
another nephew of Bhindranwale and chief of the Damdami
Taksal-backed AISSF, Avtar Singh Brahma, chief of
Khalistan liberation force and Gurdip Singh Bhatinda, a
follower of Jasbir Singh Rode, the incarcerated jathedar of
the Akal Takht. It was an impressive gathering. Atinderpal,
suspected to be involved in Indira Gandhi's assassination,
Brahma, wanted in several cases of mass killing and then
holding sway in the 'liberated' Mand area (*liberated* in the
sense that the state or central writ had ceased to run in the
area) of Majha and Malwa regions of Punjab and Gurjit
Singh, another nephew of late Bhindranwale and regarded
as the linkman between the militants and the ISI. Dhar
took them to Delhi for a 'peace meeting' with the prime
minister, where they were lodged in secured rooms of
Sushil Muni's ashram. As Dhar recounts the story:

> The Muni...wanted to interact with the youths. They
> refused. Later a suggestion came that they should
> meet Buta Singh, the Union home minister. This too
> was turned down...Sushil Muni called me aside and
> offered me a cash incentive and requested me to
> convince the youth to meet Buta Singh at least. Avtar
> Singh Brahma rejected my half-hearted proposal on
> the plea that they had no intention to meet a low
> caste Sikh. I was given to understand that the PM
> was keen to meet the youths and initiate peace
> talks...He was not against the idea of reaching a
> limited accord with the terrorist youths brought to
> Delhi...The jam lock was somewhat broken after it
> was agreed that Satish Sharma, an aide to the prime
> minister along with director, IB, would meet them. I

don't think the arrangement had pleased the home minister...The discussions conducted in the presence of Sushil Muni were not intended to evolve a clear contour for future talks...It was agreed upon that Tarlochan Singh Riyasti and I would meet them at an appointed place and date somewhere near Ludhiana. Gurjit also demanded an initial financial grant of rupees two million and it was agreed upon that the amount would be delivered at Ludhiana.

The whole exercise, code-named 'Operation Needle', would come to a tragic end when Riyasti and his driver were burnt alive in their car at Ludhiana as Satish Sharma, the PM's pointsman in the operation, refused to play the game. 'Riyasti flew down to Delhi to collect the money. He waited for two days. I shuttled between my bosses and Riyasti and was finally directed to see Satish Sharma. He hummed and chummed for a while, produced a lot of cigarette smoke and finally managed to hang a smile on his face and tell me that the prime minister was not aware of any such deal.'[5] Dhar would probably have met the same fate if he hadn't declined to go with Riyasti to Ludhiana as planned. The details of the terrorists' secret visit to Delhi to meet the PM, it seems, had reached one of the *panthic* committees through Rangreta Dal, the underground outfit launched by Buta Singh, then the Union home minister. The alarming situation in the border state had, by now, acquired a much more ominous aspect, because of the determined efforts by Pakistan to compromise the loyalty of the Sikhs, who provided the bulk of Indian troops in all Indo-Pakistan wars.

*

Surely, there must have been many other individuals or groups engaged in the so-called peace moves in the strife-torn state, not all driven by the best of motives, because of huge financial and other stakes involved. Some of them must also have enjoyed the support and patronage of top Indian leaders. Evidently, none of these moves met with much success. There was, therefore, no respite for the people from escalating violence from both sides—the state as well as the militants. We may turn again to M.K. Dhar, who was then engaged in a major undercover operation through Jasbir Singh Rode, for the reasons why all such moves failed.

Essentially, all peace initiatives were doomed from the start due to the limited vision and trivial political goals of the petty men who had been catapulted into positions of power and authority. With the local administrative and police hierarchy completely sidelined and all decision-making processes dominated by a few persons in Delhi and Chandigarh, the region continued to slide into anarchy and chaos. Delhi was fast losing credibility as most of its actions were viewed as insincere and devious, stemming from disjointed decision-making mechanisms, reminiscent of a Byzantine court.

Dhar states, 'The appointment of Satish Sharma as the pointsman was a big blunder. His knowledge about Punjab was limited to the accented Punjabi he spoke...An apolitical politician, Satish Sharma was more interested in gathering more than sufficient hay while the sun shone...Buta Singh could not be blamed for possessing the uncanny but catty sixth sense. That was the essence of his survival game in politics...As if Satish Sharma, Buta Singh and Sushil Muni were not enough to spoil the broth...the Punjab Governor, Siddharth Shankar Ray, was keen on trying his Calcutta days' Naxal elimination experiment. A section of the state police and administration too was opposed to the idea of losing a lucrative means of earning extra bucks at the cost of human misery. Some of these elements connived with a section of senior Delhi politicians and stiffly opposed the idea of negotiations with a nephew of Bhindranwale...A section of officers in the Intelligence Bureau too opposed the operation. This group of IB officials was aligned to the action plan of home minister Buta Singh, Governor Ray and the police chief K.P.S. Gill...In fact, Rajiv Gandhi's control on the divergent elements was minimal. He did not work on a centralized blueprint for his latest peace initiative and his political and bureaucratic brains trusts were not unified under one single command.'

As regards the Punjab police and administration, he thought that the top command and the various links in between firmly believed that 'brutal repression was the only remedy to contain acts of terrorism. In the process, they indulged in planned and unplanned killings of innocent youths. They detained the villagers informally and extorted money for releasing them. Even women were not spared'.

A sizeable section of the intelligentsia in Delhi and the Punjab had already come to believe that the authorities were simply not interested in a peaceful solution. However, as for Dhar's Jasbir Singh mission, his description of the nitty-gritty of an undercover operation makes interesting reading. He showed extraordinary persistence and perseverance in pursuing it until the end despite many setbacks and obvious opposition from important wings of the government. That the PM was unable or unwilling to maintain his control and interest in the project is hardly surprising, because he chose to surround himself with some of the most Machiavellian and self-serving individuals of contemporary times, whether in Delhi or in the states. The sharp rise in terrorist crime in the period after 1988 at the time when all these peace missions were underway can at least partly be ascribed to several conflicting forces pursuing different agendas and patronizing different militant groups and *panthic* committees. Then there was the all-powerful Punjab police, whose counter-terrorist strategies centred heavily around brutal repression and extortions wherever possible. Also, what is the guarantee that all the deadly weapons personally supplied by Dhar to Jasbir did not find their way into militant hands? The clashes that resulted from the arming of Rode would soon lead to Operation Black Thunder, with which we will deal presently.

*

Around mid-April 1987, which also marked the first anniversary of president's rule in Punjab, *India Today* carried a rather disquieting report about the militant situation there.

> ...notwithstanding the near commonplace occurrence of killings, Punjab had arrived at a watershed of sorts. A time of reckoning. Even Punjab's central rulers seemed to be overwhelmed by a sense of failure, perhaps, that matters were just too big for them all of a sudden. It had seemed so simple only six months ago. Terrorism had seemed to be just another numbers game. You catch them, you eliminate them, cross out their names on the police's terrorist roster and there will be less terrorism. *Bullet for Bullet.* Those were the days of an innocent wild west approach. Ray was the quintessential governor ordering his chief marshal, Julio Ribeiro, his Matt Dillon, to do battle against outlaws in Doge city. But Punjab is a hard taskmaster. It has little or no tolerance for lone rangers or verbal swashbucklers. It is perhaps this realization that has sobered both Ray

and Ribeiro. The Punjab police chief with the powers of a field marshal does not any longer offer brash statements about his successes. He now likens the fight to that in Ulster. And Ray, who had the terrorists on the run only last December, says, 'We have a long way to go. The killings are going up. Between 1980 and 1986, terrorists across the world, excluding Punjab, killed about 4,000 people. Now consider Punjab's record during the past year, since the imposition of President's rule about 2,000 innocent people have been gunned down by killers. This year, in just three-and-a-half months, some 750 people have fallen to terrorist bullets. And as the attacks grow larger and larger, official records show that terrorists with Chinese made AK47 assault rifles, have gunned down about 115 innocents in the last fortnight alone.

Even by official estimates, the terrorists were in possession of a formidable arsenal. In early 1988, it consisted of a range of armaments far in excess of what the terrorist groups had ever had. Among the victims of militant violence were two IPS officers, a state service SP and many other policemen. Extremists had set up parallel governments in some areas and were subverting the normal administrative structure through a social reform movement, while the authorities watched helplessly. President's rule had fared no better on all these counts than the Barnala government, dismissed by the Centre a year ago. Structurally, nothing had changed, only the performance had deteriorated to a grim degree. Not only had militant violence scaled new heights and police corruption and atrocities on citizens rose enormously, several areas of Tarn Taran, Patti and Harike on the Amritsar-Ferozepur border and parts of Gurdaspur and Kapurthala districts had passed under the control of parallel governments, where no government functionary dare defy the militants' diktats. Despite the presence of some 1,00,000 paramilitary personnel in the state, over and above a combined strength of Punjab police, home guards and special police officers also touching the 1,00,000 mark, Punjab officials viewed this area as de facto terrorist territory, where the government writ did not run.

The developments in 1987–88 defied all predictions made by political and bureaucratic busybodies, who claimed to speak on behalf of the central government. The new police chief had declared in May 1987 that peace would return to the state with the elimination or capture of 36 'A' category and 170 'B' category terrorists. That year, Punjab police and central forces killed 338 suspected terrorists and captured several thousand more, yet the killings continued with impunity. Later that year, the official list of top terrorists had swollen to 500.

The response of the administration to a virtual collapse of the state was hardly reassuring. Apart from the frequent visits of the Punjab Governor to Delhi, sometimes twice daily and the Union home minister's air-dash to Chandigarh every other day, all the feverish activity produced no substantive operational plan. In the meanwhile, the police and security forces responded to the crisis in the only way they were accustomed to. Fake encounters, kidnappings, disappearances, even extortions, became rampant as politicians panicked and bureaucrats were sidelined. The public had now to bear with multiple oppressors both from the militant ranks and the police. The militant groups, operating under various *panthic* committees, were rapidly reorganizing, acquiring more deadly weaponry and safe houses and building a chain of gurudwaras, in memory of militants slain by the police in (fake) encounters, along the Pakistan border for better logistical support. Such memorials attracted hundreds of Sikh devotees to participate in periodical ceremonies to pay homage to killed militants. Militants used such gatherings to induce young Sikhs to join their ranks and support their cause. Not until most militant groups turned plain and simple criminals, indulging freely in murder, extortion, rape and worse, did the community disown the militant cause and deny them the required help and cooperation. Free and plentiful flow of intelligence would now gather momentum by the day and despite numerous instances of lawless conduct by the police, the community simply refused to provide any more support to the terrorists, now turned criminals, leading in a few years to their virtual collapse. But more of this later.

*

As the end of the decade drew near, administrative and political disarray became even more glaring, the state police growing more and more unaccountable and resorting to rampant killings of innocent persons and branding them as terrorists. Even the Governor had become overly tolerant of the daily reports of brutality and extortion by the police in the name of fighting terrorism, a pretext that could justify the violation of all norms of legitimacy and propriety. In complete mockery of law and propriety, the Governor would often seek to gloss over even clear cases of lawlessness by the security forces on the plea that they were engaged in fighting the nation's war against separatists and secessionists. The police had also succeeded in silencing the print media and most human right activists. Not many retained the courage to report instances of police brutality and corruption and risk being charged with harbouring terrorists and possibly being eliminated. Even then, several such cases found their way into the media. The Governor's office was flooded with petitions alleging disappearances and false arrests.

The type of stories freely doing the rounds would have been more than enough to shake any sane person out of his still-lingering belief in the rule of law and the power of the state to render just and fair relief to the victims of police high-handedness. Some samples may be quoted. An army major comes to Chandigarh for vacation. There is a midnight knock on his door. He is arrested without being charged and taken away by a CRPF (Central Reserve Police Force) contingent. For two weeks, neither his family nor the army knows his whereabouts. Or a Sikh man from Kolkata visiting his home village in Punjab after five years is picked up by the police on account of a family dispute. He is lodged in jail and charged with harbouring terrorists.

Selective persecution of well-off persons had become a means of extorting money by a force that had virtually no checks on it. As the terrorists and police fought their desperate battles, the difference between right and wrong, law and lawlessness, vanished. Frequent reports of encounters, published in the media, claiming the elimination of wanted terrorists, only evoked skepticism and derision among the people. Two examples typical of such encounters were reported by *India Today* of 30 April 1988: A CRPF party shot dead Sukhwinder Singh of Khyali village in Amritsar district on 21 November 1986, his wedding day, because the taxi he had hired did not immediately respond when asked to stop. The driver stated that Sukhwinder and his friend Ajeet were gunned down as they alighted from the taxi a hundred yards from the CRPF picket. On 23 August 1987, contractor Sardool Singh, 35, while riding a scooter in Amritsar city, accidentally hit an old woman and tried to run away. Police officer Baldev Singh was passing by. Sardool Singh was caught and bashed up badly by the escort party accompanying Baldev Singh. In the melee, the sten gun of a policeman went off accidentally, killing one of his colleagues. This was enough for the policemen to shoot down Sardool Singh there and then. True to tradition, the police tried to pass off the incident as an encounter and Singh as a terrorist carrying a countrymade pistol. A magisterial enquiry, however, did not uphold the police version, one of the rare cases in which a magistrate dared to disagree with the police claims in those days of unrelieved police raj.

Quite often, some so-called 'dreaded' terrorist alleged to have been shot dead in a fierce encounter in which huge monetary rewards and medals had been disbursed would be found alive after several years, living a normal life. One such case reported in the *Hindustan Times*, New Delhi, of 18 February 2001, related to one Gurnam Singh Bandala, a top-notch terrorist alleged to have been shot dead in a daring encounter in July 1994. Gurnam Singh resurfaced in 1998, much to the embarrassment of the police top brass, especially as hefty cash rewards and police medals had been doled out for the 'encounter'.

*

As the situation continued to deteriorate, the authorities grew increasingly clueless about how to deal with the problem. One plan called for the re-induction of the army. Senior army commanders, however, viewed such a move as disastrous both for the army and the people of Punjab. Apart from the fact that the required number of army divisions, estimated at about seven, could not be spared at the time in view of the commitments in Sri Lanka, any further engagement of the forces in Punjab was likely to reopen the still raw wounds of operations Blue Star and Wood Rose of 1984, inflicted by an insensitive administration. The prospect of a hostile peasantry in the state was unacceptable to the Indian army, which had always received immense support from Punjab villagers in all Indo-Pakistan wars. The induction of the army on an extensive basis was, therefore, not considered a desirable option, though a sizeable army presence could be provided to supplement the police effort. Such a back-up force would prove extremely helpful later in overcoming the terrorist challenge. According to a top army commander, who also served a term as the Punjab Governor, it was these units which actually laid ambushes in the countryside, killed the terrorists spotted in these operations and delivered the dead bodies to the police for fulfilling legal requirements and letting them also claim credit and rewards for the work done. For this, the police had to devise a peculiar mechanism for claiming cash rewards, which were paid out of secret service funds, not out of the budget head for the purpose, and the dead bodies of alleged militants were not reckoned as encounter casualties but shown as deaths in inter-gang clashes.

It is not as if the political and police leadership was unaware of such furtive and illicit dealings of the security forces. Both the so-called supercops, Ribeiro and Gill, were known to have explicitly endorsed such lawless practices as the only effective way to control terrorist violence. Ribeiro stated in an interview to *India Today* of 15 September 1988, 'In fighting this undeclared war in Punjab, what matters is tracking down killers.' His successor K.P.S. Gill followed the same dictum, only he did it more ruthlessly, openly and without caring for political or bureaucratic approval. If reports are to be believed, he had secured a complete carte blanche from the highest political authority in the land to take whatever measures he considered necessary to eradicate militancy from the state. Ribeiro said of Gill, when the latter was an additional DGP with him, 'He preferred to chase the terrorists and I left this work entirely to him. He was a good organizer and a good operations man, but he did not understand the essence of terrorism, at least at that stage of the conflict.'[6] Whether Ribeiro understood this essence any better than Gill remains a matter of debate. What is obvious, however, is that the two 'supercops' who led the Punjab police during those critical times pursued strategies that tended to promote a culture of illegitimate, brutal and possibly venal policing among their subordinates. Whether they were also able to root out militancy from the region or succeeded only in eliminating the current crop of militants remains unclear. The assassination of Beant Singh, probably the most heavily-guarded Punjab chief minister in living memory a few years later, would seem to indicate otherwise.

*

With the Punjab situation showing no signs of improvement and the national media upbraiding the administration in no uncertain terms for its failure to either control militant violence or rein in the security forces, the motley group of politicians and civil servants surrounding the now somewhat more confident prime minister decided to replace the much-lionized upright 'supercop' from Maharashtra with another high-profile chief, imported this time from the north-eastern state of Assam, apparently against the advice of the former. The new chief's record of service in his parent cadre of Assam testified to his ruthless pursuit of objectives, even though the methods employed may not always have measured up to the accepted legal and procedural norms. In the kind of situation then obtaining in the state, such qualities were viewed as a vital asset and just the kind of value framework that the Punjab police chief must possess. To make the change less unpalatable to the incumbent DGP, Julio Ribeiro, he was kicked upstairs as an adviser to the Governor, an arrangement that often proved creaky, due mainly to the conflicting approaches to counterterrorism strategies between the new DGP, K.P.S. Gill and Ribeiro, now technically his superior. Punjab Governor Siddharth Shankar Ray, a former chief minister of West Bengal, who prided himself no end on ruthlessly finishing off the Naxalite movement in his home state in the 1970s, of course, fully endorsed the new DGP's no-holds-barred approach in counter-militant operations. He also went out of his way to defend his chief of police, even when the latter was clearly in the wrong, as, for example, in the notorious slap-on-the-backside episode in Chandigarh, involving a senior woman IAS officer. When the victim of the DGP's advances approached the Governor for redress, he is reported to have tried to put her off on the plea that the police chief's indiscretions needed to be glossed over 'as he was fighting the nation's war against terrorists and secessionists'. However, when she pressed her complaint, Ribeiro was asked to conduct an inquiry, in which the latter was reported to have recommended some minor action against the DGP. The non-acceptance of Ribeiro's report by the Governor led to unseemly controversies and court cases. The victim had to finally knock at the lofty portals of India's apex court to seek justice as the lower courts or the Chandigarh police would simply not record her complaint against the all powerful 'supercop'. For obvious reasons. The apex court finally convicted the 'supercop' in August 2005 but waived off the jail term for some strange reason.

It was not only the masses who felt threatened by the activities of a lawless police—even judges, magistrates and senior IAS officers were apprehensive of their safety and well-being.

*

Although the Indian authorities found no dichotomy between the requirements of the rule of law and the tactics, now freely and widely adopted by the police and allied forces, there were some honourable exceptions. Quite a few senior IPS officers of the Punjab cadre, who had held some very sensitive appointments in the past, remained sidelined throughout this period because of their principled resistance to the DGP's mode of tackling militancy. At least one of them later distinguished himself as the director general of police in another critically terrorist-affected border state. Another officer of the rank of inspector general on deputation to Punjab, by all accounts one of the finest IPS officers in the country, asked for a transfer after making his differences with the new DGP public. His services were later requisitioned by the national human rights commission of India, after his retirement from service, as an inquiry commissioner. However, the majority of Punjab officers, especially those belonging to the state police cadres, went along with the boss. Many of them would later face judicial censure and prosecutions for unlawful and improper conduct.

However, all such infringements of law and service codes of conduct were then viewed as necessary and unavoidable in the long-term interest of peace and order. Anyone trying to lay too much store by legal and human rights obligations of the police was summarily dismissed as an impractical visionary, grossly ignorant of the compulsions of 'hard' policing. Gradually, as the philosophical distinction between the means and ends in combating terrorism disappeared, so did the differences in the public mind between police parties and terrorist gangs. Senior police officers, whether in executive or other positions, were routinely accompanied by large contingents of armed constabulary, who were alleged to often extort money from villagers on some pretext or the other. Even the central paramilitary forces were not free from this malady. In at least one reported case, the security personnel deputed with a district police chief would visit a village at night posing as militants to collect large sums of money for the cause, then visit the same village the next day, this time as police and threaten the luckless villagers with an encounter death for harbouring militants, unless they paid up to buy peace.

Countless victims of police oppression and corruption, especially in the countryside, were doing the rounds of newspaper and human rights offices with their gory tales, but most such groups had already been terrorized into silence by an all-powerful security apparatus. It was left to a few media persons in Delhi and other parts of the country to bring to light the reign of state terror in the Punjab. It would only be much later that the shocking nature and scale of atrocities, extortions, disappearances and kidnappings indulged in by the police and central armed forces in those dark days would become public through investigations by human rights bodies and later by the CBI, on directions of the supreme court.

*

By the middle of 1988, the law and order situation in the Punjab had, indeed, assumed an exceedingly alarming dimension and the Golden Temple had once again become the hub of militant activity, despite strong presence of police and CRPF pickets all around as well as atop some surrounding high vantage points, thanks largely to the confused and knee-jerk policies of the central government, swinging between hard blows and soft-pedaling. The so-called peace moves initiated by IB sleuths and sundry political operators to bring the militant leadership to the negotiating table through ill-conceived and badly executed schemes in search of a political solution, had caused only confusion and uncertainty among the security force. It was under such circumstances that a decision was taken to launch another sanitization operation, this time without involving the army. So four years after the botched army operation, the police and paramilitary forces, including the specially-trained National Security Guards (NSG), launched an operation to neutralize the militants holed up inside the Temple and called it Operation Black Thunder.

Comprising of two phases, starting with Black Thunder I in May 1988, the operation comprised of laying siege to the Temple complex and cutting off water and power supply to force the besieged militants, through both physical and psychological pressure, to give up their resistance and surrender or die of hunger and thirst. Since no entry into the complex by the security forces was envisaged, there was no risk of hurting the feelings of the community. Unlike the 1984 operations, full transparency was ensured by telecasting the whole operation live and allowing the media to freely cover the episode, factors that were to prove immensely beneficial in the long run. More than 150 extremists surrendered in two batches on 15 and 18 May.

It is another matter that Black Thunder also marked the end of the ill-fated undercover operation of M.K. Dhar, involving the installation of Jasbir Singh Rode as the Akal Takht head priest and provision of sophisticated arms to him by the central government through the IB in the hope that Jasbir would then be able to neutralize the militants taking refuge in the Temple. It seems that the CRPF, a central paramilitary force, then under the command of DIG S.S. Virk, frustrated the Dhar mission, inadvertently or otherwise, by opening fire at the militant positions just as the arms consignment was about to reach the Jasbir outfit. Dhar recalls:

> Operation Black Thunder had started in all earnest after S.S. Virk took the final decision on his own to lead a reconnaissance party to a spot to the Western flank of the temple where the terrorists were ostensibly constructing new defences above the 'prasad ghar' located between the main gate of the temple and the remaining edifices of the Akal Takht... But the CRPF commander did not strategically plan the unfortunate incident that had sparked off the war shots and killed the peace process. There was no command from the top (Delhi) to resist the militants from raising defences above the 'prasad ghar'. The decision to lead the reconnaissance party was taken by the DIG CRPF.[7]

Since Dhar's undercover operation was not in the domain of public knowledge, Black Thunder was generally acclaimed as a grand success with the media carrying highly laudatory accounts of the manner in which the entire manoeuvre was planned and executed in complete transparency, with the Punjab DGP Gill receiving fulsome praise for his leadership qualities. There were some discordant notes though from some Punjab officers but more notably from the NSG, which probably felt somewhat sidelined in the apportionment of credit. Ved Marwah, then director general, NSG and later to become Governor of Manipur and Jharkhand states, claimed that Black Thunder was entirely an NSG affair, conceived and executed entirely under his personal command. Marwah's references to the then Punjab DGP, K.P.S. Gill, in his very readable book *Uncivil Wars*, are pointedly critical:

> The whole Operation Black Thunder was conceived and planned entirely in the NSG, though the help of the CRPF was taken in the initial phase to guard the parameter outside the complex. The outside force was also replaced later by the NSG special rangers groups. The Punjab police was asked to take charge of briefing the media, but were not involved in either the planning or the implementation of the operation. Their help was also sought to make the announcements on the loudspeakers for the devotees to come out of the Temple complex during the announced hours. (p.191).

Again:

> The NSG officers were operating under the direct command of their own officers. K.P.S. Gill protested, as according to him, he was the overall commander of the forces deployed there and should have the final authority to decide how an operation should be conducted. He was again told that since the task had been entrusted to the NSG, he should leave the job to them. He was not satisfied and the matter had to go to the prime minister for a decision. The PM drew a command chart in his own handwriting. The force commander of the NSG was to continue functioning directly under the director general NSG, who, in

turn, was to function under the home minister's control and direction' (p.192).

In order to press home the point regarding Gill's credibility ratings with the prime minister, Marwaha further elaborates:

> George, PS to the PM, rang me at night to summon me to the PM's House. He also let me know that the PM was in an angry mood. I was a little surprised because the PM should have been very pleased with the outcome of Operation Black Thunder. I rushed to the PM's house and as I entered the conference room, even before I could greet the PM, he asked me to go to George's room and issue orders to the NSG officers in Amritsar that they should continue their physical control of the Temple complex and not allow K.P.S. Gill or any of his officers inside the complex till further orders. I tried to say something, but he cut me short and told me to first do what I was told and then do the talking. After issuing these orders, I returned to the conference room. P. Chidambram [then minister for internal security] was already there. After I sat down, the PM asked me under whose orders K.P.S. Gill had been allowed to enter Harminder (sic) Sahib. (p.191).

Marwah also attributes the success of some other anti-terrorist measures like operations Night Dominance and Mand to the active participation of the NSG. Sarab Jit Singh, the then deputy commissioner of Amritsar, has his own views with regard to the conduct of this operation, as evident from his book *Operation Black Thunder*. This is natural as in a situation of this kind every participant would look at the affair from his own particular perspective.

M.K. Dhar, whose somewhat fanciful undercover project of arming Jasbir Singh Rode and raising an undercover contingent from Punjab's border districts to battle militancy under his command had become a casualty of Black Thunder, was understandably a bitter man. He would record many years later, 'Indira Gandhi...had allowed her maverick son and political fortune hunters like Zail Singh to play with a flaming paraffin ball called Jarnail Singh...Bhindranwale. Rajiv Gandhi had allowed another Sikh fortune hunter to meddle into the affairs of Punjab. His Home Minister Buta Singh did more harm to the nation than promoting its security by application and non-application of his contorted mind to the woes of the people of Punjab.'[8]

The achievements of Operation Black Thunder, however, proved to be transitory as the powers that be in Delhi and their minions in Punjab were simply too incompetent to consolidate the gains. While AK-47 assault rifles had become the militants' principal weapon of offence by 1987, after Black Thunder, the militant arsenal became even more lethal. For one, improvised explosive devices (IEDs) had greatly improved since the days when the Babbar Khalsa group started using their crude versions. Later, several groups would take to the use of highly sophisticated remote-controlled timer devices as well as anti-tank gadgetry and land mines, in the process considerably refining their tactics to outwit the police, which was increasingly resorting to undercover practices to undermine their credibility with the community. The militants would often use fake identity cards to conceal their identity, acquire safe houses in big cities and cultivate the underworld for such services as money laundering. The number and ferocity of extremist acts also rose alarmingly, especially those committed at night in rural areas. The army was now redeployed in bulk in the

Punjab and apart from acting as a back-up force, it was given the task of laying ambushes on all the possible vantage points on the rural link-roads, which provided safe passage to the militants and which were so far deemed to be off-limits for security forces. These ambushes would account for the bulk of militant casualties in 1989-90. Not that these operations were about to sound the death knell of militancy. In 1989, 846 incidents of militant violence were reported in which 1,168 persons lost their lives.

*

The state police and its chief K.P.S. Gill had acquired a larger than life image and role in the state administration, emasculating all state organs and political processes that could have exercised some check on the police and other security agencies. All the prescribed accountability mechanisms had been rendered ineffective as neither the state chief secretary nor the district magistrates had any control over the police. S.P. Bagla, a senior Punjab cadre IAS officer, stated in an interview to the *Tribune* on 10 June 1995, 'Since 1985, I cannot recall any chief secretary really having regained the position as head of the administration. There was a parallel man all the time, who was above the chief secretary and who did not care about the chief secretary or the home secretary or the district administration...or even the chief minister.' In a joint statement, published in the *Tribune* of 3 August 1991, the secretaries to the Punjab government protested that 'the police were perpetuating violence in the state and that...civil servants holding inquiries into complaints of police excesses were afraid of submitting their reports, apprehending danger to their lives'.

There were other voices too expressing similar views. A former IAS officer of the Punjab cadre, an officer of impeccable credentials and competence, who took over as chief secretary to the Punjab government as part of the reshuffle in senior ranks, consequent upon the Akali party assuming office in September 1985, draws pointed attention to the many distortions and deviations that characterized the administrative processes during the period when the police was enjoying almost absolute power in the state. Just one sample may be reproduced here: 'In the very first week of my joining this office, a panchayat of a certain village came to me complaining about the alleged killing of two innocent Sikh boys by the police. I asked the concerned deputy commissioner to make an inquiry immediately and report. The following day the SSP [senior superintendent of police] of that area came to my office and said, 'How can we function well in a situation, where the directives received by us from our top officers are contrary to what you expect from us?' (translated from Punjabi).

This view was further borne out by what Joyce Pettigrew noted later, 'Law and order is normally an individual state matter but in the Punjab law and order issues are controlled by Delhi. Elimination lists were drawn up not by the DGP but by the director general (Punjab) intelligence, who took his orders from the Intelligence Bureau.'[9] Julio Ribeiro too noted that (K.P.S.) Gill wanted complete control over all units including the national security guards but this had been denied to him. The IB director (M.K. Narayanan) and P. Chidambram (minister for internal security) felt that all important decisions should be taken in Delhi.'[10]

Matters came to a head in August 1992, when the police took two senior Punjab civil service (PCS) officers in custody in Jalandhar, accusing them of hindering anti-militant operations. This was a most unusual occurrence as Indian law invests these officers with powers of executive magistrates and authorizes them to hold magisterial inquiries into grave lapses of the police such as custodial deaths and professional misconduct. In a rare instance of its kind, the PCS officers went on strike and submitted a memorandum to the state Governor on 28 August 1993, citing as many as ten specific instances of police misconduct and asking for the constitution of a judicial commission to look into the massive growth of militancy during the last few years vis-à-vis the role of the police. The memorandum ended with three specific demands: the police should not be allowed to interfere in the working of other departments; the police must recognize the primacy of magisterial powers vested in the PCS officers under various laws such as the criminal procedure code, the Indian police act and Punjab police rules and the failure of any police officer to comply with magisterial orders be viewed seriously and disciplinary action taken against such officer[11].

However, the Punjab DGP was no pushover. More often than not he was able to hold his own despite determined efforts by a small group of busybodies from the Intelligence Bureau (IB), the home ministry and the political establishment, close to the prime minister, to sideline the Punjab supercop during that fateful period. Even the Punjab intelligence chief was reported to be closer to the power structure in New Delhi than in Chandigarh. In a kind of quid pro quo, he was later appointed as Governor of a north-eastern state. Though this was by no means a solitary case, IB officers were being increasingly considered for post-retirement gubernatorial assignments, which many viewed as a calculated effort to subvert their professional objectivity and integrity.

True to tradition, the ruling cliques did not feel overly perturbed even when the citizenry was writhing under unprecedented police corruption and *zulum* (atrocities). The Indian state has always taken the easy way out when faced with critical law and order situations, it simply turns a blind eye to police misdemeanours so long as the accusations can be managed in a discreet manner. The moment, however, they get out of hand and pose a danger to the ruling establishment itself, it would promptly drop the offending officials like so many hot bricks and from then on, the concerned officers would be left to fend for themselves. That is why all those officers who sought to pass off unremitting brutality and sleaze as the only effective way to end militancy were hailed as heroes during the worst years of terrorism but hauled over the coals when the full extent of police lawlessness was uncovered through the efforts of civil society and rights groups, often at the cost of their own lives and liberty.

The marked concern shown by the higher judiciary in bringing the guilty to book helped enormously in exposing the real face of the so-called police achievements. As pointed out by John Alderson, an outstanding former British officer, in his very readable book *Policing Freedom* (1979), 'In applying the law, the police officer has to have regard for the legal and ethical rules which restrict his or her powers. It is a contradiction in terms for a police officer to act illegally since he or she is appointed to uphold the law. There are particular problems in relation to the arrest, detention and questioning of people, since the police are often under pressure to achieve results, but it cannot be emphasized too strongly that no police officer is expected to act illegally to produce results. Such restrictive procedures which the law imposes are not impediments placed capriciously in the path of the police, but safeguards of individual rights and liberties, which the police exist to protect. Unethical and illegal conduct erodes the self-respect and reputation of the police, both individually and collectively, and should be studiously avoided' (pages 235-6).

*

Late that year, there was a change of government in Delhi. The new Prime Minister V.P. Singh, a grossly over-rated individual and politician, walked out of the Rajiv Gandhi ministry, accusing the prime minister of corruption in the purchase of defence stores from a Swedish firm, and rode to power on the strength of a dubious political agenda that would cause deep and lasting fissures in an already fragmented Indian society. Leading a rather discordant coalition, the new prime minister embarked upon a number of populist measures of doubtful efficacy to cope with the worsening situation in Punjab, in the process adversely affecting the overall situation in the troubled state.

The confusion and indecision prevailing in Delhi would soon get replicated in Chandigarh and Amritsar, leading to a considerable rise in militant violence. In the year 1990, 2,467 persons were killed in 2,116 incidents of extremist violence, including as many as 493 policemen and members of their families; more than three times of those killed in the previous year. Officials of other government departments like teachers, judges and magistrates too were freely targeted. 149 improvised explosive devices (IEDs) were used in 1990 as against 48 in 1989 and 34 cases of sabotage of railway track were reported that year as against only 10 in 1989. Firing in crowded places had become more common now to create panic among the minority Hindus. 289 persons were killed in 64 cases of multiple killings in 1990; as against 47 in only 3 cases in 1989. Massive acquisitions of sophisticated weaponry by the militants also came to light.

Among policemen killed was the controversial superintendent of police Gobind Ram, who was killed when an IED planted in his office in the high security PAP campus, was exploded through remote control. Such deep penetration by the militants caused widespread panic all over the state. Gobind Ram, not particularly known for possessing a high sense of integrity nor for much regard for legal niceties and propriety, had enjoyed the support and confidence of DGP Ribeiro, who planned to use scheduled caste officers to contain the largely Jutt-led militancy, because of their traditional antagonism to each other, a plan that had to be hastily abandoned when it created a host of problems of a different nature. As the police chief in Batala and Faridkot districts, Ram got embroiled in some serious acts of lawless conduct and corruption. He was also allegedly involved in the torture of the wives of Babbar Khalsa leaders Mehal Singh Dasuwal and Kulwant Singh. His name was, therefore, high on the militant hit-list.

At this point in time, the terrorists' arsenal comprised of a formidable inventory that included AK-47s, AK-74s, AK-94s, GPMGs (general purpose machine guns) light machine guns, and even rocket launchers. They were able to lay landmines and fairly efficient ambushes against vehicles, carrying police and security personnel. They could use remote control devices to detonate IEDs and operated in larger groups. On 6 June 1990, the sixth anniversary of Operation Blue Star, some 25 militants stormed Sarhali police station in Amritsar district, using rocket launchers and machine guns.

On the other hand, the militant movement was also getting fragmented. By 1988, there were as many as three *panthic* committees controlling different militant groups, although the five-member committee of Dr Sohan Singh would retain a measure of primacy until the end. Khalistan commando force (KCF), which had built up a dedicated and reasonably well-trained cadre, had again emerged as the most active group. Other outfits active at this time were Khalistan liberation force (KLF), Bhindranwale tiger force of Khalistan (BTFK), Babbars and Khalistan liberation organization (KLO). Some smaller groups comprising of lone rangers or pure and simple criminals were also operating in the guise of militants. Then there were other gangs also consisting of bad characters, crooks, felons and former militants, floated or patronized by the police. A peculiar situation now obtained in the state where it was well-nigh impossible to differentiate between a 'genuine' militant group from criminal gangs, or which particular group was taking the help of the police to harm a rival or was purely the creature of the police. The police seemed to have successfully penetrated most militant groups, apart from setting up some of their own gangs and 'armies' like the infamous Alam Sena, believed to be raised by and named after superintendent police Izhar Alam, allegedly close to both Ribeiro and Gill. In some cases, these pseudo-militants would later turn against their mentors. At least one district police chief was shot dead by one of these supposedly counter-militant gangs.

*

When faced with grave situations of militancy and extremism, security agencies all over the world seek to criminalize and penetrate the movement, a common enough tactical weapon for the containment of violent anti-state activities. The Punjab police would increasingly take to this stratagem as militancy peaked in the late 1980s. The ruling establishment was either not taken into confidence or was left with no option but to coolly accept whatever the police chief suggested as necessary and expedient for the purpose of controlling growing militant violence. A member of the *panthic* committee suggested that 'the Indian government has criminalized the movement...these elements are encouraged by the government or are even government infiltrators. They try to come inside and destroy the movement.'[12] The practice of planned induction of criminal elements into militant groups and using seized or surrendered militants as spotters initiated by Ribeiro, who thought there was nothing unusual about the use of undercover agents, was perfected by his successor K.P.S. Gill. The latter believed that 'the security forces in Punjab can do nothing without special spotters' parties and there is no question of doing away with them.'[13] The spotters or cats, as the media called them, were contacts or associates of militants, who were recruited by the police to help them identify the former. They accompanied police parties during raids and ambushes and whenever such parties came across a suspected militant, they pointed them out to the police. Conceivably, not all such identifications were above board, and very often innocent persons would get caught. The police would then put the detained person through prolonged periods of hard and brutal interrogation, regardless of age, sex or social standing. Not many persons caught in the net could ever hope for freedom, except on payment of a hefty sum. Those who survived the virtual torture chambers in Amritsar and Ladda Kothi near Patiala, officially notified joint interrogation centres, came out as virtual cripples and were liable to be called again and again for similar treatment.

Then there were special units raised by every district police chief for such undercover activity with the full approval and support of the DGP and presumably the Governor and the small coterie around the prime minister. As noted by Pettigrew, these special units were recruited from those 'dismissed for their involvement in criminal activity. One of these units was particularly infamous, the Alam Special Forces, so called after the then SSP Amritsar, Izhar Alam. All district police chiefs had such special units at their command'. Further, 'Ribeiro's separate police squads were an early attempt at counter-insurgency and worked imperfectly as they were organized by the Punjab police. Many of their operations were revealed by the Punjab police. Thereafter, the BSF and the CRPF protected the government's counter-insurgency plans.'[14] Ribeiro did not deny his role in promoting either the criminalization of the militant movement nor the practice of recruitment of spotters and special forces. He, in fact, fully justified both these strategies (see his book *Bullet for Bullet*, pages 348-349). He also provides graphic details of some cases including those relating to Izhar Alam's 'cats'.

In the early 1990s, stories abounded in both the English and vernacular press about criminal gangs operating mostly in the rural areas. These gangs came to be known as *kale kachhianwale*, as their members pursued their business clad only in black underwear. The media reports hinted that these gangs too were working for the police, because whenever they were caught by the villagers and handed over to the police, the latter would invariably set them free. Later, the villagers started handing them over to army units or, in some cases, just beating them to death.

This account will remain incomplete without referring to at least one such undercover operator, inspector Dalbir

Singh, one of the first and the most notorious of such police officers, who operated out of uniform and would become such a menace to the department in subsequent years. He rose from obscurity to win the trust and confidence of DGP Ribeiro and supposedly remained his favourite as long as he lived. Dalbir had been under suspension for a long time for professional misconduct, when he approached Ribeiro though intermediaries, promising to accomplish something spectacular in countering the rising tide of militancy, if reinstated. True to his word, he did perform remarkably well for some time, though often acting outside the four corners of law and propriety. He was then inducted into a special unit after being given two out-of-turn promotions, a jeep and two bodyguards armed with sten guns. Unofficially, two more cars had also been gifted to him. Posted in Patiala district with no fixed duties, his jurisdiction extended to all of Punjab and even nearby states. Given that kind of freedom from accountability and the support of the DGP, he soon developed other interests such as extortion and robbery, even going to the extent of becoming a gun for hire, sought out by rival gangs of smugglers of Punjab and Jammu to kidnap and terrorize opponents. *India Today* carried an article on Dalbir Singh in its issue of 15 September 1988. Ribeiro even felt that his death had created a vacuum, which would be difficult to fill.

When questioned about his mounting illicit activities by his handler, the district police chief of Patiala, inspector Dalbir Singh got so worked up that he gunned him down along with another police superintendent in a police station at Patiala, before shooting himself dead. One can be sure that several officers with poor records of service would have exploited credulous senior officers, desperate to impress the top bosses in Chandigarh and Delhi with their achievements in the anti-militancy area, and having won the confidence of the top brass stray into blatantly unlawful activities under the guise of battling terrorism and militancy, in the process freely lining their own pockets. That is why most people believe that efficiency and effectiveness in South Asian police forces is largely a matter of making compromises with legal requirements, procedural propriety and due process.

Let us turn to Joyce Pettigrew for a candid description of how the police carried out their counter-militancy operations during the period of heightened militant violence, aimed primarily at effecting widespread criminalization and fragmentation of the movement. We have already referred to the covert activities of sundry undercover players like the spotters, black cats and *kale kachhewale* gangs, some of whom joined the militant ranks to weaken them from the inside, others committed outrageous offences in their names to defame them in the eyes of the community so as to undermine their support base. This end was achieved by leaving tell-tale notes written on forged or stolen letter-pads of the militants on the spot of the crime. No prizes for guessing what purpose was sought to be achieved through such a ploy. As Pettigrew observes:

> They (the police) would issue statements on behalf of the militants. They had set up their own area commanders throughout the Punjab...give them prominence in the newspapers, saying, he has killed so many. Thereby they would keep on increasing the reward on his life that they can claim...Frequently, when these groups or organizations have been formed their alleged leaders are already in custody. They would nominate one of them as a Lieutenant General, say he has been killed after a while, and then claim

the reward money...Latterly, they have simply threatened the relatives of the boys, taken them hostage, then approached the boy, built him up, made him popular and left him in place for a while to collect information, paying him 5,000 rupees per month, but holding his relatives in custody for security.'[15] All such devious and shady transactions were accomplished through a hard core of inspectors and deputy superintendents, given quick out-of-turn promotions and promised huge monetary rewards and gallantry awards, although several middle-level IPS officers too were drawn into the unsavoury business, a few for the sheer heck of it, but largely out of baser motives. Many made newspaper headlines for using brutal force on hundreds of detainees regardless of age, gender or social standing, taken in custody on suspicion or on the basis of *source* reports. Shocking interrogative practices became more widespread as the established system of police accountability weakened and disappeared. Some of them, now in the rank of additional directors general, who spoke to me on condition that I don't identify them by name, were quite candid about the extent of functional independence they enjoyed and how proud they were of their director general, who cared for no state functionary, governor and chief minister included. Several well documented accounts of the unspeakable atrocities inflicted on the citizens by the police in the name of battling militancy during that gruesome period are now available.

Thus fighting the prolonged *undeclared war* with the militants with all sorts of devious and foul means, defying the police code, not only generated state terror and victimized the innocent citizen but also gave rise to indiscipline in the already *spoiled* Punjab police...The

Punjab police...developed vested interests in the perpetuation of violence. So much so that two attempts on DGP Mangat's life were organized by the police, although he was not guilty of any atrocity. This rule of violence not only enriched the police economically but also enhanced its political and administrative clout in the name of security of the state and its personnel...It got the licence to kill anybody, anywhere under suspicious circumstances. No inquiry commission or civil liberties group could get punishment for an erring officer (sic). But whatever happened, the DGP Gill would get him released in the name of keeping up the morale of police fighting the undeclared war.[16] (See also appendix at the end).

It may be mentioned that D.S. Mangat of the Punjab cadre had briefly replaced Gill as DGP during the short-lived rule of prime minister Chandra Shekhar. Understandably, Gill's predecessor in Punjab, Ribeiro, was not particularly supportive of Gill's handling of his subordinates accused of using excessive force against suspects and detainees. He scathingly refers to at least one such incident in his book *Bullet for Bullet* to prove the point. It relates to the highly unruly behaviour by a CRPF platoon in a Gurdaspur village, which had considerably perturbed the Barnala government. 'They (CRPF men) went round damaging the doors of the houses, and even entered some of them and belaboured the women...I recommended the prosecution of the jawan who had bitten a woman's ear and departmental punishment to the platoon commander. K.P.S. Gill was then the IG of the CRPF. He was not willing to take any action against his men. He approached the home ministry in Delhi to ensure that sanction was not accorded for criminal prosecution. Finally, the government of India did not sanction the prosecution...This was not the first time that Gill had

332 Identity and Survival

thwarted my attempts to discipline the CRPF'.

While faulting Gill on this score, Ribeiro conveniently overlooks his own role in sustaining and defending the age-old tradition of South Asian police forces for adopting harsh and brutal measures when confronted with serious law and order situations. For many historical and other reasons, the Punjab police took to practising what is commonly called hard policing from the very beginning, which left a long-term imprint on its operational modes in the times to come. Ribeiro seems to have lost no time in getting sucked into the Punjab police sub-culture. That is why unscrupulous officers like Gobind Ram were able to catch his eye so soon after he took over as the state police chief and indulge in some of the worst transgressions of law and propriety in the name of controlling militancy. The issue of troop morale in the Indian armed forces has often been the subject of widespread debate in the country and many a malefactor has escaped due retribution because of the false notions of morale and *esprit de corps*. Ribeiro's tenure as DGP Punjab is generally hailed by the media as marking the restoration of police morale in the state, although it actually coincided with a period of heightened militant activity that now enveloped the entire region.

Although a number of shocking episodes of police brutality and corruption in the conduct of anti-terrorist operations had been finding their way into the media by 1988, thanks to a few plucky journalists and human rights activists, the full impact of the reign of terror let loose by the Punjab police and central security forces during the years of total police dominance would become known only after the democratic processes were restored in 1992, then too in driblets. Sat Pal Dang, a highly reputed communist leader of long standing and generally viewed as a dependable ally of the police in the fight against militancy, too spoke out in 1994. 'It is an irony that the most superior officer of the law-enforcing authorities himself encourages the development of a lawless situation in the state. This leader of policemen has not been able to get rid of the extra-legal methods used during the fight against militancy, even during the time of peace'.[17] Dang had expressed much the same views in a meeting with me in Amritsar a couple of years earlier.

*

The Week newsmagazine published a special report in its issue of 25 January 2004, titled 'Cashing in on terror: On the sleazy art of making money in troubled times' by Vijay Pushkarna. It brings out the frightening contours of counter-terrorist operations by Indian security forces in Jammu & Kashnir, Punjab and the north-east. The portion on Punjab, charmingly called *A bloody harvest: Reaping the whirlwind was not so bad*, says:

> In one sense, the first to cash in on the Punjab militancy were politicians. They fanned the fire until it spread out of control. Analysts still maintain that Zail Singh, as Union home minister, encouraged the fire-spewing Jarnail Singh Bhindranwale, to irritate his party rival Darbara Singh, who was chief minister. Later, the Centre and the Akalis used the situation to blackmail each other. But cashing in happened in the literal sense, too. For one, there were big prices on the heads of militants. The police picked up young men at random; if two out of ten were genuine terrorists, eight probably were not. If three out of these eight innocent men were killed, five others paid a hefty ransom to be freed. The police began to smell of money or rather stank of it. One inspector in

Jalandhar built a house with a swimming pool on the terrace. A journalist who thought he had landed a scoop asked the then director-general of police about it. 'Are you talking about X?' he asked. It was an open secret. Super-rich cops were the norm rather than the exception. After the assassination of Indira Gandhi, politicians began paying protection money to terrorists. So did industrialists, who preferred this to seeking police help. 'We have paid both parties; in fact even three or four parties at a time,' said an Amritsar-based automobile agent. If one group collected the money promising protection, the other killed the protected person. This was to do with inter-group rivalry.

The racket flourished when the Punjab was under President's rule from 1987 to 1992. People paid to get out of the police's clutch. Sukhdev Singh Babbar of the Babbar Khalsa built a palatial house in Patiala. Others bought *benami* property in Punjab and helped relatives migrate to foreign countries. Many 'terrorists' used the situation to get political asylum abroad. Not many police officers were accused of having extorted people. But many earned countless awards by killing wanted terrorists. In his book *Politics of Genocide: Punjab 1984-98*, Inderjeet Singh Jaijee says that 50,000-60,000 awards were given to the police in 1991-1993. The annual outlay for awards for killing listed militants was Rs 100 million. There were unannounced awards for killing unlisted militants. He calls the award, which varied from Rs 40,000 to Rs 5 lakh, a 'cash for corpse' scheme. There was also a secret fund, used to cultivate sources who would give the correct tip-off, leading to a successful encounter. There was no proper auditing of these secret funds. In 1997, the British government informed India that many Punjabi cops had property in the United Kingdom. They made the purchases mostly during the years of militancy. The periphery of Chandigarh was full of farmhouses belonging to the relatives of police officers and bureaucrats. Terrorists had their agents. Electricians and mechanics helped them make improvised explosive devices for a fee. Ordinary men and women became couriers. The press got its share, too. Many reporters based in Chandigarh made a killing by breaking 'sexy stories' of terrorism to newspapers and agencies around the world. There is some truth in the allegation that even after terrorism died, newspapers kept it alive on their pages. When peace was restored, it was the turn of the human rights activists. Of course, there were some who were genuinely concerned about human rights. But others were in it for the money. They got the families of many who were killed in police action to move court and wrested part of the compensation. The end of terrorism was literally the end of a multi-crore industry, which left quite a few unemployed. The Gurdaspur police, in March 1998, busted a gang of dacoits which had killed a truck driver and cleaner, and looted 360 bags of cement. They were all former terrorists. They said they were forced to become dacoits because *they had lost their means of livelihood.*

*

Despite all the various measures, lawful and unlawful, overt and covert, adopted by the state police and hordes of security forces inducted into the area, many hard core militants were still very much active in the region and would remain so right into the early 1990s, In fact, it was during this period that they sought to revive the social reform movement of Bhindranwale vintage in a big way, issuing open threats to those who failed to observe the codes of conduct laid down by various *panthic* committees. They even made the use of Punjabi mandatory in all official work in the state secretariat, in addition to the lower rungs of administration, where it was already in practice, even delineating the diction and format of the language. By a decree issued on 3 December 1990, Dr Sohan Singh's *panthic* committee directed that Punjabi be used in all government and non-government offices, including educational institutions. The detailed memo covered some thirteen pages and laid down twenty-two points for observance. Apart from describing the steps necessary for the implementation of the directive, the document stressed the need for the development of a more *beautiful* Punjabi. As illustration, it suggested that:

> Punjabi must not be loaded with Sanskrit or Hindi words in any way...when we fail to find Punjabi equivalents of English words, then we must exercise utmost restraint in going towards Hindi or Sanskrit terminology. An English word should be adapted as such if it could be suitably absorbed in Punjabi...If this is not possible, then we must turn towards Urdu and Persian...Some people under the influence of Brahmanism translate (the word director) as *nirdeshak*, which is completely wrong and will not be tolerated.

Other edicts issued by the various *panthic* committees sought to regulate various social, economic and political activities, as for example, the giving or taking of dowry, ban on wearing saris and use of *bindis* and *sindoor* by Sikh women and girls, singing of the Indian national anthem in schools and other institutions and imposing certain conditions on banking operations in Punjab or 'the land of Khalistan' as they termed it. They also imposed their own seven-point code of censorship to counter the government's directives to the media against carrying advertisements and press releases of the militant organizations. Needless to say, all these directions were scrupulously carried out by all concerned.

In the meanwhile, extremist violence continued unabated. Policemen and their families now became special targets of their attacks. This was obviously meant to demoralize the force so as to ease police pressure on the militant groups, a design that seriously backfired. For it would give the entire police force a personal stake in the eradication of what had now become a looming hazard to every policeman and his family. A report in the *Hindustan Times*, New Delhi dated 11 June 1989 noted that guns continued to boom in the countryside, and 'Peace is still a far cry in the villages of the three borders districts—Amritsar, Gurdaspur and Ferozepur. Even in Faridkot, Hoshiarpur and Kapurthala, the situation is no better. Mass killings that were so rampant in 1988 and early this year, in the wake of the hanging of Indira Gandhi's assassins; have given way to kidnappings and extortion. Hired killers are having a field day as both the Sikhs and Hindus migrate from isolated farm houses to villages and from there to the islands of relative peace, the cities. Those unable to shift either pay up the terrorists or get killed'. Seven security men had been gunned down in an encounter in Tarn Taran. Murder of bus passengers in Batala and five members of a family in Ferozepur were among other depredations. Villagers also continued to be caught 'between armed bands of underground terrorists by night and over-ground looters represented by a section of uniformed men by day'. As a senior IPS officer admitted, 'people are not with the militants, but they are not with the police either'.

9

The Beginning of the End

Even as the end of the 1980s decade drew near, any prospect of restoration of normality in the state seemed to be fading fast. Despite relentless state terror and induction of a record number of central paramilitary forces, the possibility of an early end of militancy and violence looked grim. This had the authorities deeply worried. K.P.S. Gill was brought back to head Punjab police once again around 1990. Even he was of the view that militant violence was not likely to be fully contained in the near future. Outwardly though, the authorities claimed that the security forces had acquired a definite edge over the terrorists. Actually, this was not an incorrect reading of the situation in the long-range perspective in view of the fact that by the end of the year 1990, the movement had clearly become starkly fragmented and criminalized and appeared to have run its course, although the militants were still capable of pulling off some spectacular strikes. The community too had grown disillusioned and fed up with their mutual bickering and internecine clashes, more so because it was now virtually impossible to distinguish between genuine militants (*mundas* or *babas* in common parlance), plain and simple looters and police-sponsored gangs. Many over-ambitious members among the militant ranks were open to exploitation by the police, which would play upon their egos and desire for fame to make them desert their groups and engage in killing each other. Gurbachan Singh Manochahal of the Bhindranwale tiger force of Khalistan (BFTK), for example, was reported to be close to a central cabinet minister. He was also the first to walk out of Dr Sohan Singh's *panthic* committee to form his own.

Pettigrew believed that the BFTK collaborated with the police, which utilized Manochahal's services all along in return for allowing him to operate freely in the Tarn Taran area. He was not eliminated until February 1993. This was not the only case of its kind. There were others like Manochahal used by the police and then discarded and eliminated. Then there were groups created by the police itself like the Khalistan armed force of Shamsher Singh and the Khalistan liberation army of Bhai Kanwar Singh. That is how most counter-insurgent strategies are pursued all over the world.

Despite some spectacular successes achieved by the security forces, the militants still dominated the rural areas at night. This was countered by the security forces through a new operational plan called Night Dominance, actively supported by the army. When this proved inadequate, the army was requisitioned once again in strength to supplement the central paramilitary forces, already deployed in substantial numbers, in addition to the Punjab police. A massive new operation with the help of some 38 army divisions, code-named Rakshak, was now launched to cope with the still sizeable militant challenge in the countryside. Large-scale ambushes on village link roads and extensive siege and search operations succeeded in defeating any possible attempt at revival of militant activity. By the end of the year 1991, Sikh militancy appeared to have reached its nadir, having fallen prey to avarice and cupidity of the worst order. The scale of infiltration and criminalization of the movement had reached a point of no return, and although the five-member *panthic* committee of Dr Sohan Singh, now almost a permanent resident of Pakistan and the ISI tried to breathe new life into the fragmented and failing movement, the militants were clearly on the run.

Another significant factor that hastened the end was the propensity of the Jutt militant elements not to accept subordination in whichever sphere they worked. So, every militant leader of any consequence would set up his own separate militant group and *panthic* committee so as to retain a position of supremacy or *sirdari* in the new outfit. If in the process the police managed to manipulate the mutual rivalries to destroy the entire movement, so be it. The beginning of the end of Sikh militancy was now clearly perceptible and it was only a matter of time before it was defeated by the superior might, infiltration techniques and intelligence resources of the state; but more so because the militants now trained their guns against their principal support base, committing outrageous offences like murders, rapes and extortions against members of their own community. The gory tales of their misdeeds found frequent exposure in the media. One widely circulated Jalandhar daily, whose proprietor Jagat Narain was one of the first victims of the then rising tide of Sikh militancy in 1982, carried scores of such news items. Others were understandably more discreet and kept their peace. They also carried out the militants' directions in various ways. The police used every trick of the trade to sow the seeds of suspicion and hostility in the public mind and turn the bulk of the Sikh people against the militants, thus depriving them of their hiding places and safe houses.

Though the situation was still grave, the police was well on its way to gaining an upper hand. There were 71 killings in September, 84 in October and 60 in November of 1991. The flow of arms and ammunition continued through the Rajasthan and Gujarat stretches of the Indo-Pak border with the ISI as a major facilitator, though most such supplies were in the nature of commercial transactions. The ISI also helped coordinate the activities of various factions through the three groups based in Pakistan, namely Wassan Singh Zafarwal (KCF), Satinderpal Singh (ISYF) and Babbar Khalsa's Mehal Singh and Wadhawa Singh. However, there seemed little likelihood of a major resurgence of militancy in the state, because of widespread cynicism in the community about the motives and activities of the militants.

Despite huge seizures of weapons, including 539 AK series rifles, 34 rocket launchers, 22 carbines, 324 rifles, 380 guns, over 1,600 kg of explosives and large quantities of ammunition from the terrorists by the police in 1992, a Punjab intelligence report estimated that even in April 1993, the militants still held a total of 1,543 AK-47's, 106 rocket launchers, 112 general purpose machine guns and several quintals of explosives, a formidable arsenal indeed. The number of hardcore and non-hardcore terrorists operating in Punjab and elsewhere was put at 144 and 963 respectively. Fresh recruitment and realignments were also taking place, especially in the ranks of Khalistan liberation force (KLF), Khalistan commando force (KCF) (Panjwar) and Babbar Khalsa international (BKI). Although government agencies claimed to have sealed the borders, militants still managed to smuggle over 400 AK-47 rifles, 60 revolvers and pistols and 8 quintals of explosives. Even so, the bulk of the militant leadership appeared to have been either eliminated or forced to escape to Pakistan. This development, combined with holding of legislative, municipal and panchayat elections in January 1992, September 1992 and January 1993 respectively, led to a definite abatement of fear psychosis in urban areas. The rural population too was breathing easy with militant terror having faded. However, the villagers were not completely out of the woods, as they had to still live with a police force grown even more lawless and atrocious during the years of virtual freedom from external control or internal accountability. By April 1993, militant violence had practically died down and the people of Punjab were deservedly in a celebratory mood, gauged in that fun-loving state by the huge rise in the sale of liquor and other intoxicants. The extent of the lawless and oppressive behaviour of the police and security forces during that dark period was also gradually being exposed in the media. Soon, the scale and magnitude of police malfeasance and rights violations would be brought before the higher judiciary by media persons and civil society groups for adjudication.

Militant violence continued to escalate until the middle of 1992 after which it just petered off, rather inexplicably, although some groups still seemed capable of regaining their firepower and logistical ability to strike at soft targets outside the Punjab. As late as February 1995, an influential industrialist was kidnapped from Jaipur, capital of the neigbouring state of Rajasthan, by the Khalistan liberation front led by Navneet Singh Khalsa. This time, however, in a swift operation, clearly indicative of the complete police command over the situation, not only was the victim rescued in a short time; Khalsa was also shot dead. Some militant elements fled to other parts of the country, probably hoping to resurface in the future to mount a fresh challenge. The KLF, the KCF (P) of Paramjit Singh Panjwar and BKI of Wadhawa Singh seemed to have survived in a sufficiently intact position to present a considerable potential threat.

Indian intelligence sources reported that Sikh militants were still being recruited in large numbers from abroad by Pakistani agencies and trained in the handling of weapons and sophisticated explosive devices for infiltration into India with a view to setting off violent and subversive acts in important commercial and economic centres. However, the eruption of serious sectarian conflicts in Karachi and other parts of Pakistan as also the latter's total involvement with the Kashmir issue somewhat limited its active sponsorship of Punjab militancy, though, of course, it did not fully cease. Babbar Khalsa will resurface in a significant manner from time to time to stage surprise attacks on vulnerable targets. As late as June 2005, a couple of cases of bomb blasts in two Delhi cinema houses, showing a film to which some Sikh organizations had objected, led to the unearthing of quite a few dormant militant modules in Punjab and Delhi. Militant leader Jagtar Singh Hawara, the master mind in the conspiracy to kill Punjab chief minister Beant Singh in August 1995, who had later escaped from a high security jail in Chandigarh, was nabbed from a Punjab village in this connection. The police claimed to have secured much useful information from him in respect of the future plans of the still surviving Sikh militant organizations. It remains to be seen how far this will help forestall any recrudescence of Sikh militancy.

*

Sikh militancy in its earlier, roughly pre-1987 phase, could be regarded as a politically-inspired separatist movement, marked as it was by many of the well-defined militant features. Gradually, however, the movement became more and more susceptible to penetration by criminal elements and police agents, leading to a severe loss of focus and ideological purity. This set off a process of its slow but sure degeneration into pure and simple criminal terrorism, which would make it far easier for the police to devise effective strategies for its eradication than if it had retained its original character. Its relapse into criminality also turned the people against it. The flow of intelligence improved and soon became a torrent. Toning down of material and logistical support by Pakistan under international pressure (its major attention now diverted to Kashmir), sealing and fencing of the Punjab-Pakistan border and determined action against smugglers, drug-traffickers and their supporters, all contributed to the neutralization of this major challenge to the Indian state, arising out of a resolute Sikh assertion to a sub-national status in the larger Indian nation and the militant spirit that it generated. With the situation showing definite signs of improvement, normal democratic processes were resumed. The Congress was returned to office in the elections, held in January 1992, though on a minority vote, sometimes as low as 10 per cent of the electorate, since the Akalis had boycotted the elections due to some controversial decisions by the Election Commission.

Having gained political power in Punjab, the Congress

soon regained the necessary political will to bring peace and normalcy to the troubled region. Existing laws were amended, new laws enacted to plug loopholes, police allowed to enjoy unprecedented freedom from legal and democratic accountability as in the past, if they would only show tangible results. Viewed in actual terms, this required that the new government continue to overlook the shocking excesses that the security forces were inflicting upon the people in the name of ending militancy. As the people were fed up and the movement had lost its ideological appeal, not many complained. Feeble protests by some human rights and civil liberty organizations were ignored or severely suppressed.

*

Sikh militants continued to operate for some more time outside the Punjab, especially in UP, Haryana, Rajasthan and Delhi, where they were found responsible for 263 killings, including 28 security personnel in 139 incidents in 1992, as against 373 killings including 39 security personnel in 290 incidents in 1991. By the end of March 1994, incidents of militant violence dropped further, as the following table will show, the figures in brackets indicating number of killings:

1993	Punjab	UP	Haryana	Delhi
	74 (67)	34 (46)	10 (7)	7 (10)
1994	Punjab	UP	Haryana	Delhi
	6 (1)	2 (6)	1 (0)	0 (0)

The somewhat abrupt cessation of militant violence following the assumption of political office by the Congress party in Punjab caused a lot of raising of eyebrows in the country as the liquidation of almost the entire militant leadership one after the other looked too much like a command performance. One school of thought would have us believe that Sikh militancy in its later phases, the product chiefly of manipulations by certain powerful interest groups in Delhi and Chandigarh through 'plants', contact men and agents provocateurs, operated by Punjab police and central intelligence agencies, ceased to be of any use to the Congress party, once it was back in power in the crucial border state. So it just mounted more pressure on the security forces to rapidly dismantle the entire militant set-up. Another theory was that the police had earlier managed to deactivate most militant leadership through various counter-militant strategies—and when the government nod came, they just eliminated them as most of them were already in virtual custody. In an intriguing development, the police not only demolished almost the entire militant edifice, which had been a source of widespread terror to the people and the security forces for more than a decade, it also captured and killed nearly all the militant leaders between July and September 1992. Pettigrew lends considerable support to the suspicions and misgivings in the public mind on this score. She alludes to the existence of close linkages between the police and certain militant outfits, primarily the coalition of four such groups then known as *char jujharu jathebandian* or four combative organizations, led by the BKI, then being promoted by the police as the most dedicated militant group.[1]

*

The cessation of militant violence did not, however, provide much respite to the citizens from the terror let loose by an all-powerful police, owing little accountability to any state institution, which greatly augmented the sufferings and humiliations of the people. The district magistrates, who were expected to provide some relief from arbitrary police action under the Indian Police Act of 1861 and Punjab police rules, continued to be sidelined. By having subdued a major militant movement, the Punjab police had apparently achieved what seemed to be an impossible goal only a few years back. Despite a raging means-and-ends debate, numerous individuals and organizations fell over each other to confer sweeping honours and awards upon the state police chief, now immensely enjoying his 'supercop' status and defying all attempts by political and bureaucratic authorities to instill some degree of discipline and accountability in the force that he led. Even the state chief minister felt powerless to restrain the security forces from unruly and arbitrary conduct. Although the police were clearly in full control of the situation by mid-1993, there were some setbacks, by far the most serious being the assassination of the Punjab chief minister in August 1995 at the entrance of the highly-fortified civil secretariat in Chandigarh. The incident once again brought into sharp focus the inbuilt vulnerability of high-profile individuals to fatal attacks from an apparently vanquished militant network, now operating from safe houses in Pakistan and large Indian cities. Obviously, Sikh militants still possessed the ability to successfully penetrate one of the most well-guarded sites in the state capital to strike at a high-status target. Surprisingly, this time no heads rolled despite such a grave security lapse, neither the DG police nor his additional DG intelligence was held accountable. Occasional incidents of bombing of trains, public transport and religious places also continued to occur from time to time.

Unfortunately, the enormous clout that the police

enjoyed during the years of militancy bred in them a dangerous degree of indiscipline, venality, insolence, factionalism, and indiscreet and rude behaviour. A specified uniform symbolizes institutional discipline and conformity in the police and armed forces. In the post-militancy Punjab, there was a singular disregard for wearing prescribed uniform items. Individual police officials had their own versions of uniform articles, often copied from a James Bond or Bollywood film. Fake encounters, disappearances, abductions, extortions and other such unlawful activities that marked police conduct during the militancy years also did not abate even after the end of that phase. It would take a great deal of effort for successive police chiefs to bring back a measure of normalcy in the functioning of the state police.

The generous tributes showered upon the Punjab police and its chief for their singular success in containing one of the world's most lethal militant movements tended to briefly eclipse the magnitude of illegal actions and atrocities committed by the security forces during that dark decade. However, when the full facts came to public notice, there was widespread outrage, revulsion and indignation in India and abroad. For, unlike the police agencies in modern civilized societies faced with similar challenges, Punjab police had openly resorted to extra-legal methods, which could not but leave their nefarious imprint collectively on the force and, of course, gravely traumatize the people. It is not as if the political authorities were ignorant of the misdeeds of their police. In fact, they not only looked the other way when complaints were made to them, their complicity in the manner in which the police performed their duties in the post-1987 phase of militancy, was hardly in doubt.

Indian ruling classes expect their police to transcend

legal niceties and proprieties while engaged in battling serious threats to law and order, rather than change inadequate legal provisions to empower the police to act legally to defend the rule of law. An antiquated system of criminal justice, based on the mid-nineteenth century Police Act and laws of crimes and evidence, is still in force in all of South Asia in the beginning of the twenty-first century, except now with the honorable exception of Pakistan, which has replaced the outdated Police Act of 1861 with another legislation. Numerous malpractices and atrocities that the Punjab police indulged in during the years of militancy were later brought before India's higher judiciary, which would pass severe strictures against several middle level officers, many of whom were later prosecuted for grave offences like murder, kidnapping, extortion etc, generating an extensive debate in the country about the propriety and justification of a police force acting outside the law, even when faced with abnormal situations of terrorism and militancy.

Since the end of militant violence in the mid-1990s, successive Punjab police chiefs have attempted to restore a measure of functional normality in the force and regain the confidence and support of the community. Evidently, it is not an easy task, especially because, over the years, the political classes have become even more irresponsible and reckless in exploiting every possible issue of public importance in furthering their own electoral prospects. Given our politicians' fondness for fishing in troubled waters and the speed with which our law enforcement agencies are being politicized and communalized, it will be nothing short of a miracle if the region does not find itself plunged once again in a situation of acute anarchy and turmoil.

*

The account of counter-militancy operations by the police and central security forces, attempted above, contains plenty of references to the human rights situation in the region during and after the decade of militancy. However, a more focused look at the subject may be in order. Serious violation of human rights and fundamental freedoms of the citizen by security forces, engaged in tackling episodes of grave crime and extremist violence, is generally viewed with some degree of indulgence in South Asian societies. The people of Punjab, for long used to living with an arrogant and overbearing police force, are exceedingly tolerant of many kinds of excesses committed by law enforcement agencies even in normal times. Ordinarily, an aggrieved person would much rather bear with police harassment or corruption than lodge a complaint for fear of reprisals. As for the police, they are only too well aware of the enormous powers they enjoy over the lives and liberty of the citizens, whether under the law or outside it, and their ability to inflict grave hurt on any one, daring to challenge their authority.

During the last hundred years or so, the region has been witness to a string of extremist movements, occurring every ten or fifteen years. This cycle remained unbroken even after independence, when three such episodes took place one after the other e.g., the *lal jhanda* (red flag) insurgency in the late 1940s, the naxalite movement in the late 1960s and early 1970s and the Sikh militancy in the 1980s decade.

Having had to face extremist movements at regular intervals during the last half a century but armed with rather inadequate legal powers to deal with them in an effective manner, the Punjab police devised their own rough and ready methods to meet such threats. As all these three movements used violence as the principal mode of their demand articulation, the police found no difficulty in securing government endorsement for their counter-insurgency strategies, largely drawing upon encounter killings and state terrorism. Interestingly, despite deriving from vastly dissimilar ideological moorings, all three movements also had some marked similarities. For one, the infrastructure and cadre strength in all these movements came from the same stock of Jutt Sikh rural youth. One prominent example of this phenomenon is the legendary Baba Bujha Singh who remained associated with all the three aforesaid movements. He was finally killed in 1981 by the police in what they claimed to be an encounter, but was widely believed to be a custody killing. A number of former Naxalites also became leading members of Sikh militant groups right from the time of Bhindranwale, prominent among them being the Kala Sanghian group and some of the Babbar Khalsa men. All these extremist agitations were suppressed by the police with overwhelming, brute and often illicit force.

Over a period of time, the people of the region had learnt to live with an arrogant and often lawless police and grew overly tolerant of police brutality and custodial violence. Historically, rights activism and advocacy in the Punjab too has tended to be noticeably partisan and selective in nature. In other words, opposition to or condoning of human rights violations by the security forces during the militancy years in Punjab was determined not by the nature and scale of violation per se but by the particular perspective and interests of the group making the judgment.

In a well-researched essay on the incongruent nature of human rights discourse in the context of Punjab militancy and the counter-militancy strategies adopted by the state agencies, Prof. Pritam Singh of Oxford Brookes

University highlights what he calls the mode of articulation of sectarianism in human rights. 'Sectarianism in the politics of human rights in Punjab is articulated through several modes, but what unifies these diverse modes of articulation of human rights discourse is the positioning of human rights not as an end in itself but as a means to an end...The end is determined by the specific needs and strategies of the groups engaged in the human rights discourse. Such groups are aware of the moral appeal of human rights and, therefore, find it necessary, attractive and useful to use the issue of human rights to attain their specific objectives'.[2] He terms this approach to rights advocacy instrumentalist as opposed to what he calls an intrinsic worth style. The latter would, in his view, seek to inculcate a 'moral consciousness' of human rights. He further defines the instrumentalist approach as one in which human rights are merely a tool, which is available to or sought by a political party or any other institution to serve its own narrow interests rather than for the fulfillment of a higher altruistic public purpose. Thus, all the groups that were forced to engage in human rights activities or found it useful so to do during the decade-long militancy in Punjab—political parties, rights organizations or professional bodies—were generally motivated by partisan rather than humane aims.

So, while Operation Blue Star was defended by a large majority of Hindu and Congress-backed organizations, it became a searing trauma for the Sikhs. Similarly, while the brutal repression let loose in the state by the security forces in the name of controlling militancy aroused widespread revulsion and protest in Sikh groups, it was stoutly defended by Hindu and Congress-sponsored bodies, representatives of the so-called nationalist coalition as distinct from those dubbed anti-nationalist or secessionist lobbies by the former. The nationalist coalition viewed all those who questioned the grave violation of human rights by state agencies as traitors working against the unity and integrity of the country. To them, therefore, the whole concept of human rights became marginal to considerably more important issues of beating the forces of separatism and secessionism. If in the process large numbers of innocent people were subjected to unspeakable atrocities, so be it.

Thus, when a non-Congress government in Delhi mooted the idea of transferring DGP Gill out of Punjab because of rampant terror unleashed by his force in the state, Harkishen Singh Surjeet, a top communist leader, wrote a personal letter to the then prime minister strongly defending Gill. He wrote, 'There is no doubt that a section of the police and administration has contributed their bit in alienating the people from the government by their misdeeds...Taking a keen interest in the political situation in the state, I would like to caution (against) any changes in top police set-up at this moment, [as] it will encourage anti-national forces and demoralize those who had courageously come forward to fight against the terrorists'.[3] Writing in his party mouthpiece *People's Democracy* of 11 March 1990, Surjeet even rubbished the role of human rights organizations in the Punjab context. He noted that 'Another force, which is active in Punjab today is that of the human rights organization...It will not be wrong to say that it provides cover to the extremists instead of nailing down wrong actions on the part of the police administration.' Such blatantly partisan and partial approach to human rights in a situation of widespread anarchy and lawlessness, indulged in both by the police and the militants, would prove highly detrimental to the concepts of rule of law and civilized governance.

*

Asia Watch, an esteemed international human rights watch-dog, investigated the rights situation in Punjab during the last phases of militancy. A well-documented report was published by them in 1991 under the title Punjab in Crisis. Their findings make horrifying reading and fully bear out what was common knowledge in the region. 'Members of the Punjab police, the federal paramilitary troops of the Central Reserve Police Force and the Border Security Force and, to a lesser extent, the Indian army have engaged in widespread summary executions of civilians and suspected militants. Many of these executions involve persons who were first detained in police custody and then subsequently reported by the authorities as having been killed in an encounter with the security forces...The frequency with which these killings were reported to take place and the consistency of witness testimony indicate that they are not aberrations but rather the product of a deliberate policy, known to high ranking security personnel and members of the civil administration in Punjab and New Delhi.'

They also found convincing evidence that many of these killings were carried out by extra judicial forces that the police had specially recruited and trained for the purpose. New draconian laws that went against the basic scheme of Indian jurisprudence gave extraordinary powers to the security forces to violate due process with impunity, which actually promoted rights abuse by authorizing them to shoot to kill and protecting them from prosecution for such misdeeds. As in encounter killings, in cases of disappearances too, the victim was first detained in police or paramilitary custody, although such custody was invariably denied by the authorities. Such illegal detentions were believed to be in thousands. Brutal torture of suspects and their family members in custody was common and such inhuman deeds were perpetrated without regard to the victim's age, health, gender or social standing. Young girls and old women as well as old and infirm men were all grist to their mill though, of course, young Sikh men were their special targets. Their very youth was reason enough to attract police suspicion of being militant sympathizers. Family members were arrested in lieu of persons wanted by the police and detained as virtual hostages until the wanted person was produced. All such detentions and tortures were routinely used by the police for bribery and corruption of mind-boggling proportions.

No government that ruled in Delhi during the decade of militancy, regardless of its political persuasion, had any long-term and well-devised Punjab policy. Instead all their actions were determined by political expediency, not the requirements of the rule of law. According to the Asia Watch report, 'Throughout Punjab, torture is practised systematically in police stations, in prisons and in the detention camps used by the paramilitary forces. In virtually every case Asia Watch investigated, persons taken into custody were tortured. Methods of torture include:

- Pulling the victim's legs far apart so as to cause great pain and internal pelvic injury
- Rotating a heavy wooden or metal roller over the victim's thighs. Policemen frequently sit or stand on the roller to increase the weight. In some cases, the roller is placed behind the victim's knees and the legs forced back over it, crushing against the roller
- Electric shock, applied to the victim's genitals, head, ears and legs
- Prolonged beating with canes or leather straps
- Tying the victim's hands behind the back and

        suspending him or her from the ceiling by the
        arms

- Rape, threats of rape or molestation.[4]

Not many individuals and groups possessed the tenacity and courage to challenge an omnipotent Punjab police in an attempt to investigate the gruesome and barbarous episodes that marked the anti-militancy measures at the time and violated all norms of police conduct and severely trashed the laws of the land. Whatever disclosures of police brutality took place were due to the grit and resilience of a few enterprising journalists and writers. Most local human rights activists had been neutralised through various well-known police techniques. The then Punjab top cop was known to react strongly when any state functionary so much as hinted at a judicial or magisterial inquiry. So, when Punjab Governor Virendra Verma directed the deputy commissioner of Ludhiana to hold an inquiry in a case of custodial death, the police top brass expressed strong resentment at the Governor's remarks that 'a section of the police was hand in glove with extortionists and that the police of the state had become corrupt and ineffective'. According to a report in the *Tribune* of 24 June 1990, DGP Gill 'took exception to the comments of the Governor and held that the Punjab police was fighting a war of the nation and calling it corrupt or inefficient was least expected. He said that holding of inquiries into police encounters will demoralise the force and there would be laxity in the war against terrorism.' He had also strongly defended many officers under grave suspicion for corruption and brutality. In the end, it was Virendra Verma who had to make way for a more manageable Governor.

    That several vivid chronicles of the brutality and

lawless conduct of the police and paramilitary forces during that period of unquestioned police supremacy could still be put together is a remarkable tribute to stray individuals and groups, who considered the risk worthwhile, prominent among them being the indefatigable human rights activist Jaswant Singh Khalra. It was Khalra who brought to light the murky episodes of surreptitious cremation of thousands of dead bodies in Tarn Taran and Amritsar by the police and got the supreme court of India to take cognizance of the matter. That Khalra himself was kidnapped shortly afterwards in mysterious circumstances and never found again, speaks volumes about the infinite powers that South Asian police forces are still able to command to settle scores with any one who crosses their path. The higher judiciary would later intervene in a few of the thousands of cases of police high-handedness and lawless conduct, but for all those who lost their lives at the hands of the police and security forces without being arraigned before a court of law, it would obviously be a futile exercise. Khalra's murder case was finally decided in November 2005 by a Patiala court which sentenced six accused police officers to varying terms of imprisonment.

One could trace the course of progressive criminalization and brutalization of the security set-up in Punjab from the time Governors and police chiefs imported from distant parts of the country took it upon themselves to impose their own rough and ready therapies to deal with highly complex existential concerns and sub-nationality claims of a minuscule but valiant and proud community, severely traumatized by the country's partition in 1947. A senior Congress politician from West Bengal, in whose tenure as the chief minister of that state extremist Maoist elements were ruthlessly eliminated, was appointed as the Punjab Governor in the belief that he would deal with the Sikh militants in the same manner. Several inquiry reports by respected international and national level rights groups indicate that he did not belie such a belief. Not that the Punjab police was ever a model of rectitude in its functional modes and standards of conduct towards the common man. Ostensibly indiscreet statements like 'bullet for bullet' and we-will-kill-a-hundred-if-they-kill-one by some police chiefs did not mend matters much and, in fact, went a long way in lending uncalled for legitimacy to the deep-rooted unlawful practices and making an already irresponsible force even more reckless. After the dismissal of the Akali government of Surjit Singh Barnala, the Centre virtually had a free run in the state administration, unencumbered by democratic processes of checks and balances. Draconian laws were enacted but never implemented fairly, impartially and properly. They were useful in the sense that they made detention easier and manipulative, giving a handy tool to unscrupulous policemen to oppress the people and indulge in venal practices.

An alternative method of trial to ensure safety of witnesses could have strengthened the system of justice, but Indian authorities displayed neither the courage nor the initiative to change the procedural laws. Prosecution of militant elements under the existing laws and procedure was impossible, as few witnesses would like to court certain death by giving evidence. Several judges and magistrates were threatened and two were killed. Finding them powerless to meet the challenge, the state allowed the civil and judicial processes to be rendered impotent and gave the police a virtual carte blanche to deal with the situation in any way they thought fit. The removal of formal checks on police conduct opened the doors to corruption and arrogance of the worst type. Once the police acquired total freedom of action and impunity from any constitutional oversight and accountability mechanism, the state was well set on a path of unbridled police rule and the accompanying reign of state terror and police atrocity.

*

Where do we go from here and what does the future hold for the people of the region, especially the Sikhs? A decade and a half has gone by since the end of Sikh militancy, an event that brought a welcome sense of relief and deliverance to the mass of the people after a decade of acute suffering at the hands of both the militants and the police. Life was back to normal, and the characteristic Punjabi élan and verve would soon erase the ghastly memories and travails of the militancy years from their thoughts. Relations between Hindus and Sikhs were apparently on the mend and with the Akalis and the rightist Hindu Bharatiya Janata Party (BJP) sharing political power in the state as well as at the Centre for some five years, Hindu-Sikh tensions seemed to have faded, at least on the surface.

One is not so sure, though, that the subterranean antagonism between them, rooted in the years of demonisation of the entire Sikh community by the BJP's Hindu constituency as Pakistani agents, terrorists and traitors, along with the unredressed wrongs of 1984 Sikh killings, would allow mutual suspicions to completely dissipate. The Punjabi Hindu has not shed his basic prejudices against the Sikhs and their institutions nor has he shown any inclination to soften his resolute rejection of a shared language and heritage. If anything, these traits have become even more pronounced. Secure in the belief that the majority status that they enjoy at the national level will always enable them to speak from a position of strength, the Punjabi Hindus are engaged in a resolute process of religious revivalism for the last few years. Huge temples are being built in cities like Ludhiana and Amritsar and many hitherto uncommon rituals like *rath yatras* are being celebrated with great fanfare. The hard-line Hindutva philosophy of the RSS is being sought to be inculcated not only among the Hindus but attempts are also afoot to suck the rural Sikhs into the Hindutva creed through an RSS front organization, called the Rashtriya Sikh Sangat. Such goings-on do not presage a smooth and tension-free relationship between the two communities but signify a distinct pattern of preparing for possible future confrontations, involving the extremist elements in the two communities. So, the next time around, Sikh militants may not have it all their way; but may have to contend with Hindutva warriors. As for the Sikh concerns that triggered the 1980s militancy in the first place, nothing has changed. The basic grievances of the community remain unredressed with the much-acclaimed Rajiv-Longowal accord of 1985 long since dead and buried. A series of new developments have materially altered the sectarian landscape with all major political parties pulling out all the stops to lure the Hindu voter.

The Sikh killings of November 1984, the desecration of the Golden Temple and the destruction of the Akal Takht and a studied indifference to the resolution of river waters and territorial disputes between the Punjab and its neighbouring states continue to stimulate outrage and indignation in the community in addition to the deep sense of hurt arising from several post-independence developments. The restoration of normalcy in the troubled state should have provided an opportunity for a bold political initiative so as to consolidate the gains of peace and to carefully and sincerely examine the whole gamut of issues that provoked the movement in the first place. The plus and minus points of the strategies that brought to an end probably the most violent and destructive decade in the country's history, had to be carefully evaluated to draw valuable lessons for the future. Unfortunately but characteristically, however, with the restoration of normalcy, all references to innovative solutions ceased, a clear sign of political and administrative immaturity and smugness.

Let us not forget that though militancy and extremist violence have been eliminated, deep-seated political grievances remain unresolved. What was needed was a mature, informed and statesmanlike approach to unravel the root cause of the upsurge, traits in dire need of replenishment in Indian political classes. The mid-1990s ushered in an era of acute political instability in the country, which is likely to further enfeeble the capacity of the Indian political establishment in the foreseeable future to act boldly and innovatively in addressing myriad insurgencies springing from minority anxieties and concerns. In Punjab, an Akali-BJP coalition remained in power from 1997 to 2002, to be succeeded by a Congress government. Historically, the Akalis have always tended to underplay their professed concern for Sikh grievances when in power. It is only when they are out of office that they wake up to the so-called unjust and unfair anti-Sikh policies of the Indian government. However, the Akali party's capacity to effectively voice the aspirations and anxieties of the community remains severely impaired because of factionalism and personality clashes. Parkash Singh Badal, the most prominent of Akali leaders at the moment and several times chief minister of the state, is himself mired in several unseemly controversies and grave corruption charges.

True to type, at any given time, at least half a dozen factions of the Akali party claim the exclusive right to speak for the Sikh *panth*. Then there are factions aligned to, or shored up, by senior Sikh leaders in the Congress, whose main charter revolves around weakening the genuine Akali leadership and boost the extremist sentiment. In the elections to the SGPC held in September 2004 in the Golden Temple premises, Khalistani elements were again in the forefront, raising slogans against the moderate leadership, among widespread reports that the radical elements enjoyed the active support of certain highly placed individuals, belonging to the Congress party, then ruling at the Centre. Anyone who cares to read between the lines would find no difficulty in identifying the source of all such developments in the state. The Indian political landscape has itself been in a state of disarray and confusion for some time, with no single all India party in a position to form a stable government at the Centre and steer the polity through the looming credibility crisis facing the nation...It seems extremely improbable, therefore, that the Indian state is likely to come up with a positive and innovative approach in the matter of management of many modules of minority unrest in the country.

*

In the historical context, violence as a mode of political articulation, has always been considered legitimate in Punjab and, even more so, in the Sikh system of beliefs. The cultural and religious practice attributes a positive value to the use of violence to recover lost dignity and honour and to fight evil. The Sikh religious tradition legitimizes the use of violence provided it has its base in human values. However, humanist militancy may frequently be replaced with martial militancy as an instrument of political protest and agitation in a given set of circumstances. Such conditions came into being in the Punjab of the 1980s. Whether they can revive in another few decades, maybe in a different but no less fearsome dimension, remains to be seen. The Punjab has been witness to several movements in the past, which used violence to build up pressure on the establishment for demand fulfillment and the concerned sections of society responded to them very well. The Namdhari or Kooka movement of 1858 was clearly rooted in militancy and was anti-imperialist in character. The Ghadar Lehr or revolutionary upsurge, which originated in the USA and Canada (1913-18), was also anti-imperialist in nature and mainly Punjabi in composition. Many zealots of the Ghadar movement later joined the *lal jhanda* or red flag communist party and Maoist-Naxalite movements in a few Punjab districts, and continued to use violence as a mode of political discourse. Such an approach also inspired several peasant movements in Punjab. Widespread violence that accompanied independence and partition of the country in 1947 was another affirmation of the long tradition of martial militancy in Punjab.

The Sikh religion, as it developed over a period of some 200 years from Guru Nanak to Guru Gobind Singh, clearly sanctions taking up arms against unrelieved oppression and injustice. This mode of political discourse has always suffused, at least, the subaltern movements, though the decade of 1980s saw it also as a mainstream activity. This can happen again if a serious, purposeful and sincere political initiative does not check the current drift in the Indian polity with regard to the Punjab problem. The roots of such militancy could logically be traced in the relationship of both individual and state violence with the underlying social and political structure. Post-independence ruling establishments proved to be no different from British colonial rulers in promoting antagonistic and assertive communal and religious identities. In the case of Punjab, this worked against the evolution of a secular Punjabi identity. The resultant conflicting relationship between distinct identities, in the context of the partisan nature of politics and lop-sided growth of the economy, has not materially changed and will continue to present an environment for retrogressive violent articulations. Most of the factors which set off the decade-long militancy in the 1980s have not fully ceased to exist.

> The structural reality continues to produce a dwarfed Punjabi identity and a blocked economy, finding it difficult to accommodate emerging agrarian interests and create greater employment opportunities. Politics is not representative, competitive and federal. The absence of conditions for conducive human development paves the way for latent structural violence. The manifest form of violence was shaped by the opportunistic character of politics, underground economic activities, excessive reliance on the repressive state apparatus and, above all, on the external support.[5]

*

Akalis and the Hindu BJP have often come together for electoral battles against the Congress party. In all other regards, however, they vie with each other for political space on communal lines. Any *entente cordiale* between these two traditional rivals is unlikely to withstand the pulls and pressures of the ongoing Hinduization of the Indian polity for long. Also, the BJP has been primarily responsible for systematically impeding the growth of a shared identity in post-independence Punjab. Past experience also shows that whenever these two parties come together, the Hindu electorate deserts the BJP and votes for Congress candidates. This happened again in the elections to the Lok Sabha in September–October 1999 and in elections to the state legislature in 2002. With the Congress party back in power in the state in the elections held in February 2002, the Akalis started flexing their muscles once again to bring the age-old grievances of the Sikhs centrestage. However, extremely fragmented as the Akalis currently are, they are no longer capable of commanding the same degree of following in the Sikh masses as earlier.

Back in power in Delhi since 2004, the Congress has shown no special interest in chalking out a viable road map for boldly confronting the many issues that continue to trouble the Sikhs in the state. In fact, there are fairly clear signs of the resumption of the policies of divisive politics and appeasement of extremist sections in the Punjab that marked the earlier governments in Delhi. This is apt to further make the democratic methods of interest articulation ineffective and moderate politics irrelevant. In resorting to short-fuse strategies to marginalize political opponents and undermine norms of competitive politics by dismissing popularly elected governments, they will be encouraging fissiparous forces as in the past, precisely the sort of policies that are known to have precipitated separatist movements and agitations among the myriad minority groups in this nation of unparalleled diversities and feudal mindsets. According to a political analyst:

366 Identity and Survival

There is no inevitability of either violence or non-violence in the Sikh political practice. Doctrinal invocation to justify the use of non-violence or violence is also dependent upon the politico-economic and historical conditions. There is no clear preference for either violence or non-violence in the Sikh doctrine. After the traumatic period of the 1980s and the 1990s, the moderate tendency in Sikh politics has now regained ascendancy. However, the extremist tendency can re-emerge to prominence if the Sikh people feel that their identity is under threat and that their political aspirations are being thwarted in India...The fact that India has for the first time a Sikh as a prime minister and a Sikh as an army chief since 2004, is symbolic of the changed policy paradigm towards the Sikhs. However, even these significant developments can prove to be merely symbolic if the collective political aspirations of the Sikhs do not find satisfactory accommodation in the Indian political system. That is a challenge the Indian policy makers have to be constantly aware of if a return to the politics of violent conflict has to be avoided.[6]

Encouraging prospects of friendlier relations between India and Pakistan and growing American presence in the region, along with some apparently unrelated but interlinked developments, consequential to economic reforms and revolutionary advances in communication technology, would probably significantly alter the way India addressed and found solutions to the long-simmering discontent agitating its diverse minority groups, claiming a share in political power. Hopefully, such a scenario may also induce the Indian establishment to engage in some creative stocktaking to find mutually acceptable responses to Sikh discontent. As of now, unfortunately, there is no indication that such a change in stance is likely to come about any time soon. The Indian state remains a prisoner to its age-old colonial era policies, marked by lack of vision and foresight in its dealings with the countless minority groups in this vast land. As for the Sikh community, although a large majority seems prepared to let pass the traumatic events of 1984 and after and settle down to a peaceful life, the persistent failure of the government to address their principal concerns and grievances makes it possible for unscrupulous elements in the Congress and Akali parties to exploit the situation to further their own agendas.

A recent episode may be narrated here. Several Sikh organizations have been observing the anniversary of Operation Blue Star every year as a *ghallughara* week, where various Akali factions try to surpass each other in eulogizing Bhindranwale and condemning the Union government. On the occasion of its 21 anniversary in 2005, the SGPC president announced that a Shaheedi Minar would be built in the premises as a memorial to all those killed in the Operation. The *jathedar* of Akal Takht performed the *ardas* (prayer) that included the condemnation of the Indian state for Blue Star and Wood Rose. He also presented *siropas* or robes of honour to the widow and son of the late Bhindranwale. The function attracted a large number of extremists, who made highly provocative speeches amid the raising of Khalistan slogans. The same day, the high priests of the three Sikh Takhts located in Punjab together laid the foundation stone of a memorial for Bhindranwale in a village in Patiala district, with plans for a museum showcasing the atrocities committed by the army during Blue Star. Obviously, none of these events could happen without the implicit involvement of the ruling establishment. What makes the situation even more alarming is the reaction of the ultra-rightist Hindu parties, the Shiv Sena and Vishwa Hindu Parishad, which did not let go the opportunity to fish in troubled waters. While the former burnt an effigy of Bhindranwale at Sirhind in Patiala district, the latter declared that a portrait of the tenth Sikh Guru, Gobind Singh, will be put up in all prominent Hindu temples, including Ayodhya.[7] This was adding insult to injury, as the Sikhs have considered a separate identity the cornerstone of all their political campaigns.

There is reason to believe that although the concept of Khalistan was never a serious mainstream demand of a majority of the Sikh people, it has not failed to attract a sizeable following off and on in a wishful sort of way, a sentiment that has often been exploited by all kinds of political manipulators. The advocacy of Khalistan revolves around the argument that the Sikhs can enjoy the full glow of freedom only in a land of their own, regardless of the utter non-viability of such a proposition. Needless to say, Pakistan has time and again worked upon such a sentiment to create problems for its giant neighbour. The only way this argument can be effectively countered is for the Indian state to methodically set about reviewing its minority management strategies to assuage the fears and anxieties of the Sikhs and other disgruntled minority groups. If not addressed proficiently and in a timely manner, these granules of discontent and dissent will grow into so many separatist movements and insurgencies, which the state may not find possible to tackle by force alone.

According to a Pakistani scholar, it will be the discontented minorities in all the countries of the Indian sub-continent that would ultimately restructure the political geography of South Asia. 'He (Sikh) is the one who can trigger off the chain of events as, of all the regional characters, he is one who has been imbued with the most compelling human grounds for insurgency. The Sikh question in India today is not just a 'sectarian conflict' but a volcanic epicentre which, when it gets activated, could turn the political economy and the political geography of the entire region topsy-turvy once and for all'.[8] Made in 1987, the observation strikes one as a highly unlikely prognostication, unless one recognizes the dangers of increasing resurgence of Hinduism and its growing hold on the Indian state, as demonstrated by the recent horrendous events in Gujarat and some other parts of the country. The rapid rise of the fanatical rightist Hindu fringe poses immense dangers to communal peace and minority rights. The Indian state can, therefore, be expected to be far more discriminatory and manifestly unfair towards the minorities, including the Sikhs, regardless of which political party occupies the seat of power.

As for the Indian law enforcement agencies, they remain stuck in mid-nineteenth century mindsets and an archaic legal architecture. All hopes of deep and substantial reforms in the Indian police continue to miscarry because no political party is prepared to give up its control on this coercive instrument of state policy. The Punjab police has, no doubt, acquired considerable counter-militancy expertise and a vast accretion to its resource base has taken place: however, its basic culture and functional modes remain unchanged. The case of Jagtar Hawara, a prominent Babbar Khalsa leader, arrested from a Punjab village by the Delhi police in July 2005, underscores the inability of the Punjab police to maintain the utmost vigil over such militant elements capable of reviving extremist violence. Whether the end of Sikh militancy in the dark decade of 1983-92 was brought about entirely through the brutal and repressive policies adopted by the Indian security forces or the internal dynamics of the movement also contributed to its containment, remains open to debate. As does the more critical question as to whether it will resurface in some other form after a few years. For that is what we learn from the history of that turbulent region during the last many centuries. In the meanwhile, let us keep our fingers scrupulously crossed.

Annexure

Some of the more prominent reports on state terror in the Punjab during the later years of counter-militant operations are mentioned below:

1. *Punjab Andar Thahe Ja Rahe Hakumati Jabar Bare White Paper* (Punjabi)
2. *Sikh Villages Ransacked: Operation Teach Them A Lesson*, A report on torture by India's security forces, Punjab Human Rights Organization, Ludhiana.
3. *State Terrorism in Punjab: A Report*, Committee for Information and Initiative, Delhi 1989.
4. *Politics of Genocide, Punjab 1984-1994*, Inderjit Singh Jaijee, Chandigarh 1995.
5. *The Sikh Struggle*, Ram Narayan Kumar and George Sieberer, pp.297-375.
6. *Rights and Wrongs in Punjab, A Swiss Agency Report* by Hansruell Raflaub and Hans P. Spaar, published in *Sikh Review* of January 1993.
7. *Human Rights Violations in Punjab: Use and Abuse of the Law*, Amnesty International{India} 1991, pp.1-92.
8. *An Unnatural Fate: Disappearances and Impunity in the Indian States of Jammu and Kashmir and Punjab,*

Amnesty International (India), 15 December 1993, pp.1-63.

9. *Punjab Police Beyond the Bounds of Law*, Amnesty International (India) 1995.

10. *Dead Silence: The Legacy of Abuses in Punjab*, Human Rights Watch Asia and Physicians for Human Rights, May 1994.

11. *Punjab Bulldozed: A Report to the World, Operation Black Thunder II*, Punjab Human Rights Organization, Ludhiana, June 1988.

12. *Punjab Diyan Ghatnawan Te Report* (Punjabi), Jamhuri Adhikar Sabha, Ludhiana, 1985.

13. *Dehshatgard Kaun? Sikh Ke Sarkar* (Punjabi), Justice Ajit Singh Bains, Vichar Parkashan Sangrur, 1995.

14. *Punjab Kharku Lehar De Zalzale ton baad* (Punjabi), Major Singh, Vichar Parkashan, Sangrur, 1993.

15. *Truth About Punjab: SGPC White Paper*, Gurdarshan Singh Dhillon, 1996.

16. *The Sikh Case: Genesis and Solution of Punjab Problem*, Bharat Mukti Morcha, Punjab, Chandigarh 1988

17. *Punjab: People Fight Back: A Report to the Nation*, All India Federation of Organizations for Democratic Rights, Bombay 1987.

Notes

Foreword

1. For a review of the literature on the causes of the Punjab crisis, see, 'Gurharpal Singh, 'Understanding the Punjab Problem', *Asian Survey*, vol. 27, no. 2 (1987), pp.1268-77.
2. Gurharpal Singh, 'Re-examining the Punjab Problem' in G. Singh and I. Talbot (eds.) *Punjabi Identity: Continuity and Change* (New Delhi: Manohar, 1996), pp.115-39.
3. J. Pettigrew, *The Sikhs of the Punjab: Unheard Voices of State and Guerilla Violence* (London: Zed Books 1995).
4. Shinder Singh Thandi, 'Counterinsurgency and Political Violence in Punjab, 1980-94' in G. Singh and I. Talbot (eds.), *Punjabi Identity: Continuity and Change* (New Delhi: Manohar, 1996), pp.159-87.
5. See, D.P. Sharma, *The Punjab Story: Decade of Turmoil* (New Delhi: APH Publishing Corporation, 1996); Lt.-Gen. K.S. Brar, *Operation Bluestar: The True Story* (New Delhi: UBS Publishers & Distributors 1993); KPS. Gill, *The Knights of Falsehood* (New Delhi: Har-Anand Publications 1997).

6. Government of India, *White Paper on the Punjab Agitation* (New Delhi: Department of Information and Broadcasting, 1984).

7. In another brief personal anecdote he also reveals how the name Blue Star was chosen as the code name for the army operation in the Golden Temple, Amritsar.

8. C.K. Mahmood, 'Sikh Rebellion and the Hindu Concept of Order', *Asian Survey* vol. 29, no. 3 (1989), pp.326-40.

9. Paul Wallace, 'The Sikhs as a "minority" in a Sikh Majority State in India', *Asian Survey* vol. 26, no. 3 (1986), pp.363-77.

10. P. Singh, *Of Demons and Dreams: An Indian Memoir* (London: Duckworth, 1994).

11. S.S. Thandi, 'Counterinsurgency and Political Violence in Punjab, 1980-94' in G. Singh and I. Talbot (eds.), *Punjabi identity: Continuity and Change* (New Delhi: Manohar, 1996), p.162.

Introduction

1. Ranajit Guha, *The Elementary Aspects of Peasant Insurgency*, (1973, Delhi, Oxford University Press).

2. Mahasweta Devi's *Droopadi* inestimably brought to our view by Gayatri Spivak, poignantly addresses the agency of rebel woman insurgent in the context of anti-Naxal operations. See her *Breast Stories* (1993, Calcutta. Seagull Publications).

3. Jacques Derrida, 'The Mystical Foundation of Authority' in Drucilla Cornell, Michel Rosenfeld, and David Gray Carlson (Ed.) *Deconstruction and the Possibility of Justice* (1992, London, Routledge.) Concerning 'pathologies' see Jacques Derrida and Giovanna Borradori, 'Autoimmunity: Real and Symbolic Suicides," in Philosophy in a Time of Terror, ed. Borradori pp.95-96 (Chicago, Chicago University Press, 2003).

4. Ranajit Guha, Note 1, at pp.88, 108, 109 germinally alerts us to the 'ambivalence of deed' arising from the fact that insurgent violence remains 'wired to two different codes'. At its originary point, it crystallizes 'the individualistic and small group distance from the law' maturing subsequently into 'collective social defiance which adopts it' thus establishing its identity as 'public', 'destructive', and total.
Concerning 'pathologies' see Jacques Derrida and Giovanna Borradori, 'Autoimmunity: Real and Symbolic Suicides', in *Philosophy in a Time of Terror*, ed. Borradori pp.95-96 (Chicago, Chicago University Press, 2003).

5. See, concerning the relation between the 'host' and 'parasite', J. Hills Miller, 'The Critic as a Host', *Critical Enquiry* 3:439-447 (1997).

6. Id.., at 109.

7. Jonathan Xavier Inda, 'Foreign Bodies, Migrants, Parasites, and the Pathological Nation', *Discourse*: 22, 46-62 (2000).

8. See, as concerns the various languages of human rights, Upendra Baxi, *The Future of Human Rights* (Delhi, Oxford University Press, 2002, 2006).

9. Incidentally, the 'Mother of Parliaments' has just enwombed a dreadful monster, a law against 'glorification' of 'terrorism' that perhaps even criminalizes acts of historical understanding of insurgent collective violence; I do not know how far this is an exercise in 'reverse' learning whereby legislative post-colonial legislative models of the South influence the North. I have in view here the Indian law likewise criminalizing the 'glorification' of Sati. This apart, this United Kingdom legislative proposals when finally enacted, must run the gauntlet of review by the European Court of Human Rights, its own decisional jurisprudence in turn further now enthralled by the rhetoric, and realities, of the endless 'War *on* Terror'.

376 Notes

10. *A Critique of Postcolonial Reason: Towards a History of Vanishing Present* (1999, Cambridge, Harvard University Press).

11. I recourse this term, coined by the noted Hindi writer Pawan Kumar Chaudhry, concerning the recurrently produced crises of Indian governance, law and justice.

12. Rene Girard, *Violence and the Sacred* (1978, Baltimore, Johns Hopkins; P. Gregory, trs).

1. The Backdrop

1. The most prominent of these was Ghani Jafar of the Institute of Regional Studies, Islamabad, whose work on the so-called Sikh problem in the Indian subcontinent, published in 1987, under the title *The Sikh Volcano* by Vanguard Books {Pvt] Ltd. Lahore, remains a most valuable collection of extracts, culled from contemporary Indian media, to validate his projections.

2. Dr. Birinder Pal Singh, *The Logic of Sikh Militancy in Punjab in Prosperity and Violence*, Chandigarh 1998.

3. Major AE Bastow, *Sikhs* {Handbooks for the Indian Army}, Government of India Press, New Delhi—1940, pp.17, 18 and 21.

4. Prof. JS Grewal; *Sikh Identity, the Akalis and Khalistan*, an essay in *Punjab in Prosperity and Violence*, Chandigarh 1998.

5. C. Rajagopalachari {CR}, a top Congress leader, virtually endorsed the Muslim League's demand for India's partition, based on MA. Jinnah's two-nation theory, in his formula put forward in 1944. Although the Congress officially strove to distance itself from the proposal, the CR formula was widely seen as a sounding board.

6. Prof. Indu Banga, *Political Perceptions and Articulations of the Sikhs during the 1940's*, a paper presented at a seminar at Chandigarh, in February 1995.

7. ibid.

8. ibid.
9. Prof. JS Grewal; op. cit.
10. ibid.
11. Prof Pritam Singh; op. cit., *Punjab Issue in British Politics*, p.632.
12. Mark Juergensmeyer, *The Logic of Religious Violence: the Case of the Punjab*; Contributions to Indian Sociology[n.s.}, 22, 1; January-June 1988, p.73.
13. ibid.. p.77.
14. ibid. p.69.
15. Joyce Pettigrew, *The Sikhs of Punjab: Unheard Voices of State and Guerrilla Violence*; London and New Jersey; Zed Books, 1995, p.55.
16. Jasbir Singh et al. (edit.), *Invasion Of Religious Boundaries*, Canadian Sikh Study and Teaching Society, Vancouver, Canada—1995, p.27.

2. The Exposition

1. Danewalia, Bhagwan Singh, *Police and Politics in Twentieth Century Punjab*, Ajanta Publications, New Delhi—1997, p.349.
2. ibid. p.386.
3. Dr. Pritam Singh, *Two Facet of Revivalism: A Defence*, in *Punjab Today* by Gopal Singh (ed.), Intellectual Publishing House, New Delhi—1987, p.169.
4. ibid.
5. Birinder Pal Singh, *Violence As Political Discourse: Sikh Militancy Confronts the Indian State*, Indian Institute of Advanced Study, Shimla—2002, p.137.
6. For a more detailed argument on this subject, see *The Sikh Volcano* by Ghani Jafar, published 1987 by Vanguard Books (Pvt) Ltd. Lahore.
7. Birinder Pal Singh, op. cit. p.39.
8. Puran Singh, *Spirit of the Sikh: Meditations on Religion and the Spiritual Experience, Part I*, Punjabi University,

Patiala—1978, p.207, as quoted in Birinder Pal Singh, op. cit.

9. G.S. Talib, *Evolution of the Heroic Character in Sikhism and the Indian Society*—1967, pp.67-8, as quoted in Birinder Pal Singh, op. cit.

3. The Build-up

1. *Quomi Rajniti* (Punjabi), August 1983, p.51.
2. Khushwant Singh, *A History of the Sikhs*, vol. 2, Oxford University Press, Delhi—1981, p.289.
3. ibid. p.304-5.
4. Birinder Pal Singh, op. cit. p.128.
5. Mark Juergensmeyer, op. cit. *The Logic of Religious Violence*, p.86.
6. Dipanker Gupta, The Communalizing of Punjab, 1980-1985, *Economic and Political Weekly*, Vol. XX, No. 28, 13 July 1985, p.1188.
7. ibid.
8. From the taped sermons of Sant Jarnail Singh Bhindranwale.
9. *The Indian Express*, New Delhi, 27 April 1983.
10. *The Patriot*, New Delhi, 26 April 1983.
11. *The Hindustan Times*, New Delhi, 27 April 1983.
12. Ghani Jafar, *The Sikh Volcano*, Vanguard Books (Pvt.) Ltd. Lahore—1987, p.79.
13. *The Tribune*, Chandigarh, 7 October 1983.
14. *The Tribune*, Chandigarh, 7 July 1983.
15. *The Times of India*, New Delhi, 18 November 1983.
16. *The Statesman, Delhi* and *The Times of India*, New Delhi, 30 April 1984.
17. As cited in *Punjab Terrorism: Truth Still Uncovered* by Dr Pritam Singh of Oxford Brookes University UK in *Economic and Political Weekly*, Mumbai, 6 October, 2001, p.3830.

18. Lt Gen J.S. Aurora (Retd), 'Assault on the Golden Temple' in *The Punjab Story*, Roli Books International, New Delhi—1984, p.97.

4. The Conflict

1. *The Tribune*, Chandigarh, 30 April 1984.
2. As cited in AG Noorani's article 'A White Paper on Black Deeds' in *The Illustrated Weekly of India*, 22 July 1984.
3. Alexander, PC, *Through The Corridors Of Power*, HarperCollins Publishers India, New Delhi—2004, pp. 292-3.
4. ibid. p.270.
5. Tavleen Singh, 'Terrorists in the Temple', The Punjab Story, *The Punjab Story*, Roli Books International, New Delhi—1984, p.44-5.
6. *The Tribune*, Chandigarh, 14 December 1982.
7. *The Hindustan Times*, New Delhi, 24 December 1982.
8. *The Tribune*, Chandigarh, 23 January, 1984.
9. Rajni Kothari, 'The Issue', *Seminar*, New Delhi, February 1985.
10. Attar Singh, 'National Question and Punjab', *The Patriot*, New Delhi, 3 April 1984.
11. *The Telegraph*, Calcutta, 28 September 1984.
12. Bhai Gurdas was a respected companion of the Sikh Gurus, whose compositions are deferentially recited in the Harimandir, along with those of Bhai Nand Lal and, of course, the sacred hymns from Guru Granth Sahib. The line quoted above is the opening line of the first stanza, which in Punjabi reads as *kutta raj bahaliye phir chakki chattae*.
13. Birinder Pal Singh, op. cit. p.135.
14. Dipanker Gupta, 'The Communalizing of Punjab, 1980-1985', *Economic and Political Weekly*, Bombay, Vol. XX, No. 28, 13 July 1985, p.1190.

5. The Climax

1. *Indian Express*, New Delhi, 4 February 1984.
2. Alexander, Dr. P.C., *Through The Corridors Of Power*, op. cit. p.294.
3. *White Paper on the Punjab Agitation*, issued by the government of India, New Delhi, 10 July 1984, annexure XI, p.169.
4. Based on an eye-witness account given by the secretary of the Akali Dal, included in 'Genesis of the Hindu-Sikh Divide' by Khushwant Singh in *The Punjab Story*, Roli Books International, New Delhi, 1984, pp.11-13.
5. Lt Gen (retd) J.S. Aurora, 'Assault on the Golden Temple', *The Punjab Story*, op. cit. p.92.
6. ibid. p.96.
7. ibid. p.97.
8. Pritam Singh, 'AIR and Doordarshan Coverage of Punjab after Army Action; *Economic and Political Weekly*, Mumbai, 8 September 1984.
9. Alexander, Dr. P.C., op. cit. p.285-6.
10. ibid. p.297.
11. ibid. p.299.
12. ibid. p.301.
13. Kuldip Nayar and Khushwant Singh, *Tragedy of Punjab, Operation Blue Star and After*, Vision Books, New Delhi—1984.

6. The Fallout

1. Dipanker Gupta, 'The communalizing of Punjab', 1980-1985, *Economic and Political Weekly*, Bombay, 13 July 1985.
2. Birinder Pal Singh, *Violence as Political Discourse*, Indian Institute of Advanced Study, Shimla—2002, p.138.
3. Veena Das, 'Time, self and community: Features of the Sikh militant discourse', *Contributions to Indian Sociology*

(n.s.), 26, 2 (1992), p.247, as quoted in Birinder Pal Singh op. cit.

4. Birinder Pal Singh, op. cit.
5. Pettigrew, Joyce, *The Sikhs of Punjab: Unheard Voices of State and Guerilla Violence*, London Zed Books— 1995, p.148.
6. Dipanker Gupta, op, cit.

7. A Phony Accord

1. Ghani Jafar, *The Sikh Volacano*, Vanguard Books (Pvt.) Ltd. Lahore, Pakistan, 1987, p.336.
2. Kuldip Nayar, 'Punjab: Wheels Within Wheels', *The Tribune*, Chandigarh, 19 May 1985.
3. *The Tribune*, Chandigarh, 12 May 1985.
4. 'Punjab: Peace At Last?' Cover story, *Sunday*, Calcutta, 4-10 August 1985.

8. Intensification of Militancy

1. Birinder Pal Singh, *Violence As Political Discourse*, op. cit. p.140.
2. Pettigrew, Joyce, *The Sikhs of Punjab: Unheard Voices of State and Guerrilla Violence*, London, 1985, p.82.
3. Birinder Pal Singh, op. cit. p.141.
4. Maloy Krishna Dhar, *Open Secrets: India's Intelligence Unveiled*, Manas Publications, New Delhi 2005, p.279.
5. ibid. pp.325-6.
6. ibid. p.342.
7. ibid. p.343.
8. Ribeiro, Julio, *Bullet for Bullet, My life As A Police Officer*, Viking, Delhi 1998, p.305.
9. Pettigrew, op. cit. p.109.
10. Ribeiro, Julio, op. cit. p.338.
11. Jaijee, Inderjit Singh, *Politics of Genocide: Punjab 1984-94*, Baba Publishers, Chandigarh 1996. pp.196-97.

12. Birinder Pal Singh, op. cit. p.192.
13. *India Today*, 15 September 1985, p.74.
14. Joyce Pettigrew, op. cit. p.104-5.
15. ibid. p.111.
16. Pettigrew and Ribeiro as quoted in Birinder Pal Singh, op. cit. pp.195 and 200.
17. Sat Pal Dang, quoted in *Frontline*, 29 July 1994, p.123.

9. The Beginning of the End

1. Joyce Pettigrew, *The Sikhs of Punjab: Unheard Voices of State and Guerilla Violence*, Zed Books, London, 1995, p.131.
2. Pritam Singh, Prof., *Sectarianism and Human Rights Discourse: The Politics of Human Rights in Post-Colonial Punjab in Changing Concepts of Rights and Justice in South Asia*, Michael R. Anderson and Sumit Guha (ed.), Oxford University Press Delhi, 1998, p.249.
3. Harkishan Singh Surjeet, a topmost CPM leader, in *Deepening Punjab Crisis: A Democratic Solution*, Delhi 1992 pp.365-6.
4. *Human Rights in India: Punjab in Crisis*, An Asia Watch Report, New York, 1991, p.5.
5. Pramod Kumar, *Violence in Retrospect: Punjab in Prosperity and Violence*, Institute of Punjab Studies, Chandigarh, 1998, p.133.
6. Pritam Singh of Oxford Brookes University, UK, in an unpublished paper presented at the 50th Anniversary Conference of the British Association for the Study of Religions at Oxford on 11 September, 2004 and at the 21st Annual Conference of the Association of Punjab Studies (UK) on 25 June 2005 at Oxford.
7. Malkit Singh, *Mainstream*, Delhi, 23 July 2005, pp.17-8.
8. Ghani Jafar, *The Sikh Volcano*, Vanguard Books, Lahore, 1987, 450.

Select Bibliography

Alexander, P.C. *Through The Corridors Of Power: An Insider's Story*, HarperCollins Publishers India, New Delhi—2004.

Butalia, Urvashi, *The Other Side of Silence: Voices from the Partition of India*, Penguin Books, 1998.

Dang, Satyapal, *Genesis of Terrorism: An Analytical Study of Punjab Terrorists*, Patriot Publishers, Delhi—1989.

Dhar, Maloy Krishna, *Open Secrets: India's Intelligence Unveiled*, Manas Publications, New Delhi—2005.

Birinder Pal Singh, Dr; *Violence As Political Discourse: Sikh Militancy Confronts The Indian State*, Indian Institute of Advanced Study, Shimla, 2002.

Brar, Lt Gen K.S. *Operation Blue Star; The True Story*, UBS Publishers' Distributors Ltd. New Delhi—1993.

Chakravati, Uma and Nandita Haksar, *Delhi Riots: Three Days In the Life of a Nation*, Lancer International, Delhi—1986.

Citizens for Democracy, *Report to the Nation: Truth About Delhi Violence*, Citizens for Democracy, Delhi—1985.

Citizens' Commission, *Delhi: 31ˢᵗ October to 4ᵗʰ November, 1984*, Citizens' Commission, Delhi—1985.

Danewalia, B.S. *Police And Politics In Twentieth Century Punjab*, Ajanta Publications, Delhi—1997.

Duggal, KS; *The Akal Takht and other Seats of Sikh Polity*, UBS Publishers' Distributors Ltd. New Delhi—1995.

Ghani Jafar; *The Sikh Volcano*, Vanguard Books {Pvt.} Ltd. Lahore, Pakistan—1987.

Gill, KPS, *The Knights of Falsehood*, Har Anand Publications, Delhi—1997.

Grewal, Prof J.S. *The Akalis: A Short History*, Punjab Studies Publications, Chandigarh—1996.

——*From Guru Nanak to Maharaja Ranjit Singh: Essays in Sikh History*, Guru Nanak Dev University, Amritsar—1972.

——*Miscellaneous Articles*, Guru Nanak Dev University, Amritsar—1974.

Grewal, J.S. and Bal S.S. *Guru Gobind Singh: A Biographical Study*, Punjab University, Chandigarh—1967.

Grewal, Prof J.S. and Banga, Prof Indu{ed.}; *Punjab In Prosperity And Violence*, Institute Of Punjab Studies, Chandigarh—1998.

Gupta, Dipanker, *The Context of Ethnicity: Sikh Identity in a Comparative Perspective*, Oxford University Press, Delhi—1996.

——*The Communalizing of Punjab, 1980-1985*, Economic and Political Weekly, Vol. XX, No. 28, 13 July 1985.

Jaijee, Inderjit Singh, *Politics of Genocide: Punjab 1984-1994*, Baba Publications, Chandigarh, 1995.

James, Lawrence; *Raj: The Making And Unmaking Of British India*, Little, Brown and Company, UK—1997.

Jasbir Singh Mann, Surinder Singh Sodhi and Gurbaksh Singh Gill {ed.}; *Invasion of Religious Boundaries: A Critique*, Canadian Sikh Study and Teaching Society, Vancouver—1995.

Juergensmeyer, Mark, *The Logic of Religious Violence: the Case of the Punjab, Contributions to Indian Sociology* {n.s.} 22{1}, 1988.

——*Religious Nationalism Confronts the Secular State*, Oxford University Press, Delhi—1994.

Khushwant Singh, *A History of the Sikhs* in two volumes, Oxford University Press Delhi—1981.

Lawrence James, *Raj: The Making and Unmaking of British India*, Little, Brown and Company, Great Britain, 1997.

Marwah, Ved; *Uncivil Wars: Pathology of Terrorism in India*, HarperCollins Publishers India Pvt. Ltd.—1995.

Minocha, Vivek Sagar, *The Punjab Problem*, Delhi 1989.

Mohammed Ayoob; {ed.}; *The Politics of Islamic Reassertion*, Vikas Publishing House, New Delhi—1982.

Oberoi, Harjot; *The Construction of Religious Boundaries: Culture, Identity and Diversity in the Sikh Tradition*, Oxford University Press, New Delhi—1994.

——*Orphans of the Storm: Stories on the Partition of India*, Selected and edited by Saros Cowasjee & K.S Duggal, UBSPD—1995.

Pandey, Gyanendra, *The Construction of Communalism in Colonial North India*, Delhi—1994.

Paul Wallace and Surendra Chopra (eds), *Political Dynamics of Punjab*, Amritsar—1981.

Pettigrew, Joyce, *The Sikhs of Punjab: Unheard Voices of State and Guerrilla Violence*, Zed Books, London—1995.

——*Punjab in Crisis: Human Rights in India*, An Asia Watch Report.

Kohli, Atul, *Democracy and Discontent: India's Growing Crisis of Governability*, Cambridge University Press—1991.

Ram Narayan Kumar and Amrik Singh, *Reduced to Ashes: The Insurgency and Human Rights in Punjab, Final Report; Vol. One*, South Asian Forum for Human Rights, Kathmandu—Nepal, 2003.

Sarab Jit Singh; *Operation Black Thunder: An Eyewitness Account of Terrorism in Punjab*, Sage Publications, New Delhi—2002.

Talib, Gurbachan Singh, *Evolution of the Heroic Character in Sikhism and the Indian Society*, 1967.

——*The Punjab Story*, {Ed.} Roli Books International, New Delhi—1984.

——*The Sikhs in their Homeland: India*, a government of India publication, 1984.

White Paper on the Punjab Agitation, issued by the government of India, 10 July 1984.

Index